COUPLET PAIR REBUS

The Principle of Cause and Effect in Art

COUPLET PAIR REBUS

The Principle of Cause and Effect in Art

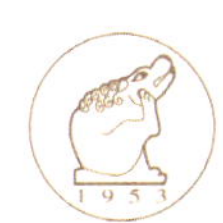

University Museum and Art Gallery

The University of Hong Kong

Florian Knothe

Foreword and Introduction

Foreword

The University Museum and Art Gallery (UMAG) is delighted to present **COUPLET PAIR REBUS The Principle of Cause and Effect in Art**, based on the 2024 UMAG exhibition that illustrates the concept of "call and response". This artistic interchange between artworks is interpreted within the galleries in myriad ways, based on the context and intention of the curator and individual artists. As the exhibition illustrates, and this accompanying publication documents, the integration of the fundamental principle of harmony through couplets, pairs and rebuses in visual art can result in visually compelling, conceptually rich and engaging compositions that invite individuals to explore, interpret and interact with artworks on multiple levels. These interconnected elements create a sense of unity, balance and depth, fostering a dynamic and immersive viewing experience.

This exhibition brings together objects from UMAG's collection of Chinese art as well as some European artworks on loan from private collectors and artists, some of whom carefully, creatively and generously produced work following the exhibition's atypical theme. We would like to thank all of the artists and lenders for their cooperation and partnership.

It is crucial to note that the layout of each artifact was meticulously considered, as the theme of balance and harmony was generated through the meaningful arrangement of both individual and paired artifacts that developed a uniquely created "Gesamtkunstwerk"—a complete work of art highlighting the connections between artworks and the thought-provoking associations within the larger group.

The thoughtful curation of this exhibition is guided by the understanding that while the concept of harmony is a universal principle in art, Chinese and Western artistic traditions approach and manifest harmony in distinct ways. While Chinese art routinely emphasizes unity with nature, balance, cultural symbolism and calligraphic expression, Western art tends to focus on classical proportion, perspective, color theory and individual expression. Visitors to the exhibition galleries and readers of this publication are therefore introduced to Chinese and Western forms of engagement with the concept of harmony, a key element in creating visually compelling and aesthetically pleasing artworks.

While the exhibition and this catalog are intimately related and similar in scope, they differ fundamentally in character, as the former benefits from the visual experience of visitors in the gallery. The publication COUPLET PAIR REBUS limits engagement with the art objects due to the inherent strictures of the book format.

Introduction

In both exhibition space and book chapters, the introductory section presents a series of couplets in a space for reading, contemplation and resonance. The poems offer a multitude of voices with which nature and the world can be described, while the various calligraphic styles visualize the contents. The paired artworks are dedicated to balance and symmetry—playfully juxtaposed to form a three-dimensional equilibrium. This concept is supported by the objects of applied art that illustrate humanity's constant striving to create objects in symmetrical harmony across creative genres.

Additionally, the rebus puzzles offer a space of associations, forming a network of various content-related references that connect the artworks. These works have been curated to create and highlight the relationship between works that are potentially related by content or presentation, and enrich the context by emphasizing the similar or complementary nature of the artworks. The motif of the pair connects like or unlike elements, represents sequences in time or space and enables serial storytelling.

In the gallery, symmetry is a crucial element, which was seen in the numerous objects of applied art, while the abstract works relied on the idea of balance and equilibrium. Beyond the individual works, the exhibition space displayed artifacts that were not originally intended to be paired together, but were carefully aligned to face each other in a "curated" balance within the three-dimensional space. This catalog demonstrates a different set of qualities, though it still relates to the exhibition by presenting the associated artifacts as much as the book format allows. The crucial task of documenting the exhibition and its reflective juxtapositions helps to explain the concept in more detail and describe the objects made, or curated, as couplets, pairs or rebuses, and then analyzes their cultural value. As the catalog takes into account and reflects on the curator's experiences, this publication is a so-called "reflexive catalog".

Couplets and pairs, known as *lian* (聯) in Chinese, bear significant importance in Chinese art and culture by emphasizing harmony, balance, unity and symbolism; they enhance visual impact and reflect cultural traditions. Their use in various art forms adds depth, meaning and aesthetic appeal, highlighting the interconnectedness of ideas and the beauty of complementary elements. These matched sets, often displayed together, are commonly found in various art forms, including calligraphy, painting and poetry, and they are believed to bring harmony and balance to the composition. In Chinese art and aesthetics, the concept of Yin and Yang, balance and symmetry, are highly valued. Displaying pairs or couplets together creates a sense of visual equilibrium and completeness, reflecting the harmony of opposites. The visual impact of the artworks is enhanced by creating a sense of rhythm and repetition. The repeating of motifs, characters or colors in a paired format can draw the viewer's attention and create a cohesive visual statement. This repetition adds a sense of rhythm and flow to the composition.

Couplets and pairs are also used to express a unity and connection between two related ideas, themes or images. They can represent complementary concepts, such as heaven and earth, past and present, or joy and sorrow, emphasizing the interconnectedness of duality in life. Each part of a pair or couplet often carries symbolic meanings or conveys a specific message. When displayed together, they create a layered and nuanced expression of ideas, emotions or wishes. In Chinese calligraphy and poetry, pairs and couplets are often used to convey literary or poetic expression. The matching of characters or phrases in a structured format adds a poetic rhythm and elegance to the written text. The pairing of words or phrases creates a sense of completion and unity in the literary composition. The combination then of words or images in pairs can evoke deeper meanings and associations that enrich the viewer's understanding. Couplets are commonly used in auspicious contexts, such as celebrations, festivals or important ceremonies. Displaying pairs or couplets is believed to bring good luck, prosperity and blessings, making them an essential element of traditional Chinese art and decor.

A rebus is a form of visual art that uses images or symbols to represent words, phrases or sounds. This technique is often playful and relies on visual puns or wordplay to convey a message or meaning. Rebuses have a long history in visual art and communication. The form was widely used in Egyptian hieroglyphics as well as in medieval manuscripts and heraldry. By combining images that phonetically or conceptually correspond to parts of a word or phrase, artists create a playful and engaging visual puzzle for viewers to decipher. A rebus allows artists to exercise creativity and wit in conveying messages or ideas through visual means. By cleverly combining images, symbols and text, artists can create layered and nuanced compositions, whereas curators display juxtapositions, all of which invite viewers to interpret and engage with the artwork on multiple levels.

Rebus art can be both educational and entertaining. In educational settings, rebus puzzles can be used to teach language skills, phonetics and visual literacy. In a more light-hearted context, a rebus can be a fun and engaging form of visual entertainment, challenging viewers to decode the hidden meanings within an artwork. However, they often also carry important and long-lasting cultural or symbolic meanings, depending on the context in which they are used. Traditionally, artists have infused their rebus art with layers of meaning and significance by incorporating cultural references or symbols. Today, rebuses continue to be a popular artistic technique in contemporary art, graphic design and advertising.

In this exhibition, the curatorial concept expanded on the traditional meaning of the rebus and used it to combine several works of art into an overarching theme that the visitor must interpret. The artworks themselves, and their arrangement, became part of a 3D puzzle. Through the constellation of works, the original interpretation of the individual artwork intended by the artist is joined by another, this time inspired by the curator. For example, six paintings depicting pine trees becomes "6 Ways to Live a Life". Or, architecture, nature, a cage and a scale symbolize humanity's fragile relationship to the world and ongoing global change. The basic idea of the exhibition, which can be described as "call and response," can also be seen in this interplay of constellations and extended interpretations.

"Call and response" is a concept borrowed from music that involves a dialogue or interaction between two or more participants. In visual art, the idea of the call and response can be interpreted in various ways, depending on the context and intention of the artist. It can refer to a dialogue between different elements within an artwork, or it can involve the repetition or variation of motifs, colors, shapes or textures to create a sense of rhythm and interplay. The artist may introduce a visual "call" or stimulus that elicits a "response" from another element in the composition, creating a dynamic relationship between different parts of the artwork. In so doing, the call and response engages the viewer in a dialogue with the artwork.

Artists and curators may use visual cues or prompts to invite viewers to actively participate in the interpretation or completion of the artwork. This interactive approach encourages viewers to respond in a personal and subjective manner, fostering a deeper engagement with the piece.

Furthermore, the call and response in visual art can be used to reference or reflect cultural, historical or artistic traditions. Artists can incorporate symbols that evoke specific cultural contexts, prompting viewers to make connections with familiar visual language. This interplay between the artist's creation and the curator's exhibition enriches the layers of meaning. Therefore, the technique can also be explored in terms of formal and conceptual relationships. Exhibitions can present visual contrasts, juxtapositions or parallels between various elements to provoke a dialogue between complementary ideas. This tension or harmony between visual elements can create a dynamic and engaging viewing experience.

The exhibition included a variety of artifacts of Chinese and Western origin spanning thousands of years, from Neolithic earthenware and Chinese Shang dynasty bronzes to contemporary Asian and European paintings, objects and interactive installations. Here, the call and response also encompasses a range of interactions, dialogues and relationships within an artwork, between the artist and the viewer, or cultural, historical and formal considerations. This dynamic and interactive approach to artmaking and the display of art enhances the richness and complexity of visual compositions, inviting viewers to engage with the artwork and contemplate the creative process. By selecting a significant number of collection items that had rarely been shown, and never before juxtaposed in this manner, the curatorial concept allowed visitors to experience how couplets, pairs and rebuses relate to harmony; interconnected concepts that create visually engaging and meaningful compositions.

Harmony in visual art refers to the balance, unity and coherence of elements within an artwork. It involves the arrangement of colors, shapes, textures and forms in a way that creates a sense of visual unity and cohesion. By incorporating harmonious elements in a composition, artists can create a sense of aesthetic pleasure and balance. Harmony can be achieved through the careful selection and arrangement of visual elements to create a cohesive and visually appealing whole, and it can extend to the overall concept or theme of an artwork or exhibition, where the interconnectedness of ideas, symbols or motifs contribute to a unified and harmonious visual narrative.

Chinese art often emphasizes harmony with nature, reflecting the interconnectedness between humanity and the natural world. Artists in Chinese art strive to capture the essence of nature, incorporating elements such as mountains, rivers, trees and animals in their artworks to convey a sense of unity and balance with the environment. They frequently incorporate symbolic motifs and imagery that carry cultural and philosophical meanings. These symbols, such as the dragon, phoenix, pine tree and bamboo, are used to convey auspicious messages, virtues and beliefs, adding layers of meaning and harmony.

Calligraphy is considered a highly expressive and harmonious art form in Chinese culture. The fluidity and rhythmic brushstrokes are believed to capture the energy and vitality of the artist, creating a harmonious fusion of form and meaning in written characters.

Chinese art values balance and symmetry, drawing on the principles of Yin and Yang within compositions. The harmonious arrangement of elements, such as colors, shapes and lines, creates a sense of visual equilibrium and completeness in Chinese art.

Western art has a long tradition of emphasizing classical proportion and composition to create a harmonious arrangement of elements. Artists often employ principles of symmetry, balance and perspective. They thrive within the tradition of depicting realistic representations of the world, using techniques such as perspective and chiaroscuro to create a sense of depth and spatial harmony. The accurate depiction of light, shadow and form contributes to the overall harmony of the compositions. In the Western tradition, artists and curators routinely experiment with color combinations and contrasts to create visual harmony and balance through complementary, analogous and harmonious color schemes. They value unique artistic voices and styles, individual expression and innovation. Though harmony remains an important principle in Western art, there is a greater emphasis on personal interpretation and creative freedom.

The object selection for the exhibition COUPLET PAIR REBUS adhered to a principle that creates a thematically stimulating concept uniting art and artifacts from East and West, spanning from antiquity to the present. Its immersive character encouraged visitors and readers to actively engage with the exhibition items by deciphering rebuses and becoming participatory agents.

Harald Kraemer 孔慧銳

Some Thoughts about the Principle of Cause and Effect in West and East

Cause > Effect >
(The Perspective of the West)

Cause > < Effect
(The View of the East)

Cause O Effect

Cause > Effect >
(The Perspective of the West)

"Nihil est sine ratione [sufficiente]
cur potius sit, quam non sit."
"Nothing is without a reason
for why it is rather than is not."

Wolff cited by Schopenhauer, 1813, § 5.

The Western principle of cause and effect is based on the standard of sufficient reason (lat. principium rationis sufficientis) (Ritter 2001). This states that everything must have a reason or cause. The first discussions on this interplay can be found in the writings of the **Presocratics**, for example, in Anaximander, Democritus and Parmenides (Hankinson 1998; Losee 2011). They were searching for the primordial substance, the origin of the all-encompassing principle of being, which they called Archē (ἀρχή). As a primordial first cause, Archē offers a conclusive answer to the question of the whence. It is interesting to note that the noun Archē is closely linked to the verb árchein (ἄρχειν), meaning "to begin, to precede, to be the first, to rule" (Lumpe 1955). The first is therefore the cause of what follows and what follows necessarily joins the first and expands upon it.

By referring to cosmogonic myths, the Presocratics were attempting to explain the origin of the world holistically. Their aim was to create a basic order in which man could find his role and position (Angehrn 2007). Cosmogony describes the emergence of diversity from a single primordial principle. This can be found in numerous origin myths, with the image of the world as an egg playing a distinctive role.

Whether imagining a male-female creator god associated with Dionysus, as the Greeks believed, or the giant Pángǔ (盤古), as in China, both entities emerged from an egg containing primordial chaos in the form of the complementary poles of Yin and Yang. In this construct, the one always precedes the many, from which the many then develop (see *Tao Te Ching*, chapter 42). However, the temporal succession of the first and the subsequent many does not mean that the initial is displaced by the latter. Rather, the two coexist and the original retains its place as the starting point.

The complexity and flexibility with which the principle of causality was understood and interpreted in ancient Greece can be deduced from the fact that "an event can be determined by factors human and divine, visible and invisible, present and past, as well as proximate and remote, both in spatial and temporal sense." (Collins 2008, 47). While **Democritus** (460/459–370 BCE) was one of the first philosophers to advocate for the idea of comprehensive causality in the sense of cause and effect, **Aristotle** (384–322 BCE) went a significant step further by following the question of why something occurs to a thing or an event ("Because of what?"). He divided these causes into four types according to form (causa formalis), purpose (causa finalis), material (causa materialis) and effect (causa efficiens) (Hankinson 1998, 132–135; Losee 2011, 3–6). Aristotle used his doctrine of the four causes to explain the change in the formation of a substance or the change in a substance and their interaction:

> "Of things which are generated, some are generated naturally, others artificially and others spontaneously; but everything which is generated is generated by something and from something and becomes something. When I say 'becomes something' I mean in any of the categories; it may come to be either a particular thing or of some quantity or quality or in some place."
>
> Aristotle, *Metaphysics*, VII 7, 1032a.

This was a decisive step in the differentiation of multiple causes and provided the basis for the general principle of sufficient reason (principium rationis sufficientis); that every being or cognition can be traced back to another in an appropriate manner. Aristotle used the four causes to explain change.

Marcus Tullius Cicero (106–43 BCE) also followed the causal principle formulated by Aristotle. In his work *De Divinatione*, written around 44 BCE, Cicero dealt with the question of whether or not prophecies can be based on reality. He defined "divination" as the ability to perceive and understand signs presented to humans by the gods and to explain them to outsiders. Finally, in chapter XXVIII, Cicero encourages his readers to look for the causes of omens and phenomena in nature—be they earthquakes, shooting stars or comets—and not to understand them as signs from the gods:

> "Not to be too verbose, all portents have one and the same explanation and it is this: whatever comes into existence, of whatever kind, must find its cause in nature; and hence, even though it may be contrary to experience, it cannot be contrary to nature. Therefore, explore the cause, if you can, of every strange thing that excites your astonishment. If you do not find the cause, be assured, nevertheless, that nothing could have happened without a cause, and employ the principles of natural philosophy to banish the fear which the novelty of the apparition may have occasioned. Then no earthquake or opening of the heavens, no showers of stones or blood, no shooting stars or comets, will fill you with alarm."
>
> Cicero, *De Divinatione*, book 2, 60.

To affirm that there must be a cause for every phenomenon that can be explained by the laws of nature, Cicero brings into play the soothsayer Chrysippus (280–207 BCE), recording him as saying:

> "Nothing can happen without a cause; nothing actually happens that cannot happen; if that has happened which could have happened, then it should not be considered a portent; therefore there are no such things as portents."
>
> Cicero, *De Divinatione*, book 2, 61.

With this statement, which is often quoted in its abbreviated form as "Nothing can happen without a cause," Cicero prepared the groundwork for subsequent debates, as the clarification, refinement and application of Aristotelian categories determined the philosophical discourse over the next few centuries.

Thomas Aquinas (1225–1274) and the philosophical and theological school of Thomism established a hierarchy of Aristotelian causes and defined a first cause (causa prima) that preceded all others: God as the creator of the world (May 1970).

This irrefutable truth remained for several centuries, and it was only at the beginning of the modern era, when modern science slowly broke away from natural philosophy, that the debate about cause and effect began to intensify. In his book

The Causation Debate in Modern Philosophy 1637–1739, Clatterbaugh describes this debate, which was about considering the principle of causality as a metaphysical problem and as a scientific problem (Clatterbaugh 1999). Based on the works of **René Descartes** (1596–1650), in particular his publications *Discourse on the Method* of 1637 and *Meditations on First Philosophy* of 1641, a fundamental discussion of the principle of causality took place over the next few decades (see Cottingham et. al. 1984–1991). Philosophers such as Benedictus de Spinoza, Thomas Hobbes and David Hume, but also physicists such as John Locke, and polymaths such as Isaac Newton and Gottfried Wilhelm Leibniz were involved in this debate. And at the same time, something unforeseen happened.

When the first reports about China were published towards the end of the 16th century, it came as a great shock to Europe. It was not merely the chronological age of China, which far surpassed the literal dates established by the biblical creation of the world, but also the absence of the Flood that aroused interest in this foreign culture. As a result, Jesuit missionaries decided to learn the Chinese language in order to familiarize themselves with the culture, philosophy and history of the Middle Kingdom (Rowbotham 1966). After initial successes as early as 1692, Emperor Kāngxī

(康熙) issued an edict of tolerance that allowed more than 300,000 Christians in China to practice their religion freely. The so-called *Rites Controversy* between the rival Catholic missions in China led to a ban on the practice of traditional customs by Chinese converts to Christianity and, as a result, to the prohibition of Christianity in China by Emperor Yōngzhèng (雍正) in 1724 (Gernet 2012).

Several publications from those years testify to the inspiring exchange between the two worlds (Harris 1966, Lundbæk 1992).

With the publication of his book *On Friendship* (Jiāoyǒu Lùn 交友論) in 1595, the Italian Jesuit **Matteo Ricci** (1552–1610) introduced Chinese readers to Western ethics and ideas on friendship. This work became one of the most widely read Western books in China during the late Ming dynasty, acquainting Chinese literati with ancient moral concepts concerning various types, values and natures of friendship (Ricci 2005).

With *The True Meaning of the Lord of Heaven* (Tiānzhǔ Shíyì 天主實義), published in Beijing in 1603, Ricci also addressed scholars trained in the teachings of Confucius, and in so doing created a controversial publication that was to have a decisive influence on the exchange between Europe and China (Ricci 1985). The conversations between a scholar from the West and a Chinese scholar reproduced in dialogue form are to be understood as a synopsis of the conversations that Ricci had with numerous Chinese literati.

As early as 1687, the book *Confucius Sinarum Philosophus, sive, Scientia Sinensis Latine Exposita* (Confucius, Philosopher of the Chinese, or, Chinese Knowledge Explained in Latin) was published in Paris as a translation of three of the four canonical books of the Confucian doctrine (Intorcetta et. al., 1687; Lundbæk 1992). In the preface, the authors' enthusiasm for Confucius becomes clear when they write:

"One might say that the moral system of this philosopher is infinitely sublime, but that it is at the same time simple, sensible and drawn from the purest sources of natural reason . . . Never has reason, deprived of divine revelation, appeared so well developed nor with so much power."

Hobson, 2004, 194.

The Flemish Jesuit **François Noël** (1651–1729) published his anthology *Sinensis Imperii Libri Classici Sex* (Six Classics of the Chinese Empire) in Prague in 1711, which made two more classics accessible in addition to the four (Noël 1711; Lundbæk 1991). The classics compiled by the New Confucian Zhū Xī (朱熹) in the Song dynasty, the so-called *Four Books* (Sìshū 四書), include the *Great Learning* (Dàxué 大學), *Analects* (Lúnyǔ 論語), *Doctrine of the Mean* (Zhōngyōng 中庸) (see

Confucius / Legge 2006) and the works of Mencius (Mèngzǐ 孟子) (see Legge 1895; Bloom 2009). Noël added translations of the *Classic of Filial Piety* (Xiàojīng 孝經) and *Elementary Learning* (Xiǎoxué 小學). The former focuses on the benefits of always remaining obedient towards parents, elders and superiors, which is considered a cardinal virtue according to Confucian ethics (Legge 1879). The latter, written by Zhu Xi around 1150, is a collection of doctrines, dialogues and anecdotes in the Confucian sense with roots in ancient sources.

The following books constitute the *Five Classics* (Wǔjīng 五經): *Book of Rites* (Lǐjì 禮記), *Book of Documents* (Shūjīng 書經 Shàngshū 尚書), *Classic of Poetry* (Shījīng 詩經), *Spring and Autumn Annals* (Chūnqiū 春秋) and the *Book of Change* (I Ching, Yijīng 易經).

A first partial translation of the *I Ching* into Latin was also produced in 1687 by the Flemish Jesuit Philippe Couplet (1623–1693). However, it was his French colleague Joachim Bouvet (1656–1730) who recognized the formal relationship between binary arithmetic and the hexagrams of the *I Ching* after the invention of the calculating machine by **Gottfried Wilhelm Leibniz** (1646–1716) in 1672 (completed in 1694). Inspired by the simultaneous complexity and binary simplicity of the *I Ching*, Leibniz finally published his paper in 1703 under the title *Explanation of binary arithmetic, which uses only the characters 0 and 1, with some remarks on its usefulness, and on the light it throws on the ancient Chinese figures of Fuxi* (Leibniz 1863, Lach 1992a, 105–108). However, as Ryan has shown in his study, it was not Fúxī (伏羲), the mystical creator of the Chinese characters, who is responsible for the diagram of the *I Ching*, but Shào Yōng (邵雍 1012–1077). Shao, who shares similarities with Leibniz, was of the opinion that the cosmos was created according to a binary system and that this binary system is reflected in all things and their relationships (Ryan 1996, 59). Leibniz hoped that by analyzing the *I Ching* he could arouse interest in Western science and thus also in Christianity in China.

The impression that the Chinese classics made on European scholars, which were now available in Latin, can be seen in the fact that Gottfried Wilhelm Leibniz, for example, produced four publications on the subject of China: *Novissima Sinica* (1697/1699), *On the Civil Cult of Confucius* (1700), *Remarks on Chinese Rites and Religion* (1708), and *Discourse on the Natural Theology of the Chinese* (1716) (Leibniz 1994; Leibniz 2011).

It was obvious to Leibniz that "we could learn from the Chinese a 'practical philosophy' in order to apply it to European ethics and politics with great benefit." (Leibniz, *Novissima Sinica*, 11).

When Leibniz considers, in view of the moral decline in Europe, whether Chinese missionaries could "[...] teach us the application and practice of a natural theology" as he wrote in *Novissima Sinica* (19), he is also expressing the fact that, in contrast to Europe, ethics and morality in China are supported to a significant degree by politics, and thus a well-being can be created that serves both the individual and the general public. (Cook; Rosemont 1992).

In his complex philosophical system, Leibniz attempted nothing less than to reconcile the Aristotelian categories with the Christian doctrine of creation and the causal laws of physics (Lyssy 2016). To explain his principle of sufficient reason he wrote in his *Monadology* of 1714:

"In the sense of sufficient reason, we find that no fact [fait] can be considered true or existing and no statement [enonciation] can be considered correct without there being a sufficient reason [raison suffisante] for it being so and not otherwise, although these reasons may not be known to us most of the time."

Leibniz, *Monadology*, 1720, § 32, see Lyssy 2016, part 1.

Leibniz had already commented on this topic ten years earlier in his *Theodicy*. In this book he contrasted the later concept of "sufficient reason" (raison suffisante) with the concept of "determining reason" (raison déterminante).

> "[...] nothing happens without there being a cause or at least a determining reason [raison déterminante], i.e. something that can serve to justify a priori why something exists rather than does not exist and why something exists just as it does rather than in a different way."
>
> Leibniz, *Theodicy*, 1710, § 44,
> see Lyssy 2016, part 1.

For Leibniz, therefore, every event can be explained both in terms of its cause and purpose, i.e. it is causally and finally determined at the same time, even if the reasons that led to an event are often unknown to us (Jost 2019; Wang 2012).

Christian Wolff (1679–1754) was a German polymath and one of the most important philosophers of the Enlightenment between Leibniz and Kant. In his two main works, *Vernünfftige Gedancken von den Kräfften des menschlichen Verstandes und ihrem richtigen Gebrauche in Erkäntnis der Wahrheit* (Rational Thoughts on the Powers of the Human Understanding and Its Proper Use in the Cognition of Truth), also known as the *German Logic*, published in 1713, and the philosophical textbook *Vernünftige Gedanken von Gott, der Welt und der Seele des Menschen, auch allen Dingen überhaupt* (Rational Thoughts on God, the World and the Soul of Man, and on All Things in General), also known as the *German Metaphysics*, published in 1720, Wolff developed a conception of knowledge and science based on reason and on mathematics. Wolff thus proves to be a representative of rationalism and a specifically modern metaphysics whose highest principles are the theorem of excluded contradiction ("It cannot be that the same thing is and is not.") and the theorem of sufficient reason ("Nothing exists without a sufficient reason why it exists and does not exist.") (Wolff 1720; Wolff 2019, see 5.1 Ontology). Wolff interprets the facts of reality as an ordered expression of universal harmony, as a linking of the coexistence of things in terms of a philosophy divided between efficient and final causes.

Wolff played a special role in the Western and Eastern understanding of the principles of cause and effect. Wolff's intensive reading of the works of Confucius and Mencius inspired him to deliver his "Speech on the Practical Philosophy of the Chinese" at the University of Halle in 1721 (Lach 1992b, 119–120). Wolff was looking for a philosophy that traced the truth of faith back to rationality, which brought him into conflict with theologians who insisted on the inscrutability of revelation. In his speech, he recommended the virtuous life of the non-Christian Chinese as exemplary. The Confucian tradition served him as living proof of an ethic that had characterized an advanced civilization for thousands of years, independent of Christian faith and religious morality. The speech was not without consequences and caused a major scandal.

His pietist opponents subsequently accused Wolff of atheism; they forced him to resign from his office in 1723 and to leave the city of Halle within 48 hours by order of the Prussian King Friedrich Wilhelm I (Lach 1992b, 121–128).

However, Wolff's speech was also well received and seen as the culmination of a wave of enthusiasm for China that had gripped large sections of the critical European intelligentsia. China played a crucial role in the reorientation of the world view that took place during the Enlightenment, because what was reported from the East fundamentally and lastingly upset the entrenched ideas of history, morality and religion. Wolff countered his opponents' accusation that the Confucians were atheists with the conviction that nature, created by God, was so perfect that one only had to conform to it in order to be a good person. Goodness is achieved through the independent realization of nature and not through external instruction.

The findings recorded in the *Four Books* (Sìshū 四書) and the *Five Classics* (Wǔjīng 五經) provide Wolff with empirical evidence for the assumption that the law of nature can be recognized and obeyed even without revelation. China, "free of all religion," shows in purity "how powerful nature is." Morality is "written in people's hearts" so that "they can see for themselves what is good." Virtue does not require the "fear of an overlord" (Wolff 1720). All external motives for right behavior, as provided by religions, count for little compared to the inner moral feeling and the search for justice and truth that lie within man himself.

Wolff studied the Chinese classics in Noël's translation until his death in 1754, and his entire body of work, especially his series of *Reasonable Thoughts*, is permeated with quotations and allusions to this reading, which can be regarded as evidence of the most fruitful encounter between Western and Chinese philosophy. It is only in recent years that this great mediator between East and West has been rediscovered by researchers. His China speech has been recognized as one of the rare great moments of forward-looking cosmopolitan philosophy.

The Scottish philosopher and historian **David Hume** (1711–1776) firmly opposed the prevailing belief in fixed causal principles and Leibniz's principle of sufficient reason. In his publications *A Treatise of Human Nature* (1739–1740) and *An Enquiry Concerning Human Understanding* (1748), Hume argued that all human ideas were based on sensory perceptions (Hume 1882; 1777).

Following the spirit of skepticism at the time, Hume denied the fundamental principles of causal relationships and concluded that we can only perceive cause and effect if they occur one after the other and are directly related (May 1970). By casting doubt on the existence of causality, Hume shifted the focus to an empiricist theory of knowledge in which the subjective sensory impressions of the individual override the assumption of the universal lawfulness of cause and effect (Losee 2011, 29–35).

In contrast to Hume, the German philosopher **Immanuel Kant** (1724–1804) saw the principle of causality as a necessity that manifests itself in the logical and chronological sequence of time (Watkins 2005; Losee 2011, 37–39). Kant contrasted a causality based on the laws of nature with a causality of free will guided by reason, which he called the categorical imperative. His instruction was published in the *Critique of Practical Reason* in 1788. His "Act in such a way that the maxim of your will can at all times be regarded as the principle of a general law" can be understood as an extension of the principle of cause and effect and at the same time as a fundamental principle for moral behavior. (Kant, *Critique of Practical Reason*, 1, Book 1, § 7, AA V, 30).

In this context with Kant, we should briefly refer to the principle of ethical causality or the ethics of responsibility, which can be found in all world religions (Lucas 1993). In simplified form, this states that evil leads to evil and good leads to good. This means that the principle of causality from the physical world can also be applied to ethical and moral actions, even if the actions go beyond life into future forms of existence. Hans Jonas transferred the idea of Kant's categorical imperative to an ethics for the technological age in his essay *The Imperative of Responsibilty*, when he demands: "Act so, that the effects of your action are compatible with the permanence of genuine human life." (Jonas 1984, part 1, ch. V).

The explosive nature of Kant's writings were made tangible by his *Critique of Pure Reason* (1781) being placed on the *Index of Prohibited Books* by the Catholic Church in 1827, in the wake of neo-scholasticism and the associated rediscovery of the writings of Thomas Aquinas. Kant's motto "Sapere aude," which can be translated as "Have courage to use your own reason" leads back to the Roman poet Horace and shows the power of this motto of the Age of Enlightenment. Kant's work continues to have a strong influence on contemporary philosophers, even in Asia (Palmquist 2010). Móu Zōngsān (牟宗三) is considered to be the most influential Kant scholar in China. His translations of Kant's writings can also be seen as an attempt to bring Western and Chinese philosophy closer together (Chan 2006).

"Nothing is without a reason for why it is rather than is not." (Schopenhauer, 1903, § 5). **Arthur Schopenhauer** (1788–1860) used this simplified motto from Christian Wolff as the starting point for his dissertation *Über die vierfache Wurzel des Satzes vom zureichenden Grunde* (On the Fourfold Root of the Principle of Sufficient Reason), which he wrote at the University of Jena in 1813. For Schopenhauer, this theorem forms the key foundation of all scientific knowledge. Starting with the history of philosophy from Plato and Aristotle, via Cartesius (also known as René Descartes), Baruch Spinoza, Christian Wolff and David Hume to Immanuel Kant, Schopenhauer concluded that credit for establishing the definitive formulation of the theorem "as the main principle of all knowledge and science" should go to Gottfried Wilhelm Leibniz (Schopenhauer 1903, § 9 Leibniz). In order to explain the four components of the theorem, Schopenhauer developed a system of four classes. The first class—the proposition of the sufficient ground of becoming—denotes "vivid, complete, empirical ideas" and represents the physical level of natural science, in which every effect is preceded by a cause or, if a cause is given, must be followed by an effect (Schopenhauer 1903, IV, § 17–§ 25). The second class is governed by the theorem of the sufficient ground of cognition. This concerns abstract ideas and the linguistic-formal level, i.e. presuppositions such as premises that precede subsequent conclusions, i.e. judgments (Schopenhauer 1903, V, § 26–§ 34). The causal relationship between location (position) in space and chronological sequence in time is represented in the third class by the proposition of the sufficient ground of being (Schopenhauer 1903, VI, § 35–§ 39). In the fourth and final class—the proposition of the sufficient cause of action—man stands as a subject who wants something objective, so to speak "the Subject in volition, which is the Object for the Knowing Subject." The cause here would correspond to the motive to want something and the effect would consist of the action to obtain that which is desired (Schopenhauer 1903, VII, § 40–§ 45, here § 40). Schopenhauer now assigns a "subjective correlate" to each of the four classes: understanding (1st class), reason (2nd class), sensuality (3rd class) and the inner sense or self-consciousness (4th class) (Schopenhauer 1903, VII, § 42).

"Everything that can be thought at all can be thought clearly.
Everything that can be said can be said clearly."

Wittgenstein, *Tractatus*, 4.116.

"Whereof one cannot speak,
thereof one must be silent."

Wittgenstein, *Tractatus*, 7.

With these sentences, which appear in chapter 4 and at the end of his *Tractatus Logico-Philosophicus*, written in 1918 and published in 1922, **Ludwig Wittgenstein** (1889–1951) describes two different worlds (McManus 2006). One world can be represented by language and is therefore logically and rationally comprehensible. This world consists of a reasoning based on causal chains and deterministic sequences that leads to exact conclusions. The other world is a world without language. Its contents are visible but cannot be grasped by us conceptually. We do not understand it because language is not sufficient to grasp this world. While the first part seems like the legal conclusion of a long chain of arguments and definitions on the principle of causality, the second part refers to a knowledge beyond reason. A knowledge that eludes our language and logic.

Cause > < Effect
(The View of the East)

知忘是非，心之適也
"When the heart is right,
'for' and 'against' are forgotten."

Chuang Tzu 莊子, 13; Merton, 1965, 112.

The previous chapter outlined the philosophical and historical development of the "Principle of Sufficient Reason". Whether a cause is based on a reason, occasion or condition does not play a significant role, as the decisive factor is the relationship between cause and effect, or the sequence of events and states that relate to each other. For example, an event can lead to a state, which in turn can lead to the next event as an initial position, which in turn leads to a state, and so on. This sequence is encapsulated in the concept of transformation.

The basic idea of dualism, and the element of transformation as a principle of order, resides at the core of ancient Chinese philosophy and its writings (Suzuki 1914, 14). Among the *Four Books* and *Five Classics* (Sìshū Wǔjīng 四書五經), including the *Book of Rites* (Lǐjì 禮記), *Book of Documents* (Shàngshū 尚書), *Book of Songs* (Shījīng 詩經) and *Spring and Autumn Annals* (Chūnqiū 春秋), the *Book of Changes* (I Ching, Yìjīng 易經) occupies a special position.

Before discussing the particular significance of the *I Ching*, the challenge of translating these classics will be briefly addressed. The fundamental problems with the translation of the Chinese classics into Latin by the Jesuit missionaries of the 17th and 18th centuries were the attempts to interpret the content in terms of Christian doctrine (Gernet 2012, see Chapter 1, *Errors and Misunderstandings*, 40–52).

In the 19th and early 20th century, a second wave of translations of the Chinese classics into modern languages took place. Behind this were authors such as the Scottish linguist James Legge with his series *The Chinese Classics* (1861–1872) (*Confucian Analects, the Great Learning, and the Doctrine of the Mean* 1861) or the *Sacred Books of the East* (*The Yî King* 1882; *The Tâo Teh King* 1891) as well as the translations *Tao Te King* 1910 and *I Ching* 1924 by the theologian and sinologist Richard Wilhelm. These translations must be understood in terms of the authors' religious and socio-economic backgrounds. In general, they had a classical humanist education based on Christian values, believed in the principle of causality, grew up in the Industrial Age and were heavily influenced by a form of colonialism promoted by the nation state. Of course, the peculiarities of the Chinese language and thought also played an important role (Zhang 1939; Granet 1963; Hansen 1983; Roetz 2006; Trauzettel 1990).

If one reads the translations of the classical Chinese writings of Lǎozǐ (老子), Kǒngzǐ (孔子), Mèngzǐ (孟子), Mòzǐ (墨子) and Zhuāngzǐ (莊子) against this background, two things stand out. Firstly, all the authors have a philosophy of the way things are. Or in the words of Daisetz Teitaro Suzuki in his *Brief History of Early Chinese Philosophy*:

"The philosophy of the Chinese has always been practical and most intimately associated with human affairs. No ontological speculation, no cosmogonical hypothesis, no abstract ethical theory, seemed worthy of their serious contemplation, unless it had a direct bearing upon practical morality."

Suzuki, 1914, 13.

There is almost no speculation; the world is there and we must live in it. This sets them apart from the philosophers of the West who question many things and are often plagued by doubts.

The second point can be understood from a pragmatic view of the world. The almost excessive use of so-called conditional sentences, which often appear in translation as if-then sentences. A conditional sentence expresses that an action only takes place or would have taken place under a certain condition. Therefore conditions and their consequences are described. This can also take place as a question posed to oneself with a corresponding answer in a fictitious dialogue or as advice on a previously described situation. All these authors have a highly pragmatic attitude towards the world and one can say that there is not "so much of pure philosophy as of moral sayings." (Suzuki 1914, 13). The use of conditional sentences corresponds to the aspect of conveying knowledge through one's own experience and reflection and thus reinforces the content of the statement.

Here are two examples. If we take the updated version of the *Tao Te Ching* (Dàodéjīng 道德經) translated by Richard Wilhelm in 1910 and published in 1998, the following picture emerges: In the 81 sections of the book, 32 conditional sentences are used ("If... , then..."). Just as often, a situation is described and a conclusion drawn or advice given ("Therefore"). Nine times the author asks himself a question and answers it. In the *Doctrine of the Mean* (Zhōngyōng 中庸) attributed to Kǒngzǐ (孔子), we also encounter conditional sentences in 25 places in the 33 chapters.

With this accumulation of conditional sentences, the translations of the classics prove to be a sequence of causal conclusions. However, to deduce from this that the principle of cause and effect disguised as a conditional sentence only found its expression through the form of the translations would have to be investigated and proven in the writings of the other classics. Regardless of this, the writings of the old masters Lǎozǐ (老子),

Kǒngzǐ (孔子), Mèngzǐ (孟子), Mòzǐ (墨子) and Zhuāngzǐ (莊子), and in particular the *I Ching*, still appear today as a compass to assess our behavior in changing situations according to ethical and moral guidelines.

Numerous philosophers and teachers took their inspiration from the *I Ching*, the *Book of Changes*, and created complex models to explain the world, the interplay of visible and invisible (heavenly) forces and our fate. Suzuki describes the *I Ching* as "the most unintelligible, most enigmatical, document ever found in Chinese literature" (Suzuki 1914, 14)—for which there were already over 1,500 commentaries by the end of the 18th century, and has been understood and used in vastly different ways. In the 4th century BCE, scholars such as Shào Yōng (邵雍) regarded the *I Ching* as a manual of divination, while others such as Zhèng Xuán (鄭玄) or Wáng Bì (王弼) endeavoured to interpret it philosophically. For the latter, the *I Ching* was the source material for philosophizing on cosmological, philosophical and political topics.

In Europe, sections of the *I Ching* were first translated into Latin in 1687 in *Confucius Sinarum Philosophus* (Intorcetta et. al. 1687). In his 1697 *Novissima Sinica* (The Latest News from China), Gottfried Wilhelm Leibniz made reference to the *I Ching* (Leibniz 2011). The first complete Latin translation was published in 1834–1839 by the

Jesuit priest Jean-Baptiste Régis; in 1882 a translation into English was made by James Legge.

However, it was not until 1923 that the German sinologist Richard Wilhelm, with the assistance of the scholar Láo Nǎixuān (勞乃宣), created a version that was eventually translated into many languages (Wilhelm 2005; Zhao 2021).

The commentary, in which Wilhelm incorporated quotations from the Bible, ancient Greek writings, numerous Western philosophers and poets such as Johann Wolfgang von Goethe, is worthy of special mention. This was strongly criticized by Wilhelm's contemporaries in the 1920s, but his unusual method revealed numerous parallels in the philosophy of East and West. Wilhelm's achievement lies in describing the ambiguity of the texts in such a way that this ambiguity was preserved and is still stimulating for us today.

Its popular use as an oracle largely fell into disuse as a result of the Cultural Revolution and it is only in recent decades that the *I Ching* has experienced something of a renaissance.

The *I Ching* is the oldest Chinese text, traditionally dating back to the 3rd millennium BCE. It is based on eight three-part half-characters, the so-called trigrams, which in turn are based on Yin and Yang as the starting position. In order to understand the *I Ching*, the interplay of Yin and Yang and thus the aspect of change must be understood, because:

"Change is a predominant characteristic of all activities; and this is caused by the interplay of the male (Yang) and the female (Yin) principle of the universe. Owing to this interaction of these opposite forces, which in the I Ching proper are called chien [qián 乾] and k'un [kūn 坤], and respectively represented by a whole line and a divided line, beings now come into existence, and now go out of it, and a constant transformation in the universe takes place."

Suzuki, 1914, 15–16.

The challenge was to capture this constant change and depict the transformation. A binary model was used for this purpose:

"Change has an absolute limit: This produces two modes; The two modes produce four forms; The four forms produce eight trigrams; The eight trigrams determine fortune and misfortune."

I Ching, transl. by Cleary, 1992, xi.

The eight trigrams or primordial signs (bagua 八卦) are juxtaposed in pairs and often depicted as a kind of compass rose in Taoist cosmology. In the Shuo Gua (說卦), the explanatory section of the I Ching, the eight trigrams are described as follows:

"(The symbols of) heaven [Kien] and earth [Kun] received their determinate positions; (those for) mountains [Gen] and collections of water [Dui] interchanged their influences; (those for) thunder [Zhen] and wind [Sun] excited each other the more; and (those for) water [Kan] and fire [Li] did each other no harm. (Then) among these eight symbols there was a mutual communication. The numbering of the past is a natural process; the knowledge of the coming is anticipation. Therefore in the Yi we have (both) anticipation (and the natural process)."
天地定位，山澤通氣，雷風相薄，水火不相射，八卦相錯。數往者順，知來者逆，是故《易》逆數也。

Legge, 1882, see *Shuo Gua*.

The sequence of trigrams contains a double movement that can emphasize either the passing or the future, depending on how the course of time is read. These eight trigrams can be paired to create 64 hexagrams, which form the foundation of the *I Ching*. Based on the 64 images, which describe 384 situations, a total of 64 x 64, i.e. 4,096 interpretations, can be achieved by utilizing all the lines.

In view of this wealth of possibilities for understanding the past and interpreting what is yet to come, it is understandable that users of the *I Ching* assumed that all possibilities of changes could be captured. What happens in the visible world does not occur by chance, but is rather the manifestation of an idea that has its origin in a superior invisible celestial order.

In this respect, the *I Ching* is an ideal instrument for understanding the principle of cause and effect.

"The Book of Changes also shows that all changes take place according to fixed laws. The Book of Changes contains the view that the whole world of phenomena is based on a polar opposition of forces [...] which bring about all change and transformation. For these forces must not be imagined as dormant primal principles. The view of the Book of Changes is far removed from any cosmic dualism. Rather, these forces themselves are in a state of constant change."

Wilhelm, 2003, *The Tao*, Commentary, I.

While the idea of transformation on which the *I Ching* is based takes place between the two polar, i.e. binary elements of Yin and Yang, the meanings of the 64 hexagrams follow mythological models and ethical rules of behavior from antiquity. Furthermore, there is a connection between the recurring and yet changeable processes (sky) caused by the lunar rhythm and the human being dependent on these natural events (Fiedeler 1988). In the field of tension between these forces, the potential of the *I Ching* can be understood as an experimental simulation, which can help to find one's way in changing conditions in order to make correct decisions.

Cause O Effect

"All truths wait in all things. [...]
(What is less or more than a touch?)"
Walt Whitman, *Song of Myself*, 1855, 30.

In order to visualize the fundamental difference between the interrelated linearity of the principle of cause and effect in the Western understanding and the interwoven and alternating forces in the Eastern understanding, Richard Wilhelm should be quoted again at this point:

"These eight signs [the eight trigrams of the *I Ching*] were taken as images of what was going on in heaven and on earth. The prevailing view was of a constant transition of one into the other, just as in the world there is a constant transition of phenomena into one another. Here we have the decisive basic idea of the changes. The eight signs are signs of changing transitional states, images that are constantly transforming. The focus was not on things in their being—as was mainly the case in the West—but on the movements of things in their change. Thus the eight signs are not images of things, but images of their tendencies to move."
Wilhelm, 1923, V.

After this fundamental difference between West and East has been worked out by Wilhelm, he expands his observation of continuous change to include the possibility of how people are influenced by this and can interact with it through their own actions.

"In addition to the law of change and the images of the changing states, as given by the 64 signs, there is now another one. Each situation demanded a particular way of acting in order to be able to adapt to it. In every situation, one course of action was right, another wrong. Obviously, the right course of action brought good luck, the wrong one bad luck. So which course of action is the right one in each case? This question was the decisive one. [...] When for the first time someone was found in China who was not satisfied with the signs announcing the future, but asked: what should I do? it happened that the book of fortune-telling had to become a book of wisdom."
Wilhelm, 1923, VII.

For Wilhelm, this ongoing process of "change" or "transformation" formed the basis of Chinese philosophy, ethics and religion. As he explains in the preface, the *I Ching* describes how changes take place in humans and in nature. It was only through this step of understanding the given not as inevitable, but as an option that can be influenced by people's own actions, both positively and negatively, that the *I Ching* became the basis for ethical and moral principles for the ruling system and then for society as a whole. Through their behavior, people are responsible for shaping their own destiny and their actions contribute to change. Lao Tzu, Confucius and all subsequent teachers build on this. It is up to people themselves to help determine and organize these changes through their actions. If we do this, we are jointly responsible for the success of our lives. The *I Ching* therefore also serves to stimulate reflection on one's own life and to offer guidelines with which people can control, change and improve their actions. With so much self-responsibility and freedom to determine one's own destiny, it is no wonder that the proponents of the Enlightenment such as Leibniz, Kant and Wolff were so greatly impressed by the Chinese writings and also took up these new ideas in their reflections.

In the *I Ching*, the all-encompassing idea of transformation is at the center. However, the idea that everything is connected to everything else can already be found in the founding myths of the earth. In his *German Metaphysics* from 1720 Christian Wolff explains: "The world is a collection of changeable things that stand next to each other, follow each other, but are connected with each other as a whole." To emphasize this interconnection, Wolff used the term "extended composite." (Wolff, *German Metaphysics*, § 544; *Wolff 2019*, see 5.2 Cosmology).

$$\text{☯}$$

<table>
<tr><td align="center">— —</td><td align="center">———</td></tr>
<tr><td align="center">YIN</td><td align="center">YANG</td></tr>
</table>

8 TRIGRAMS

Earth	Mountain	Water	Wind	Thunder	Fire	Lake	Heaven
坤 (Kūn)	艮 (Gèn)	坎 (Kǎn)	巽 (Xùn)	震 (Zhèn)	離 (Lí)	兌 (Duì)	乾 (Qián)

8 x 8 combinations of Trigrams = 64 HEXAGRAMS.

Based on the 64 hexagrams, which describe 384 situations, a total of 64 x 64, i.e. 4,096 interpretations, can be achieved by using all 6 lines.

Lake Hexagram 49 (see p. 74)
Fire 革 (Gé) = change

By this Wolff means a cosmology, the study of the world as a whole which is depicted in either a general sense or through the interaction of macrocosm and microcosm, and also how these are in a state of eternal change with each other. Although Wolff recognized the interplay of "changeable things," he did not doubt the principle of causality for a moment, as already explained (Wolff 1720; Wolff 2019, see 5.1 Ontology).

It was not until more than two centuries later that studies were carried out that brought the *I Ching* into the focus of the natural sciences. For the context of our exhibition, the writings of **Carl Gustav Jung** (1875–1961), who described the influence of the *I Ching* on the development of modern depth psychology, and developed the idea of synchronicity from this, should definitely be mentioned here (Jung 2023). The founder of analytical psychology was extremely interested in the myths and mysteries of past cultures. Apart from his patients, he used them to research archetypes and develop his theories of the collective unconscious and the principle of synchronicity. Jung became familiar with the *I Ching* through the translations of James Legge and later Richard Wilhelm. A friendship developed between Wilhelm and Jung, so that the latter not only contributed the foreword to the English translation of the *I Ching*, but also wrote an obituary after Wilhelm's

death, which was published in 1930. In this obituary, Jung used the term synchronicity publicly for the first time:

"The science of the I Ching is not based on the causal principle, but on a hitherto unnamed principle— because it does not exist among us—which I have tentatively labelled the synchronistic principle."

Jung, 2011, 63.

By distinguishing the *I Ching* from the causal principle and describing it as a "previously unnamed and non-existent principle," Jung makes it clear that, separate from the millennia of development in the West, an independent principle has emerged in the East that fundamentally differs from the Western model. In the foreword to his 1952 publication, Jung warns the reader of the "still obscure area, which is, however, of the greatest importance in terms of worldview" (Jung 2023, 8). Jung refers to causality as a "philosophical principle that underlies our view of natural law" and concludes that if "the linking of events is of a nature other than causal under certain circumstances," this calls for a different "explanatory principle". (ibid). Furthermore he goes on to note that such non-causal events can occur sporadically and are then regarded by scientific research as a "reaction disorder" or coincidence. But what would happen if non-causal events were to occur

more frequently and simultaneously as a "meaningful coincidence"? (ibid). Would these non-causal events still be perceived as something connected and related to each other?

Jung describes synchronicity as the temporal coincidence of an inner event in the form of an idea, vision or dream with an external, physical event, which is a manifested reflection of the inner event. For him, synchronicity by no means replaces the causal principle, but rather he sees synchronicity as an extension of the causal principle in that an event contains a meaningfully related antipole. Synchronicity gains its symbolic power through the perception of the relationship between the two events. The second external event is understood as a resonance of the first internal event and causes the person concerned to derive consequences for their own behavior.

What does the principle of synchronicity mean for working with the *I Ching*? Based on the 64 images, which describe 384 situations, a total of 64 x 64, i.e. 4,096 interpretations, can be achieved by using all the lines. The question asked before using the *I Ching* receives a possible answer through the arrangement of the hexagram, which is interpreted by the person who asks the question and leads to a change in behavior. Subsequent external events ultimately reinforce the impression that this new behavior is recognized as meaningful.

The use of the *I Ching* thus changes from an instrument for consulting an oracle to the application of ethical guidelines that can significantly influence one's own behavior.

In conclusion, by following the usual clichés, one can state that the West's thinking is based on logos, reason and the principle of causality, while the East focuses on feelings and the holistic. However, this distinction is now far too short-sighted and oversimplified. The West also has its own holistic view of the world and the East has its rationalistic thinking.

What is certain is that the success of modern technology has helped to break the world down into calculable units, allowing rational, causal, digital, calculating thinking to prevail. This applies to both East and West.

Rational-logical thinking has an exclusive character. There is only one truth and it is either/or. From this conflict between thesis and antithesis, the synthesis emerges victorious and makes one forget the opposites of thesis and antithesis. But truth has no claim to exclusivity; it is also contradictory and challenging. This dialectic of competition is contrasted with a dualism of simultaneity, interdependence and dependent relationships. Thesis and antithesis are not mutually exclusive, but are related to each other in a fruitful interplay. The balance of forces takes the place of exclusivity. This balance can also be understood as unity in contradiction. Considering the processes of nature, chance takes its place alongside causality and rational-logical thinking is only one way of understanding the world.

It is the task of man to keep these opposing forces in balance in order to tread the path of the center. This realization is the basis of classical Chinese philosophy and is aptly expressed in the short foreword to the *Book of Rites* (Lǐjì 禮記) by the philosopher Zhu Xi 朱熹 (1130 -1200):

"Leaning to no side is called centre, allowing no wavering is called moderation. Centre denotes the right path that all under heaven should follow, measure denotes the principle that applies to all under heaven."   Wilhelm, *Li Gi*, 2015, 9.

Exclusivity is thus replaced by a balance of power. This balance can also be understood as unity in contradiction. Causality is replaced by synchronicity. In addition to logical, linear thinking, there is thinking in images, in constellations and relations. Instead of either/or, we find both/and. The *I Ching* as well as the writings of Lao Tzu, Confucius, Mengzi and Zhuanghzi are by no means to be understood as dogmatic teachings, but rather as instructions for a lifelong training of the self that is true to life.

The *Book of Changes* is still justified today as a universal guiding principle for responsible behavior, as the *Book of Rites* (Lǐjì 禮記) so aptly puts it: "He who can be creatively active like heaven and earth forms a great trinity with heaven and earth." (XXII).

"The next stage is to cultivate the disposition for good and thus come into possession of the truth. Truth becomes reality, and reality becomes visible. Visibility creates clarity, and clarity sets things in motion. Movement creates change, change becomes reorganisation. Only those who possess the highest truthfulness on earth can reshape something."

Wilhelm, *Li Gi*, 2015, XXIII.

How the principle of causality and its various manifestations can be translated into the languages of this exhibition is the subject of the second part of this publication.

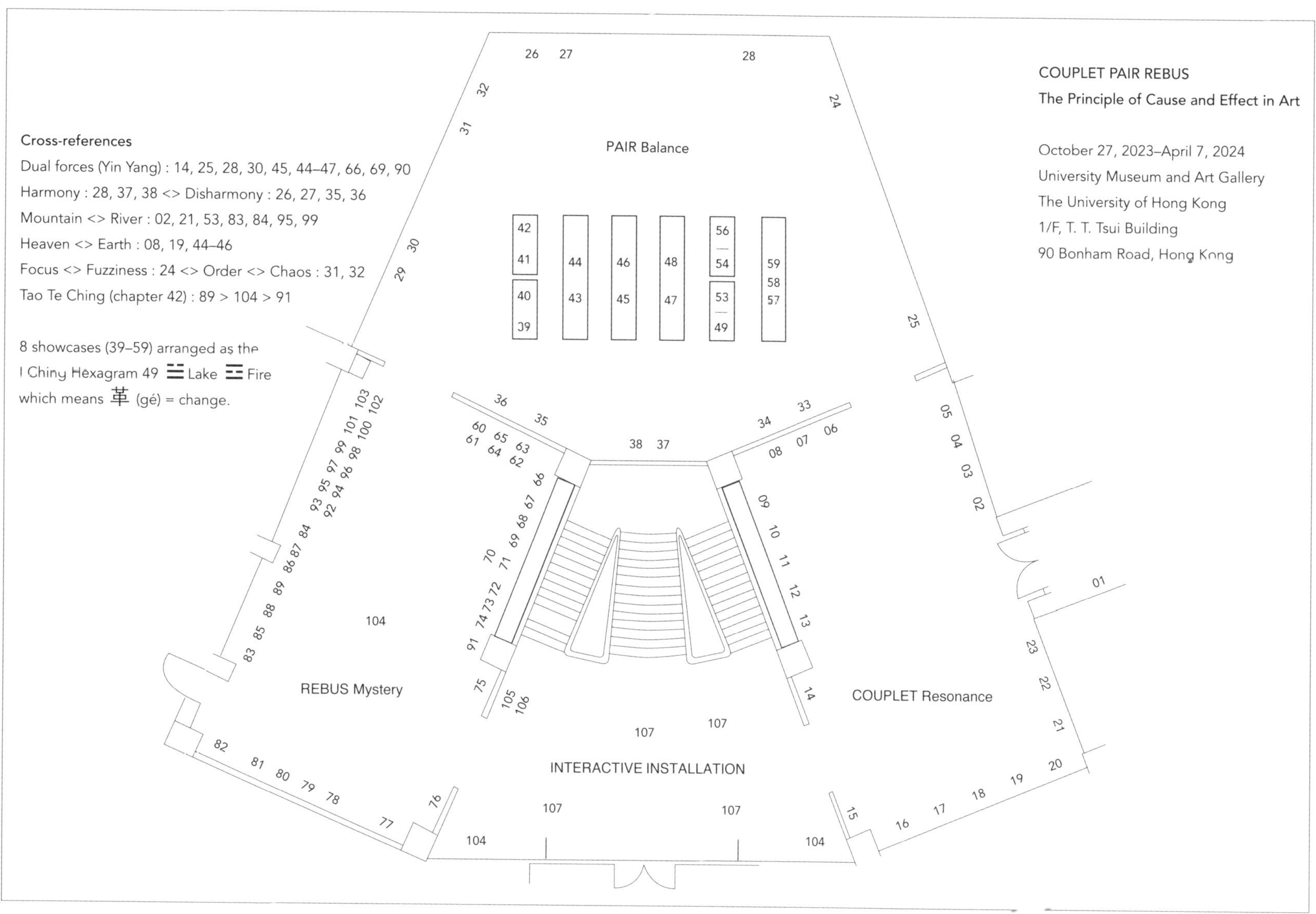

COUPLET PAIR REBUS
The Principle of Cause and Effect in Art

October 27, 2023–April 7, 2024
University Museum and Art Gallery
The University of Hong Kong
1/F, T. T. Tsui Building
90 Bonham Road, Hong Kong

Cross-references
Dual forces (Yin Yang) : 14, 25, 28, 30, 45, 44–47, 66, 69, 90
Harmony : 28, 37, 38 <> Disharmony : 26, 27, 35, 36
Mountain <> River : 02, 21, 53, 83, 84, 95, 99
Heaven <> Earth : 08, 19, 44–46
Focus <> Fuzziness : 24 <> Order <> Chaos : 31, 32
Tao Te Ching (chapter 42) : 89 > 104 > 91

8 showcases (39–59) arranged as the
I Ching Hexagram 49 Lake Fire
which means 革 (gé) = change.

PAIR Balance

REBUS Mystery

COUPLET Resonance

INTERACTIVE INSTALLATION

COUPLET Resonance

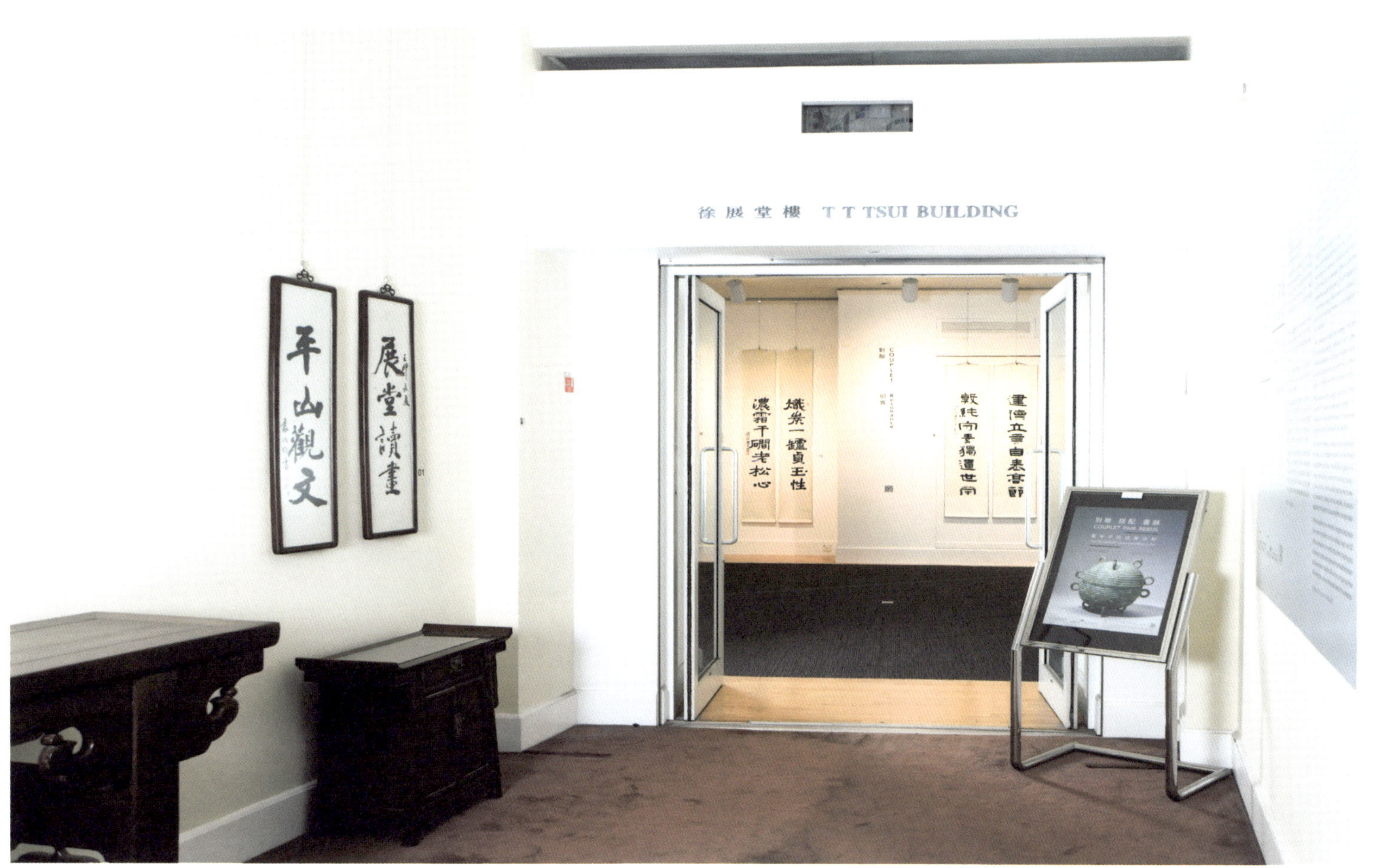

^ COUPLET

01
YUEN Hung Shue
袁鴻樞

Introduction

"Antithesis and parallelism in thought and speech, by virtue of their quality of symmetry, are aesthetically satisfying to the human mind." Lai, 1976, V.

With these lines, MA Meng describes the fascination emanating from couplets in his introduction to the first English-language publication on the subject. T.C. LAI, the publication's author, also points out in his foreword that

"Couplets are emblematic of Chinese thought, or at least the Chinese way of thinking. They are poetic and lend themselves (however grudgingly) to translation." Lai, 1976, XIV.

Antithesis, parallelism and symmetry are the structural principles of couplets, while the prerequisite of understanding the Chinese way of thought is the primary challenge. The fascination with "regulated verse" (Lùshī 律詩) appears in texts as early as the *Book of Documents* (Shūjīng 書經), the *Classic of Poetry* (Shījīng 詩經) and the *Elegies of Chu* (Chǔcí 楚辭), among others. TO Yeuk Hung 杜若鴻—expert in Chinese poetry—takes a closer look at the history and structure of couplets in his following excursus.

Ever since Liú Xié 劉勰 (465–522) published his critical work, *The Literary Mind and the Carving of Dragons* (文心雕龍), couplets have been recognized as a literary genre in China (Liu 1983).

To explain the basic structure of couplets, Liu Xie wrote:

"Nature, when endowing living things with limbs, does so in pairs. Man's imagination, in its function, never sees things in isolation. In the creation of rhetorical language, the mind shapes and polishes a hundred thoughts that cluster around it, and by balancing the high with the low, produces antithesis and parallelism without apparent effort."

Lai, 1976, VI.

However, it is not only the couplets that follow a natural and, in a certain sense, cosmic order, but also the 50 chapters of *The Literary Mind and the Carving of Dragons*, which are structured according to the numerological principles of the *I Ching*.

What accounts for the popularity of couplets? MA Meng identifies three characteristics. Many of the monosyllabic characters are well suited to creating antithetical constructions, and Chinese words often have an emotional quality as images. This visual language has an immediate effect on the reader, who also becomes a viewer, "[...] namely that in these compositions, the unique Chinese art of calligraphy finds a happy match in the language itself." (Lai 1976, XIII). Except for the oldest form of Chinese writing, oracle bone script (Jiǎgǔwén, 甲骨文), the other common styles of Chinese calligraphy are represented in this publication.

Couplet number 16 (fig. 16) by **YIK Yuet Sek** 易越石 (1912–2007) is written in the style of stone-drum script (Shígǔ Wén 石鼓文), based on the *Stone Drum Poems* (Shígǔ Shī 石鼓詩) of the late Spring and Autumn or early Warring States period.

Numbers 03, 09, 12 and 17 (figs. 03, 09, 12, 17) are written in seal script (Zhuànshū 篆書), which was widely used during the Qin dynasty and is characterized by a symmetrical structure of thin, even lines executed with balanced movements.

During the Han dynasty, the clerical script (Lìshū 隸書) was frequently used for the creation of official records and documents. It is a simplified version of seal script; numbers 13, 14 and 20 (figs. 13, 14, 20) are made in this style.

The numbers 19, 21, 22 and 23 (figs. 19, 21, 22, 23) are written in cursive script (Cǎoshū 草書), which is also known as grass script. This developed towards the end of the Han dynasty (220 CE). The individual strokes within a character are simplified and shortened, often resulting from a single brush movement.

Running script (Xíngshū 行書) or semi-cursive script, used for number 10 (fig. 10), came into fashion immediately after the Han dynasty. Running script is considered the most popular form for everyday use thanks to its simplicity and legibility. Individual characters can be joined by connecting strokes and individual strokes can sometimes even be omitted or condensed.

Standard or regular script (Kǎishū 楷書) also emerged after the fall of the Han dynasty in 220 CE. The characters of this commonly used script are balanced and easy to read, but can also take on sophisticated and complicated forms, as seen in numbers 01, 02, 04, 05, 06, 07, 08, 11 and 18.

Number 15 is the exception, which was written by SHE Xueman (佘雪曼) in the Shoujin style of Emperor Huizong of Song.

The 23 couplets displayed at UMAG can be roughly divided into two categories: nature and aphorisms. Behind both of these are philosophical observations which can be categorized as observations and experiences made using nature or as the reproduction of knowledge by teachers and writers. The transitions between the two groups are fluid. The exhibition space containing the couplets was designed as a reading room.

Two tables from the Qing dynasty, each with four stools, were placed in the room so that visitors could study the couplets in peace and allow the messages to sink in.

A guest book placed on a table invited visitors to try their hand at writing couplets or simply to leave their observations as comments in the exhibition. Some of the visitors, especially some of the younger ones, used the guest book to make drawings.

During the Qing dynasty, the writing of couplets was so widespread that the test of a person's education was often assessed by giving them a suitable line to complete. Couplets are read from top to bottom, first the right column (head) and then the left (tail). The number of characters in both sections must be the same. However, the content of the characters in the head is usually the direct opposite of the content in the tail characters. The syntactic arrangement of words and phrases must match exactly in both. One challenge that is unfortunately omitted in the translation, and in the form of the text, is the pronunciation of the characters. The tone of the words in the two sections can be different, but the sounds can also be similar.

In addition to parallelism, both the idea of antithesis and the principle of causality are elements of the couplets. When examining the couplets, it becomes apparent that some artists have used calligraphy to transpose couplets handed down from earlier poets, as is the case with numbers 11, 12, 14, 15 and 22, while other calligraphers have composed and drawn their own lines.

In some, such as 03, 04, 05, 06 and 15, there are references to historical persons, geographical places, past events, famous literary works and paintings. Others, such as numbers 07, 09 and 10, read like moral doctrines. And couplets such as numbers 02, 08, 13, 16, 17, 19, 20 and 23 hide their often philosophical message behind a deliberately ambiguous statement. Numbers like 11, 12, 18 and 22 describe observations of nature.

The fact that decoding couplets requires considerable prior knowledge can be seen in number 15 (fig. 15). SHE Xueman 佘雪曼 (1903–1993) has selected a work by the calligrapher and seal carver DENG Shiru 鄧石如 (1743–1805) and written it in the Shoujin style of Emperor Huizong of Song. The head on the right contains the names of famous sites, along with the sun, moon and rain. The left side contains the names of famous literati and mentions the titles of some of their poems, paintings and historical events. Read together, this couplet is a tribute to nature and to those who use nature as inspiration for their works of art:

> "Powerful heroes with great strength come
>
> from north of the Huanghe River [Yellow River]."
>
> "Great literature and good calligraphy come
>
> from the region of Wu."

These lines used by LI Zanzhi 黎湛枝 (1870–1928) in his couplet in running script (fig. 6), refer to the chapter Kung Yung [Zhong Yong], also titled "The State of Equilibrium and Harmony" in the *Book of Rites* (Lǐjì 禮記):

> "Dze-lû [Zi-lu] asked about fortitude.
>
> The Master said, 'Do you mean the fortitude of the South, the fortitude of the North, or your fortitude?
>
> To show forbearance and gentleness in teaching others; and not to return conduct towards one's self which is contrary to the right path: this is the fortitude of the South, and the good man makes it his study.
>
> To lie under arms, and to die without regret: this is the bravery of the North, and the bold make it their study.
>
> Therefore, the superior man cultivates a (friendly) harmony, and is not weak; how firm is he in his fortitude! He stands erect in the middle, and does not incline to either side; how firm is he in his fortitude! If right ways prevail in (the government of his state), he does not change from what he was in retirement; how firm is he in his fortitude! If bad ways prevail, he will die sooner than change; how firm is he in his fortitude!'"

Legge, 1885, vol. 2, book XXVIII, 15–19.

While Legge speaks of "fortitude" in his translation and the term "strength" is found in Wilhelm, Sturgess translates 強 as "energy." Despite the inconsistent translations, all three authors agree on one thing: "He [the superior man] stands tall in the middle, and does not incline to either side."

The superior man, or the noble one, as he is called by Wilhelm, stands for someone who does not bend in any direction and represents the center's moral-ethical point of view. In the spirit of the exhibition, balance is once again the theme.

In times of crisis, we need the soldiers and military, in times of peace we need culture; i.e. artists, poets and musicians. No state can exist if one of these groups is missing. While the strong are not mentioned in the following text, the noble are described in great detail. The superior man describes a person who is helpful and good. The superior person stands for moral integrity. It is about strength of character and exemplary behavior and formulates a value system that combines duties towards oneself and others through timeless virtues that are desperately needed today.

In number 14 (fig. 14), the antithesis becomes acutely apparent. Here, the painter and calligrapher FANG Zhaoling 方召麐 (1914–2006) quotes a couplet by HAN Wo 韓偓 (ca. 842 or 844–ca. 923), a poet of the late Tang dynasty:

> "My spirit is as pure as the stove's burning coal."
>
> "My heart is as firm as the pine tree in deep frost."

What beautiful images and strong contrasts: spirit vs. heart, pure vs. firm, burning coal vs. deep frost. The clarity of mind, which burns brightly, contrasts with the heart's firmness, which overcomes even the strongest frost. Or is it perhaps someone who is no longer accessible to logic because he is furious with anger or someone who is emotionally cold and heartless. Taken on their own, both point to extremes. It is only in the combination of elements that the noble one described becomes visible, which succeeds in bringing mind and heart into balanced harmony to resist both heated discussions and emotional coldness. The pine tree is considered a symbol of a long life, and also of constancy and self-discipline, which requires a clear will and a strong heart. Together with plum and bamboo, it is one of the three friends of winter (Eberhard 1983, 153–154).

The principle of cause and effect is well illustrated in number 21 (fig. 21). The artist **TING Yin Yung** 丁衍庸 (1902–1978), also known as the "Matisse of the East" for his colorful paintings, was known for drawing highly expressive calligraphy.

> "So much wind and rain in a cup of wine."
>
> "Ten thousand miles of rivers and mountains in my heart."

In the upper part of the head, wind and rain blur the ink. In the center, as a single drop of falling rain, and at the bottom, as an implied vessel containing the wine.

On the other side of the tail a river is visible through the two banks, while in the case of the mountain, an arduous path to the summit. This multiplicity of one thousand contrasts with the one. And the heart acts like a reflection of the wine. What at first glance has nothing to do with the other in terms of content turns out to be a finely tuned couplet in which knowledge made and reflected through experience resides at the center. Just as the right mix of sunny, windy and rainy days helps the grapes ripen to produce an exceptional wine, overcoming the challenges of our lives, known as rivers and mountains, helps us gain sufficient experience throughout our lives to achieve wisdom and serenity. The metaphor of the image of rivers and mountains is reflected in the works of **FUNG Yee Lick Eric** 馮以力 (fig. 83) and **LI Jing** 李淨 (fig. 84) in the third exhibition room, REBUS. The latter is located in the visual axis opposite the couplet of **TING Yin Yung**.

The art of reading couplets is to discover the multi-layered meanings of the unwritten in the space between the head and tail, and for most of the couplets, the observation that MA Meng aptly described applies: "Read as a whole, the lines have a force, derived from the antithesis, which it is enough to appreciate." (Lai 1976, X).

Through antithesis, two opposing points of view emerge in the couplets as individual statements, and the interplay of the two results in a third position that is accessible to the reader. This forms the totality of the two statements. One could almost assume that the unlocking of the message is a procedure that is described in a reverse form in chapter 42 of the *Tao Te Ching*:

> "The Tao produced One; One produced Two;
>
> Two produced Three; Three produced All things."
>
> Legge, 1891, book XVIII, Kung Yung, 42.

In the exhibition this process is visualized in the axis of the works by **THÍCH Nhất Hạnh** 釋一行禪師 (fig. 89), **Joseph LEUNG Mong Sum** 梁望琛 (fig. 90), and **Christoph DAHLHAUSEN** (fig. 91). But here, it is the Head and Tail as the two antitheses of the Yin and Yang that make One, the Invisible, visible as a common thing arising from the two. And together the two form the three from which the ten thousand things finally come, as it is written in the *Tao Te Ching*.

In a figurative sense, ten thousand things could also be used to describe all the experiences and insights that the readers of the couplets bring with them. It is only through the process of reading the two parts and interpreting them through their own experiences that the space between is filled with life and the messages become comprehensible.

In addition to their concentrated form, the couplets also captivate with the timelessness of their content, as the messages can be deciphered by future generations. The prerequisite for this is that the viewer sees him/herself as a resonance, a response of the call of the couplet and engages in the inspiring play of antitheses as a synergy.

TO Yeuk Hung 杜若鴻

The Aesthetics of Chinese Couplets

Literary Pearls:

From Talismans to Couplets

The earliest known couplets (Duìlián 對聯) in Chinese culture have been traced to the Han dynasty (202 BCE–9 CE, 25–220 CE). According to historical records, the practice of writing couplets began in the Eastern Han with individuals posting "Peach Talismans" written on peach wood boards (Táofú 桃符) during the Spring Festival. The name of celestial figures such as Shén Tú (神荼) and Yù Lěi (鬱壘) were inscribed and hung on door gates to ward off evil spirits. Shén Tú and Yù Lěi were two gods celebrated for their ability to drive away plagues.

This custom shifted after the Five Dynasties and Ten Kingdoms (907–960 CE), with the rise of the Hou Shu kingdom (934–965 CE). The Hou Shu emperor, Mèng Chǎng (孟昶, 919–965), is said to have written the couplet:

新年納餘慶；嘉節號長春
"The New Year is filled with celebrations, the festival is called Long Spring."

By the time of the Tang (618–907 CE) and Song (960–1279 CE) dynasties, couplets had become extremely popular and their forms had grown quite diverse. People regularly used the format to write regulated poems which expressed a range of emotions. The jaw couplets (3–4 sentences) and neck couplets (5–6 sentences) in the rhymed poems of Dù Fǔ (杜甫, 712–770) are regarded as model forms by later generations. Later on, literati used cleverly opposed tones and rhythmic phrases to form couplets that demonstrated their literary ability and wisdom.

Though writing couplets became a common way for the literati to communicate with each other, the folk custom of hanging talismans during the Spring Festival remained well into the Northern Song dynasty. Wáng Ānshí (王安石, 1021–1086), the poet, philosopher and famed prime minister of the Northern Song (960–1127 CE), offered the following couplet for New Year's day:

千家萬戶曈曈日；總把新桃換舊符
"Ten thousand households with bright days ahead, replacing old peach talismans with new charms."

During the Ming (1368–1644) and Qing (1636–1911) dynasties, the subject matter of couplets gradually became more secular and focused on daily life. Spring Festival couplets (Chūnlián 春聯), congratulatory couplets (Hèlián 賀聯), elegiac couplets (Wǎnlián 輓聯) and other related formats permeated everyday life. According to historical records from the Ming and Qing dynasties, couplets were quite common in the early Ming period.

When Ming emperor Zhū Yuánzhāng (朱元璋, 1328–1398) ascended to the throne and established Nanjing as the capital, he issued a decree that during the Spring Festival, every household should affix couplets on both sides of their doors or hall pillars. Couplets placed on pillars are commonly referred to as Yínglián (楹聯).

破虜平蠻 功貫古今人第一；
出將入相 才兼文武世無雙。
"His military achievements transcend
all eras and rank him first among men.
As a general and prime minister
his talents remain unmatched."

Hanging talismans and posting spring couplets signify the desire to ward off disaster by preparing for times of misfortune and welcoming good fortune, happiness and longevity, with the hope that the upcoming year will be better than the previous.

Even in today's more modern and commercially oriented communities, couplets continue to play a significant role. Merchants seek prosperity and wealth through popular couplets such as

生意如春意；財源似水源
"Business like the vitality of spring,
wealth flows like a river."

Visiting a department store will reveal an abundance of themed couplets, highlighting how they have evolved into a phenomenon within Chinese culture.

Form and Function of Couplets

A Chinese couplet is a literary form composed of two corresponding and parallel sentences arranged in a pair. The two sentences contain an equal number of Chinese characters, maintaining a well-balanced rhythm and presenting a concise antithesis, all while exuding a distinct poetic flavor.

In traditional society, couplets were typically featured during the Lunar New Year, weddings, birthdays and at other special occasions where people used them to convey blessings, celebrations and praise. In addition, couplets were used as a form of dialogue between literati and scholars, as well as literary exchanges and cultural displays.

A key aspect of a couplet is antithesis, where the two sentences correspond rhythmically; they also must utilize the same type of prosody and the tones must be in opposition to each other so that the words create a symmetrical relationship. It is generally accepted that prosody has the greatest effect on rhythmic beauty.

The sentences also must have the same or similar structure, such as an equal number of Chinese characters and opposite parts of speech, to form a balanced construction. This requires the parallel alignment of nouns, verbs, adjectives, quantifiers and vocables.

Moreover, prosodic features such as poetic rhythm, emotional states, intonation and stress are the "invisible hands" that trigger the couplet's beauty. Utilizing poetic modes of prosody and presenting them through rhythmic recitation is one of the most effective ways to create and demonstrate the aesthetics of couplets. This complements the technical approach of pure grammatical or rhetorical analysis as demonstrated in a couplet (fig. 14) by FANG Zhaoling (方召麐, 1914–2006) using a poem of Han Wo (韓偓, ca. 842 or 844–ca. 923).

熾炭/一鑪/貞玉性；濃霜/千碉/老松心。
2/2/3；2/2/3 in prosody

1. burning – heavy
2. charcoal – frost
3. one – thousand
4. stove – valleys
5. pure – old
6. jade – pine
7. character – heart

"My spirit is as pure as the stove's burning coal.
My heart is as firm as the pine tree in deep frost."

The meaning of the sentences must be similar, or in opposition to each other, and should read so that the words' meanings present a symmetrical relationship and form an aesthetically appealing construction. Based on their formal beauty, couplets often encompass profound meanings, incorporating simultaneous references to nature, philosophy and enlightenment. This provides an allegorical beauty to the thoughts being expressed through words:

芝蘭君子性；松柏古人心
"Irises and orchids are the nature of the sages.
Pines and cypresses are the hearts of the ancients."

As this couplet (fig. 20) by an anonymous author and calligraphed by LI Jing 李淨 (*1972) demonstrates, couplets often feature Chinese characters related to natural scenery or historical events presenting a rich tapestry of beauty. We also can find this in the embroidered calligraphic panel (fig. 18) by WENG Tonghe (翁同龢, 1830–1904):

雲蒸山骨秀；花孕樹身濃
"Steaming clouds that rise from the hills illustrate the spirit and resonance of graceful mountains.
Flowers nourish luxuriant trees."

Based on the combination of formal beauty and profound meaning, couplets frequently exude a specific poetic flavor. This charm and appeal impart a sense of aesthetics to the words. In summation, the literary features of couplets are reflected in the beauty of their form, profound meaning, allegorical symbolism and poetic imagination.

The Beauty of Symmetrical Balance

The resonance and balance of a couplet reflects a symmetrical beauty. In terms of form, the couplet requires that the words have an equal number of Chinese characters, opposing parts of speech and a well-balanced rhythm. This symmetrical relationship forms a balanced aesthetic.

Secondly, both sentences of the couplet require an identical rhythm and opposing tones. The other requirement is the use of contrasting levels and oblique tones in parallel to uphold the rhythm. In particular, the final Chinese character of the couplet's first line should use an oblique tone while the second line uses a level tone. Such a symmetrical pairing of rhythm creates the harmony of Yin (陰) and Yang (陽).

Finally, the couplet's two sentences must correspond in meaning. This symmetrical form can evoke an appreciation for the conceptual content. The beauty of couplets is realized through the symmetrical relationship between form, rhythm and meaning. This balance evokes integrity and harmony.

How to Write a Couplet

Though writing couplets is inherently content-specific, the importance of individual skill is crucial.

Choose a suitable theme: Couplets are generally used to express blessings, describe nature and explore thoughts. Before writing, you must choose a subject for the theme.

Pay attention to meaning: Couplets are meant to bear profound meaning, often containing references to nature, philosophy and education. Close attention should be paid to presenting the deeper meaning to establish ideological depth and value.

Choose beautiful words: When writing couplets, the choice of Chinese characters is extremely important. Each character must be precise, corresponding in meaning and poetic nature.

Pay attention to the number of words and structure: The couplet's two phrases must contain the same number of Chinese characters, similar or relative parts of speech, and have the same or similar structure to create a sense of harmony.

In addition, pay attention to the antithesis of level and oblique tones. The antithetical lines of the couplet require the same rhythm and antithesis so that the words will present a sonically symmetrical relationship.

Writing couplets requires a certain level of

literary achievement and cultural literacy. Attention must be paid to the selection of Chinese characters, the number and structure of words, rhythmic confrontation, profound meaning and allegorical symbols.

Consider DENG Shiru's 鄧石如 (1743–1805) couplet (fig. 15), which was written by SHE Xueman 佘雪曼 (1908–1993). This masterpiece combines nature, geography and rhythm. Various connotations such as literature and thought are presented in an ideal format.

Interaction between Couplets and Calligraphy

There is an inextricable relationship between couplets and calligraphy. The formal beauty of couplets and the artistic beauty of calligraphy share common elements. Both require artists to consider format and meaning and to express emotion and talent through the use of writing brush and ink. In the following couplet in cursive script (fig. 19) by SUN Xingge 孫星閣 (1897–1996), the style of the calligraphy follows the words and looks like a flying dragon or dancing phoenix—free and unrestrained.

花放水深處；龍飛鳳舞時
"Flower blossoms in deep water.
Dragon flying while the phoenix dances."

Calligraphy is a crucial element of any couplet.

The calligraphy must be beautiful, smooth, rigorous in structure and harmonious in layout. Therefore, the calligraphic style directly affects a couplet's artistic value and aesthetic feeling.

Secondly, calligraphers often use couplets to demonstrate their artistic achievements and talents. When writing couplets, calligraphers need not only strength and spirit, but also skillful arrangement and various styles such as Cursive Script, Running Script and Regular Script to express their talent and creativity. All five main styles of Chinese calligraphy are represented in the exhibition. These are, following the chronological order of appearance: Seal Script (Zhuàn shū 篆書), Clerical Script (Lìshū 隸書), Cursive or Running Script (Cǎoshū 草書), Semi-Cursive Script (Xíngshū 行書), and Standard Script (Kǎi shū 楷書). Couplets and calligraphy are in a relationship that complements and promotes each other. Couplets need the assistance of calligraphy and calligraphy requires couplets to present their artistic value. Both are regarded as central elements of traditional Chinese culture. In the interweaving of calligraphy and couplets, people experience the profound heritage of rich and colorful forms of artistic interaction.

Realms of Mystery

The Chinese characters in couplets are often representative symbols of both natural scenery and ideological thought. These symbols typically carry profound and symbolic meanings that evoke a sense of mystery between words and images. Couplets are considered a mysterious form with multiple layers of meaning.

The first of these layers is moral spirit. Couplets often contain profound meaning related to nature and enlightenment, inspiring contemplation, cultivating moral sentiment and leading people to delve into the cultural layers. Due to the poetic aesthetics inherent in couplets, they have the power to spark imagination and appreciation for their mysterious and lofty thoughts, as shown in this calligraphy in Clerical Script (fig. 13) by ZHANG Huaqing 張華慶 (*1959):

建德立言自表高節；敦純守素獨遺世榮
"To establish noble principles
through eloquent speech.
To remain modest and frugal
so as to leave behind worldly glory."

The second layer of mystery refers to artistic beauty. The rhythm and aesthetic beauty derived from antithesis hold a specific charm that can illuminate a balanced point of view and parallel beauty between divergent objects. Together, these layers can assist individuals in comprehending the pursuit of artistic life, along with the beauty of nature and Chinese thought.

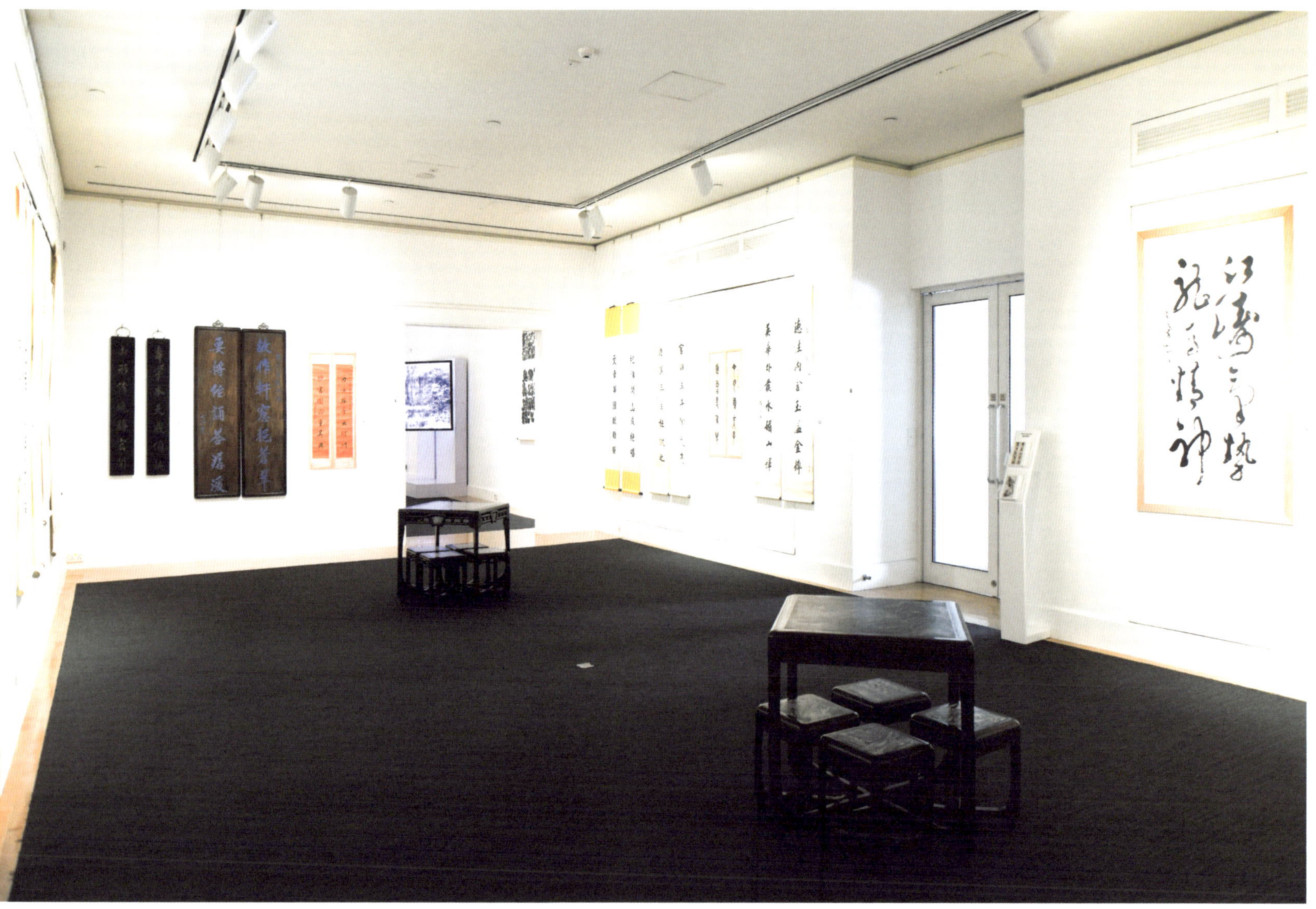

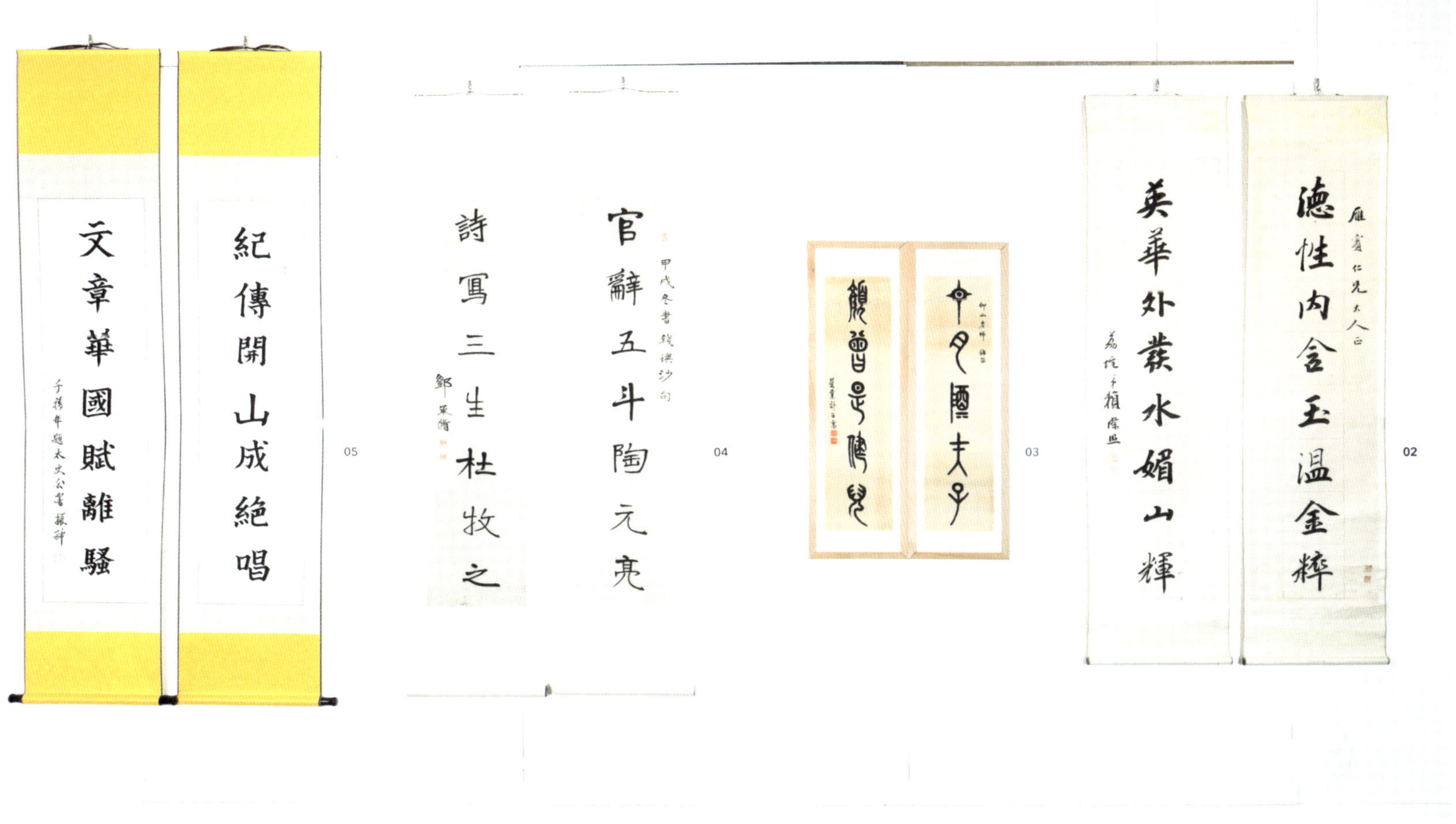

05

TU Chen Tsui

杜振醉

04

DENG Chengxiu

鄧承脩

03

JI Zigao

計子高

02

LAI Jixi

賴際熙

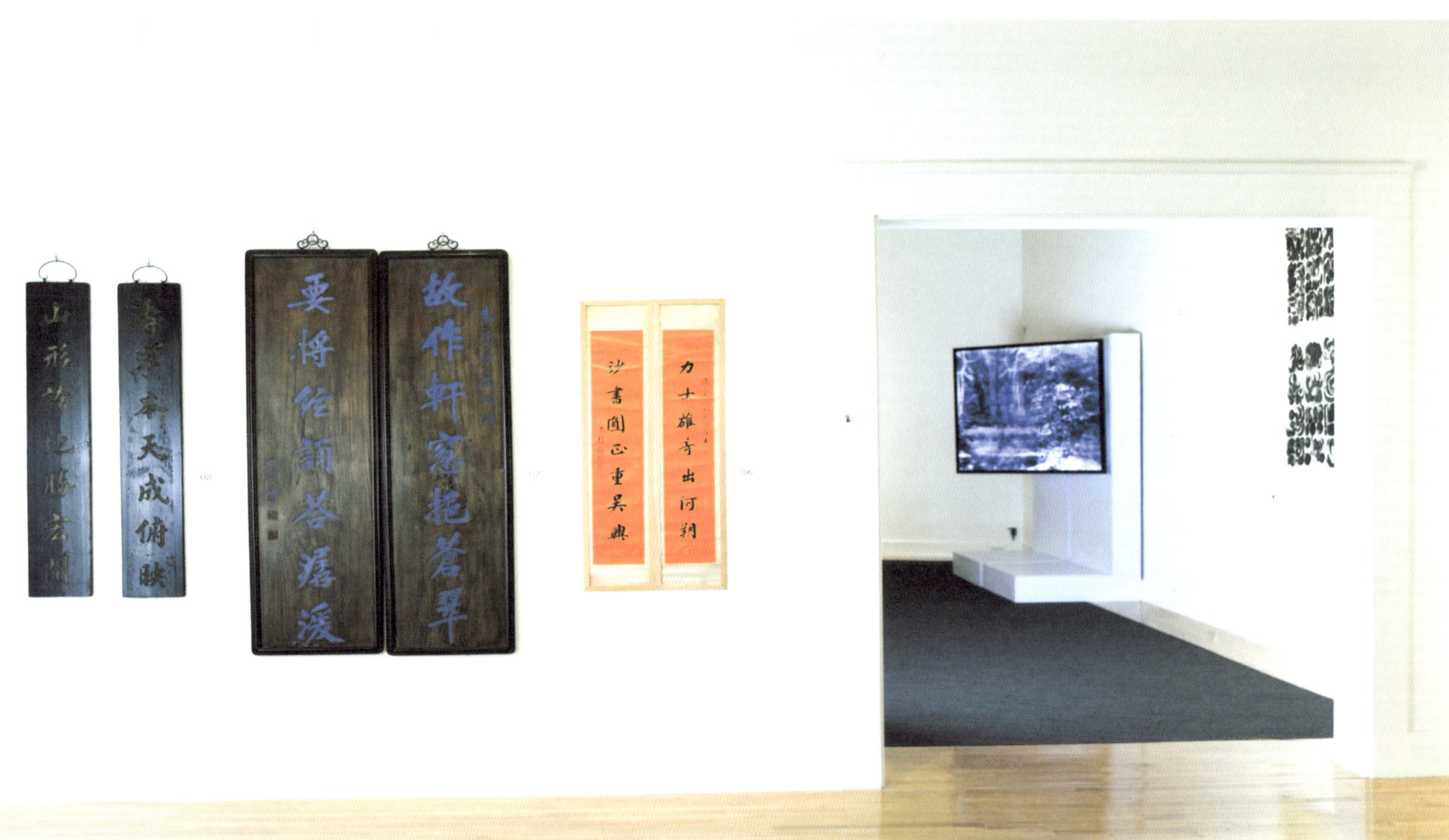

08	07	06	24	25
Artist Unknown	ZHANG Zhidong	LI Zhanzhi	Tobias KLEIN	LI Ki Kwok Victor
佚名	張之洞	黎湛枝	簡鳴謙	李其國

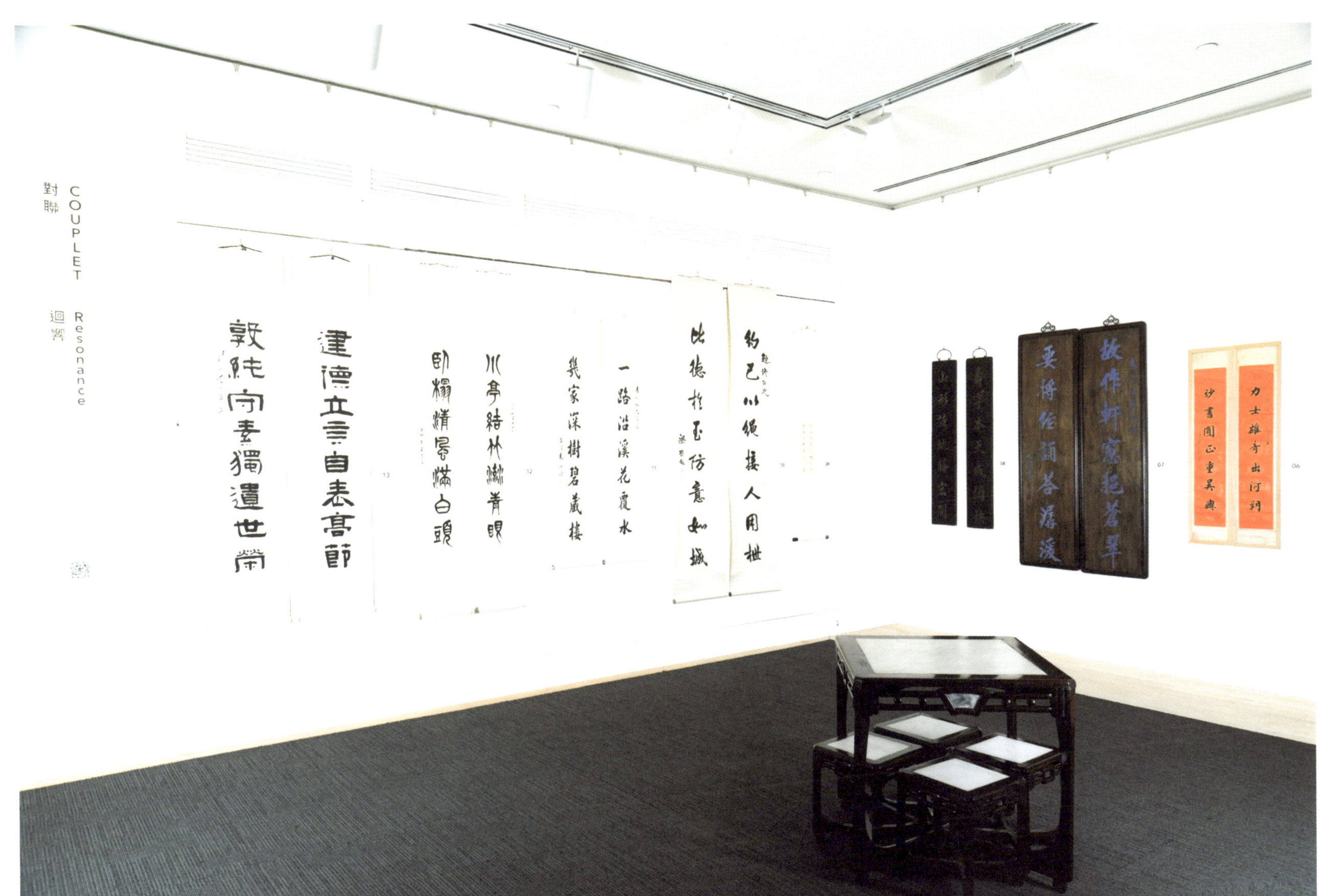

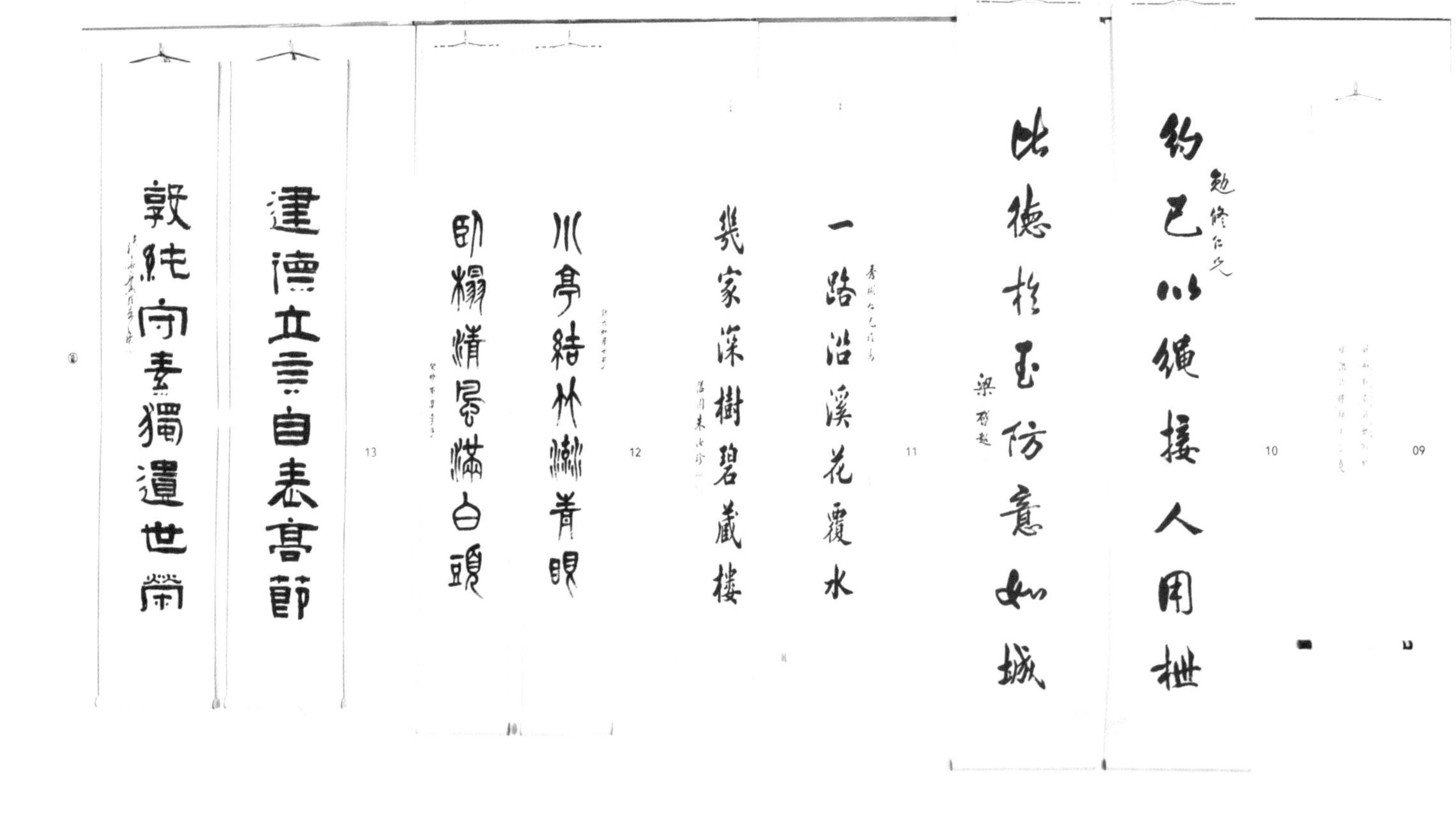

13	12	11	10	09
ZHANG Huaqing	LI Jing 李淨	ZHU Ruzhen 朱汝珍	LIANG Qichao	JAO Tsung-i
張華慶	TANG Yin 唐寅	YUAN Jiagu 袁嘉谷	梁啟超	饒宗頤

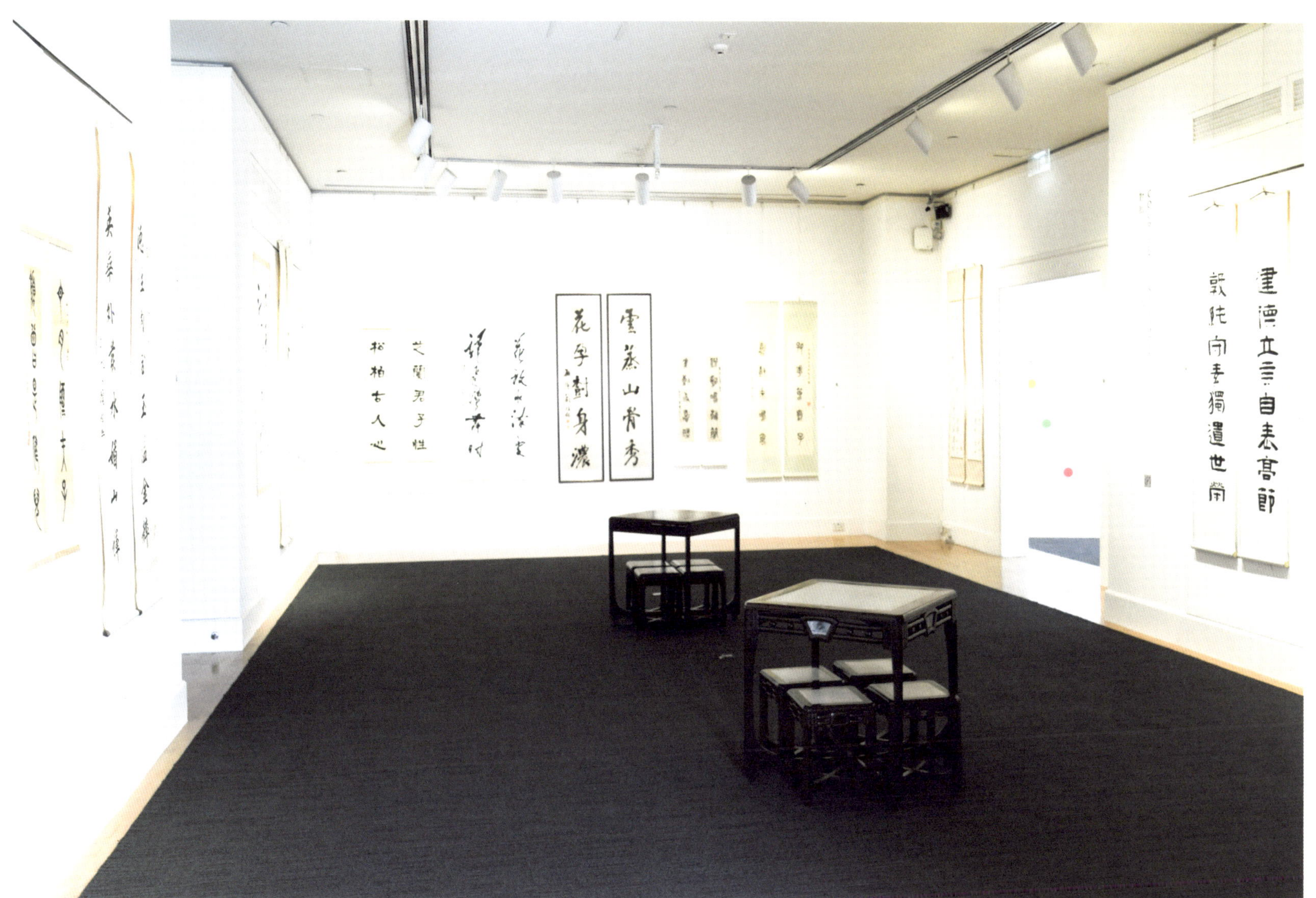

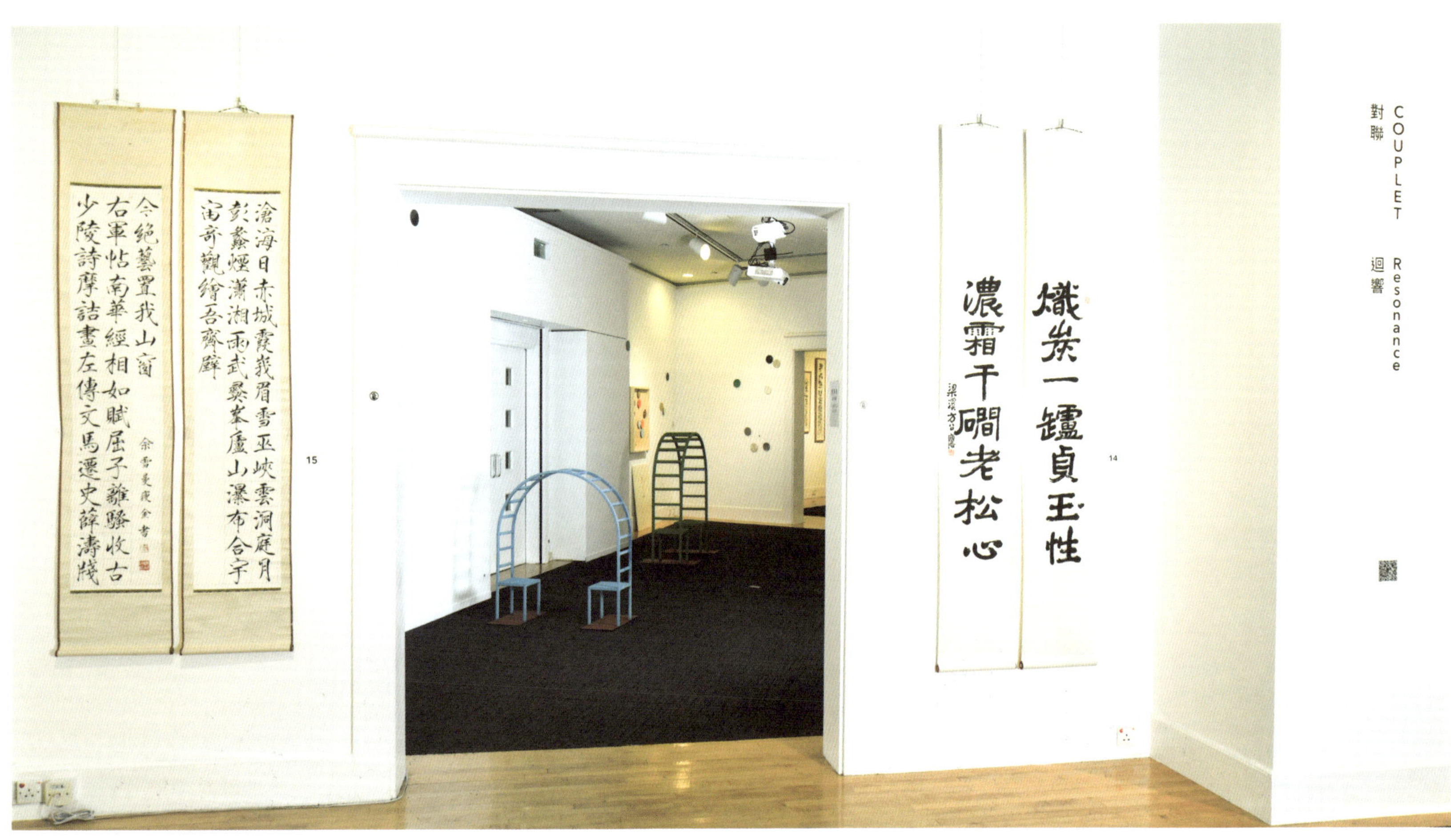

^ INTERACTIVE INSTALLATION

15

SHE Xueman 佘雪曼

DENG Shiru 鄧石如

107

Debe SHAM

岑愷怡

104

Christoph DAHLHAUSEN

14

FANG Zhaoling 方召麐

HAN Wo 韓偓

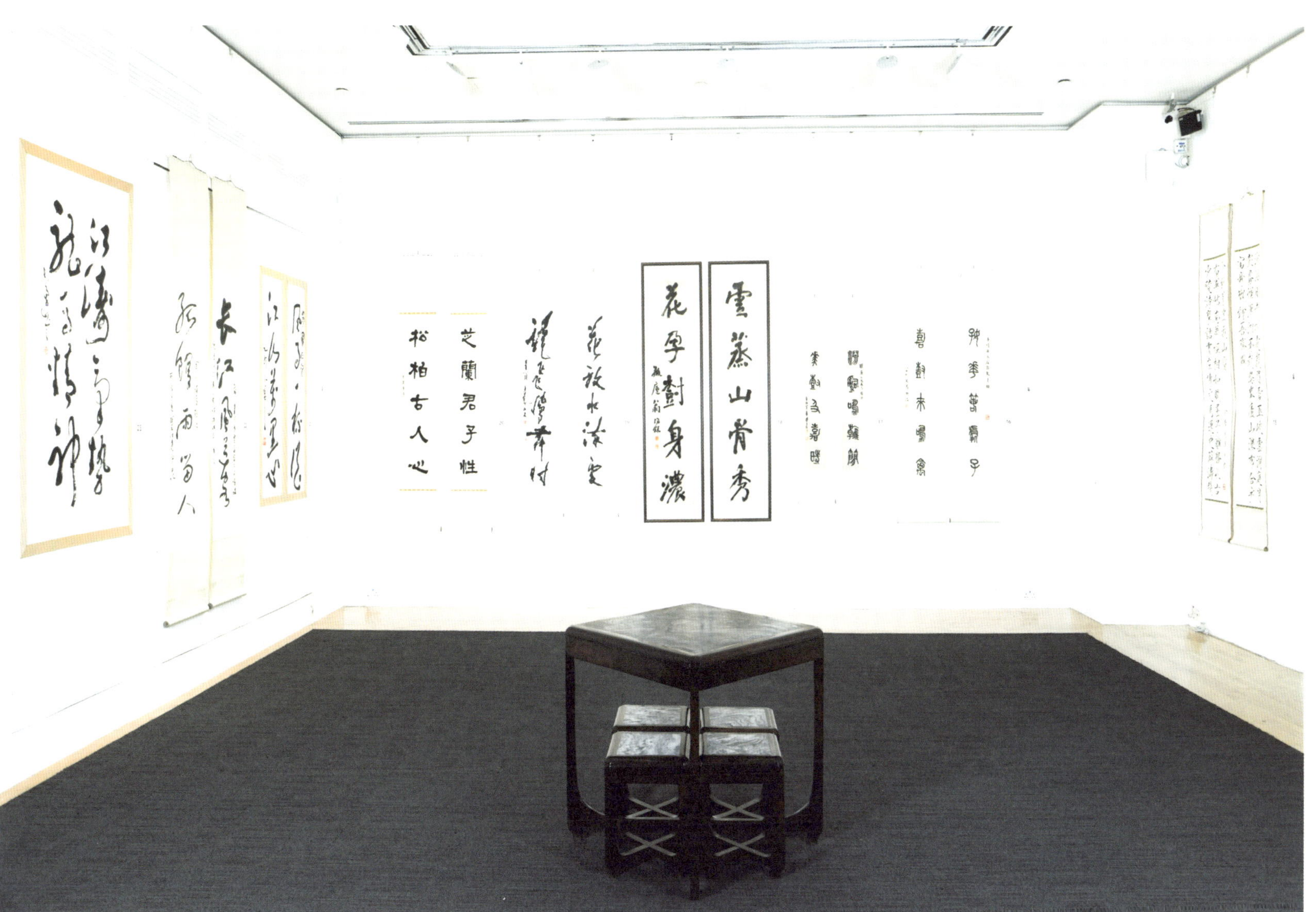

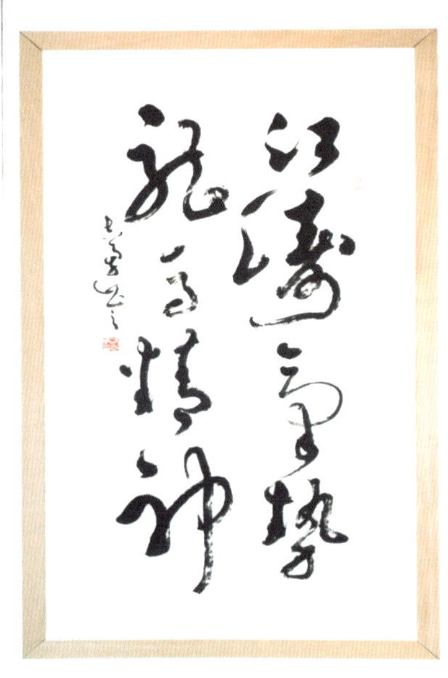

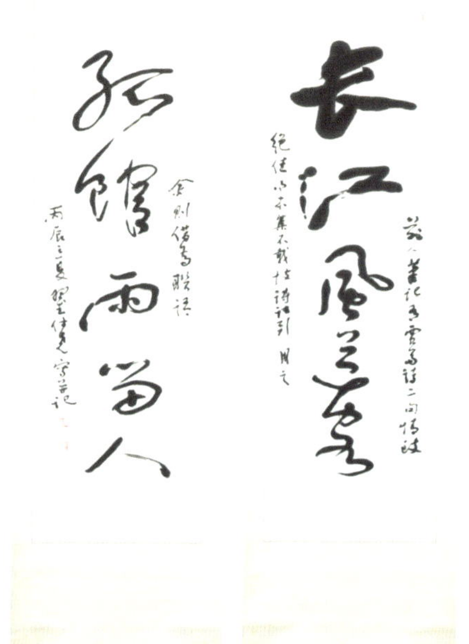

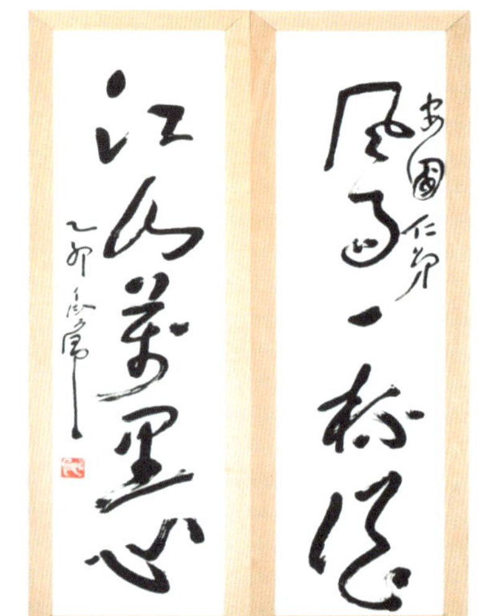

23

FANG Zhiyong

方志勇

22

JAT See Yeu 翟仕堯 |

JIA Dao 賈島

21

TING Yin Yung

丁衍庸

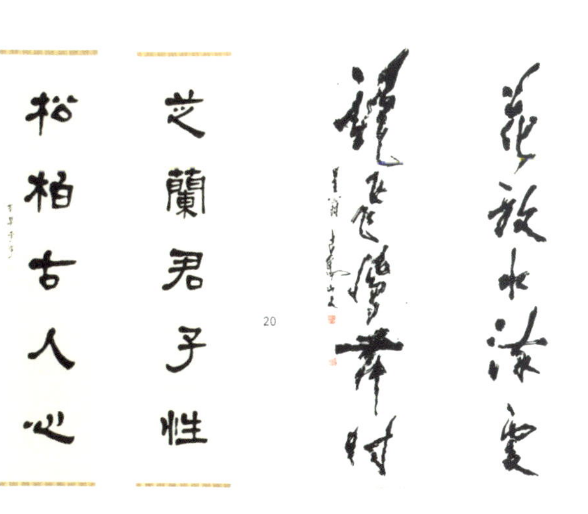

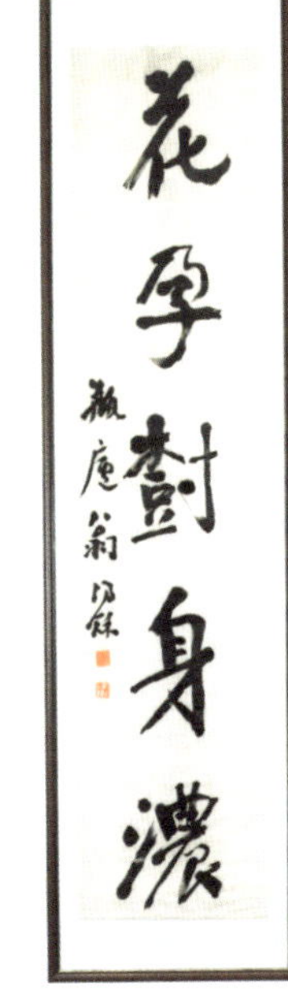

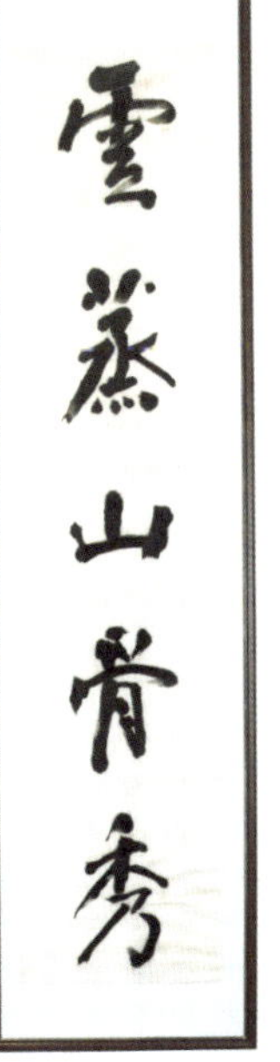

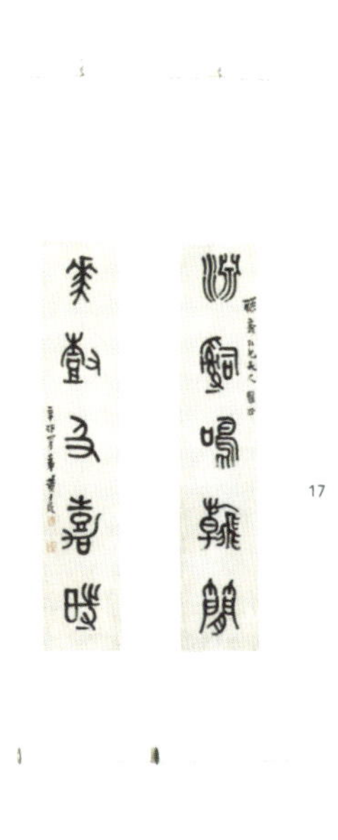

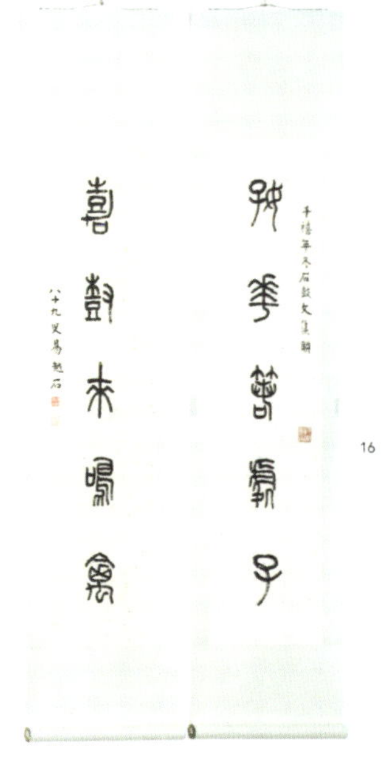

20

LI Jing

李淨

19

SUN Xingge

孫星閣

18

WENG Tonghe

翁同龢

17

HUANG Shiling

黃士陵

16

YIK Yuet Sek

易越石

COUPLET

List of Works

平　1
山　2
觀　3
文　4

Ping　1
Shan　2
read　3
article　4

"Read books in
Fung Ping Shan Library."

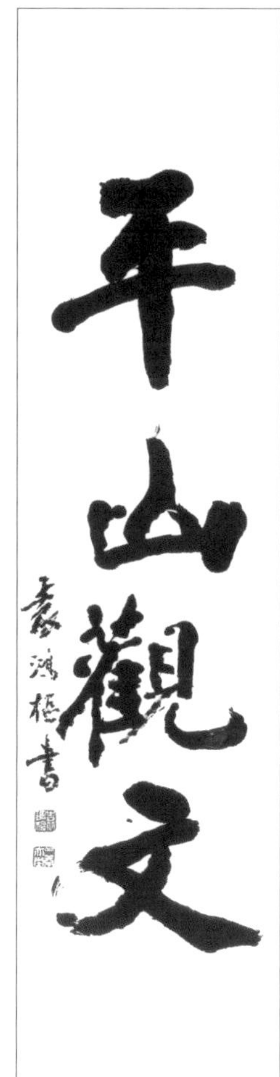

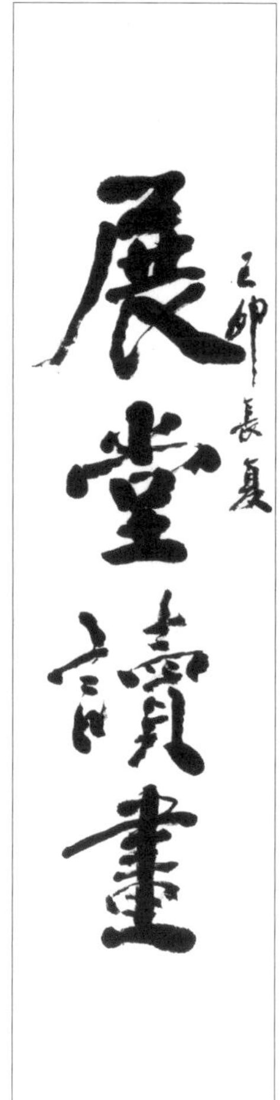

1　展
2　堂
3　讀
4　畫

1　Tsin
2　Tong
3　appreciate
4　painting

"Appreciate paintings in
Tsui Tsin Tong Building."

01

YUEN Hung Shue 袁鴻樞 (1910–2012) | Couplet in Regular Script | 1999 | Vertical scroll, ink on paper | Each L 100 x W 25 cm

HKU.Ca.2015.2144 a, b | Gift of YUAN Hongshu

英 1
華 2
外 3
發 4
水 5
媚 6
山 7
輝 8

glamorous 1
aura 2
external 3
spread 4
water 5
beautiful 6
mountain 7
shiny 8

"The aura spreads out like water
and shines like a mountain."

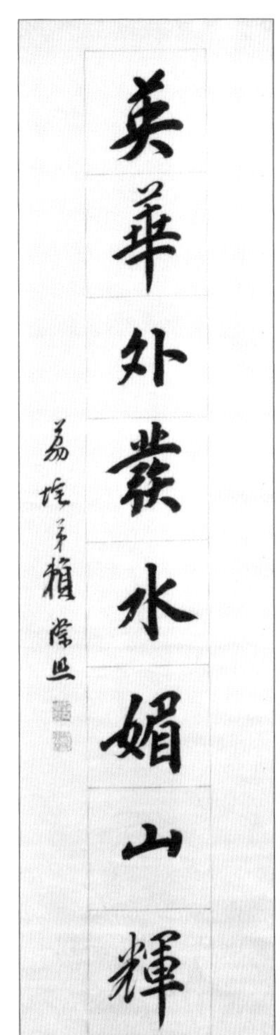

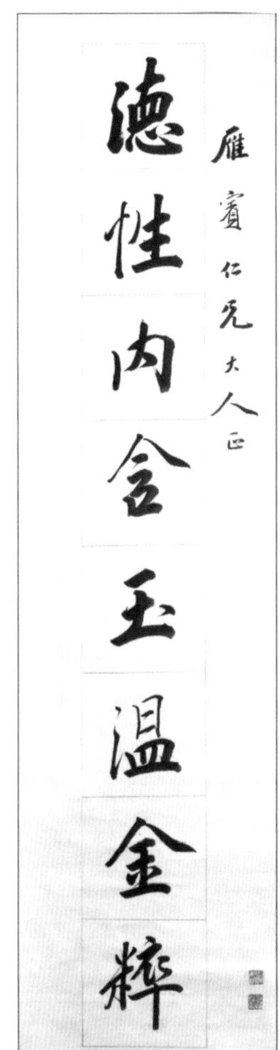

1 德
2 性
3 內
4 含
5 玉
6 溫
7 金
8 粹

1 moral
2 personality
3 internal
4 contain
5 jade
6 warm
7 gold
8 pure

"The inner virtue is warm like jade
and pure like gold."

02

LAI Jixi 賴際熙 (1865–1937) | Couplet in Regular Script | Late 19th/early 20th century | Vertical scroll, ink on paper | Each L 150 x W 40 cm

HKU.Ca.2015.2132 a, b

顏 1
曾 2
是 3
健 4
兒 5

[student name] Yan Hui 1
[student name] Zeng Shen 2
is 3
gentleman 4
guy 5

"Yan Hui and Zeng Shen
are like sons."
[Confucius' students]

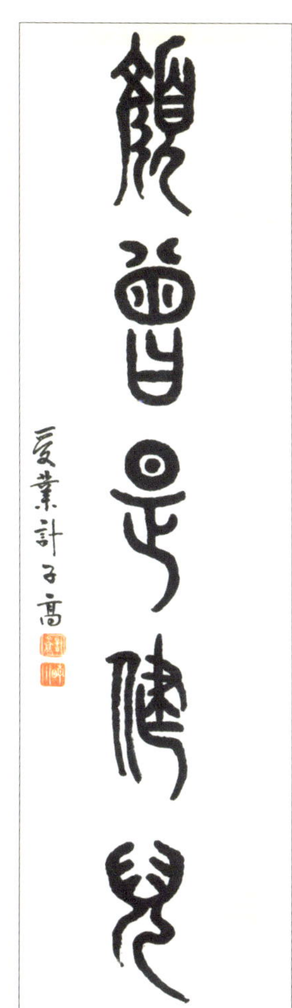

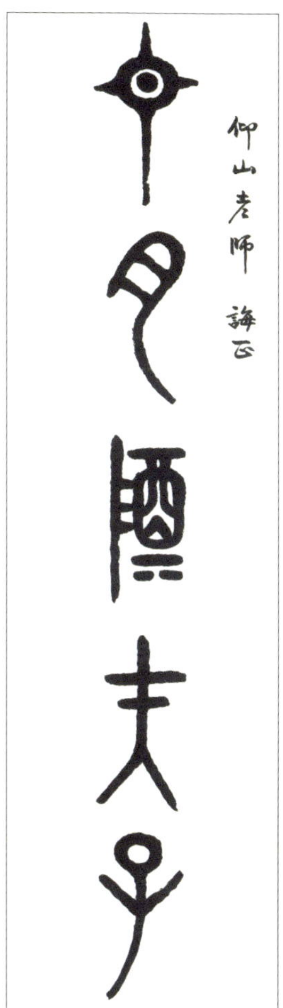

1 日
2 月
3 猶
4 夫
5 子

1 sun
2 moon
3 like
4 literati
5 respectful man

"Sun and moon
are like the master."
[Confucius]

03
JI Zigao 計子高 (1910–1984) | Couplet in Seal Script | 20th century | Vertical scroll, ink on paper | Each L 86 x W 22 cm
HKU.Ca.2015.2125 a, b

詩 1
寫 2
三 3
生 4
杜 5
牧 6
之 7

poetry 1
compose 2
three 3
life 4
Du Muzhi [poet's name] 5
Du Muzhi [poet's name] 6
Du Muzhi [poet's name] 7

"The poetry of Du Mu
spans the past,
present and future."

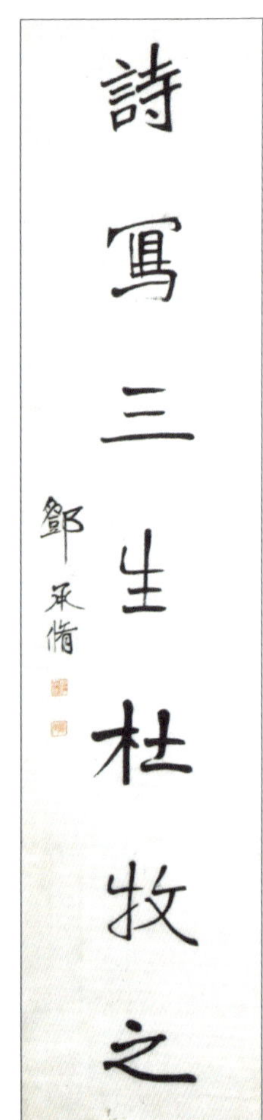

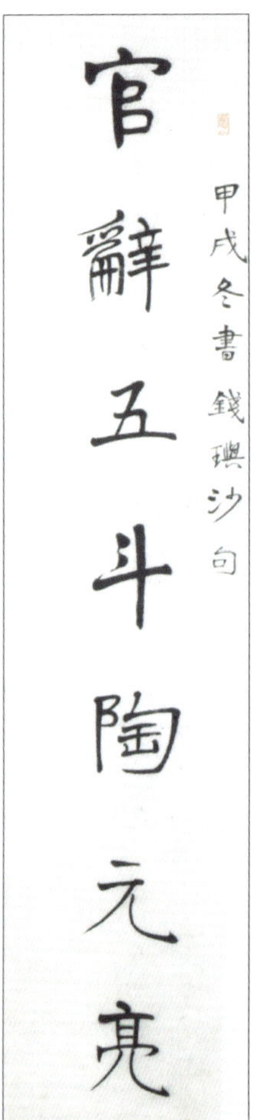

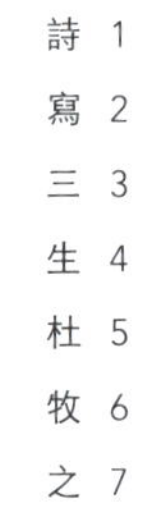

1 官
2 辭
3 五
4 斗
5 陶
6 元
7 亮

1 officer
2 resign
3 five
4 Chinese peck [to measure grain]
5 Tao Yuanliang [poet's name]
6 Tao Yuanliang [poet's name]
7 Tao Yuanliang [poet's name]

"Not even for five pecks of grain would
Tao Yuanliang
withdraw his resignation."

04

DENG Chengxiu 鄧承脩 (1841–1892) | Couplet in Regular Script | Late Qing dynasty (1644–1911) | Vertical scroll, ink on paper | Each L 137.5 x W 31.4 cm

HKU.Ca.2012.1972 a, b | Gift of TANG Cho Fung and LEUNG Wai Yee

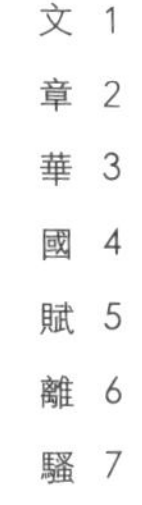

文　1
章　2
華　3
國　4
賦　5
離　6
騷　7

article　1
structure　2
decoration　3
nation　4
express　5
Li Sao　6
Li Sao　7

"Eloquent words praise
the nation
in the poem Li Sao."

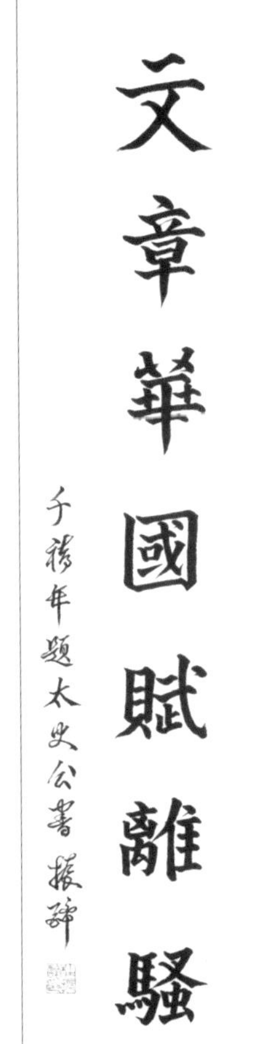

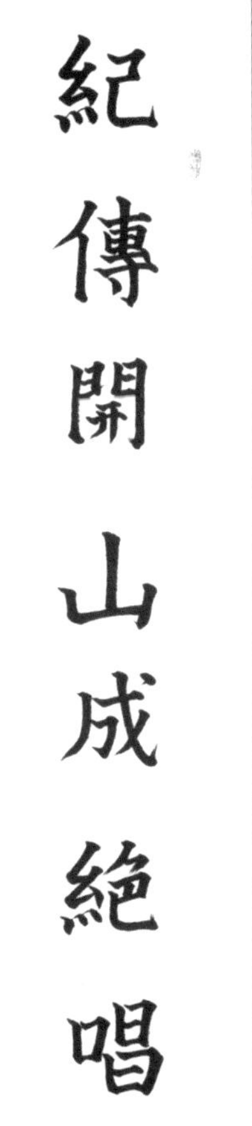

1　紀
2　傳
3　開
4　山
5　成
6　絕
7　唱

1　history genre based on
2　biography
3　open
4　mountain
5　accomplishment
6　the best
7　product

"Past chronicles lay bare
the mountains,
singing the glories of history."

05
TU Chen Tsui 杜振醉 (*1942–) | Couplet in Regular Script | 2000 | Vertical scroll, ink on paper | Each L 136 x W 33 cm
HKU.Ca.2023.2644 a, b | Gift of TU Chen Tsui

妙 1
書 2
圓 3
正 4
重 5
吳 6
興 7

good 1
calligraphy 2
circular 3
regular 4
repeatedly appearing 5
Wuxing 6
Wuxing 7

"Great literature and good calligraphy come from the region of Wu."

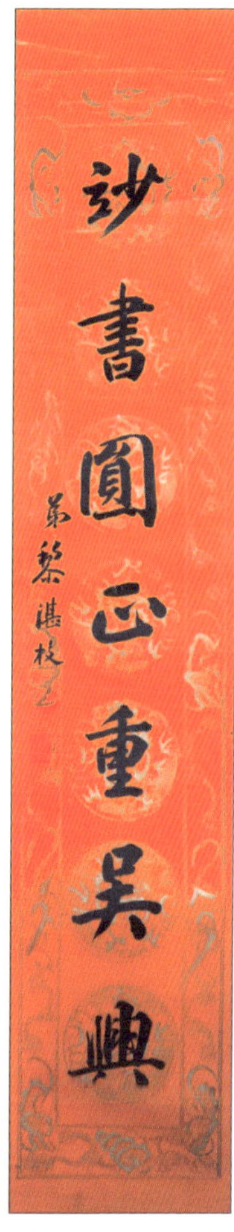

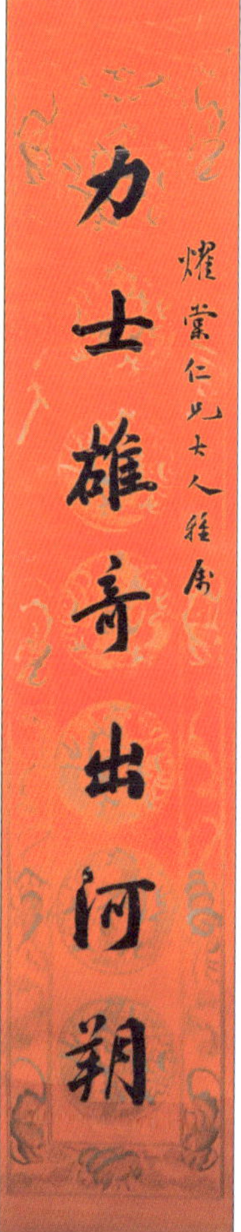

1 力
2 士
3 雄
4 奇
5 出
6 河
7 朔

1 powerful
2 hero
3 heroic
4 great
5 come from
6 Huanghe River
7 north of Huanghe River

"Powerful heroes with great strength come from north of the Huanghe River." [Yellow River]

06

LI Zhanzhi 黎湛枝 (1870–1928) | Couplet in Regular Script | Late Qing dynasty (1644–1911) | Vertical scroll, ink on paper | Each L 101 x W 20 cm

HKU.Ca.2015.2138 a, b

要　1
將　2
絃　3
誦　4
答　5
潺　6
湲　7

want to　1
will　2
string　3
recite　4
respond to　5
sound of slowly flowing water　6
sound of slowly flowing water　7

"To play the strings
one must first learn
the sound of flowing water."

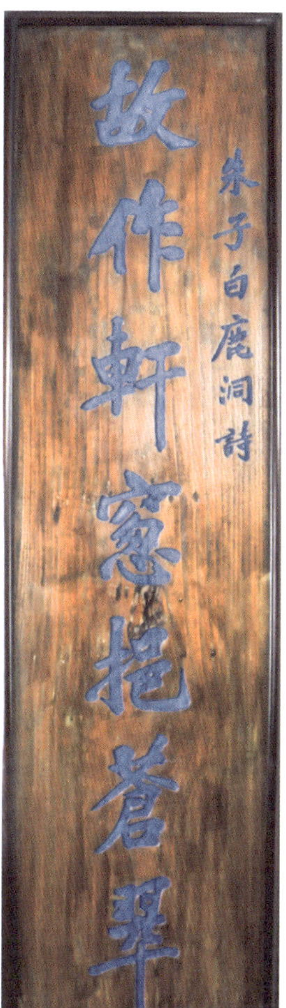

1　故
2　作
3　軒
4　窗
5　挹
6　蒼
7　翠

1　pretend
2　act
3　balcony
4　window
5　ladle out
6　dark green
7　bluish green

"To exhaust the green of nature,
one must leave
the balcony window open."

07
ZHANG Zhidong 張之洞 (1837–1909) | Couplet in Regular Script | Late Qing dynasty (1644–1911) | Wood, blue color | H 167 x W 43.5 x D 1.2 cm / H 173 x W 49 x D 2.5 cm
HKU.W.2024.2657 a, b

山 1
形 2
誇(跨) 3
地 4
勝 5
宏 6
開 7

mountain 1
shape 2
across 3
territory 4
be equal to 5
spacious 6
open 7

"The mountains create
an open void."

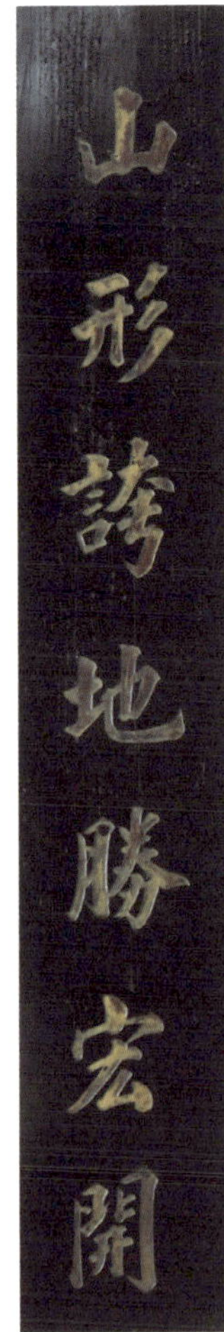
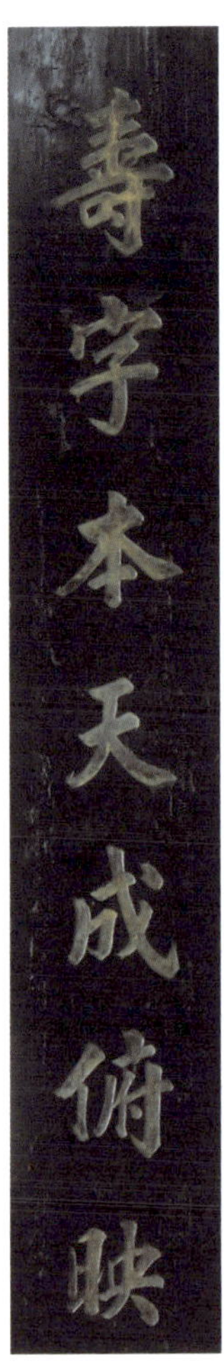

1 壽
2 字
3 本
4 天
5 成
6 俯
7 映

1 longevity
2 word
3 according to
4 heaven
5 become
6 look down
7 to mirror

"Longevity is given
by the heavens."

08

Artist Unknown 佚名 | Calligraphy Couplet in Regular Script | Late 19th–20th century | Wood, carved decorations | Each H 134 x W 22.5 cm

HKU.W.2001.1381 a, b

持　1
酒　2
以　3
禮　4
持　5
才　6
以　7
愚　8

hold　1
wine　2
by　3
courtesy　4
bear　5
talent　6
by　7
humility　8

"Drink wine
with courtesy and
treat your talent
with humility."

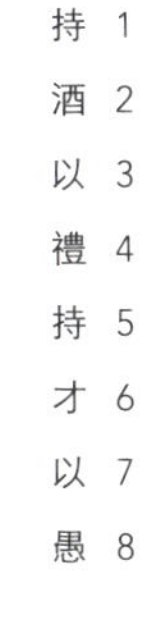

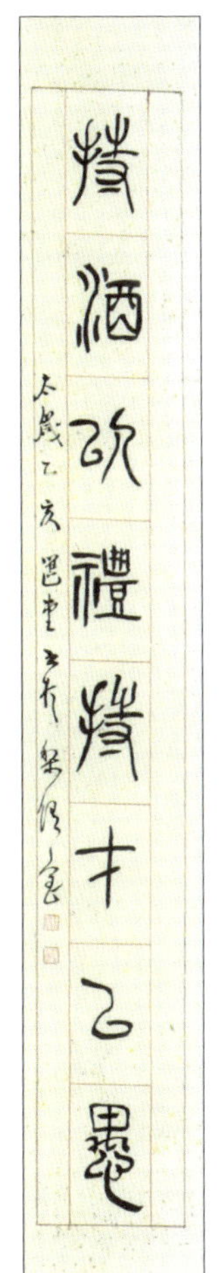

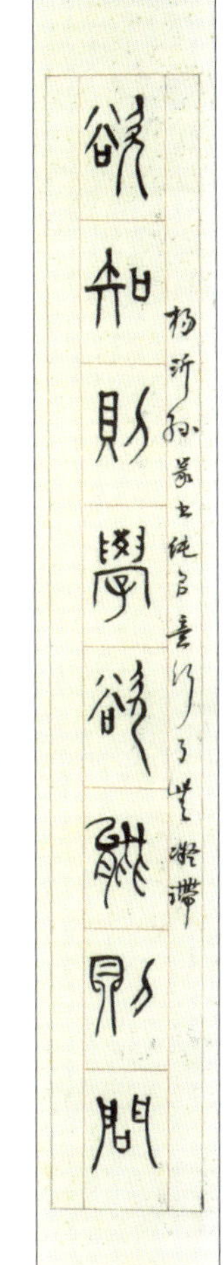

1　欲
2　知
3　則
4　學
5　欲
6　能
7　則
8　問

1　want
2　know
3　then
4　learn
5　want
6　capable
7　then
8　ask

"If you want to know,
you must learn;
if you want to learn
you must ask questions."

09

JAO Tsung-i 饒宗頤 (1917–2018) | Couplet in Seal Script | Late 20th/early 21st century | Vertical scroll, ink on paper | Each L 45.5 x W 16.7 cm

HKU.Ca.2015.2074 a, b

比 1
德 2
於 3
玉 4
防 5
意 6
如 7
城 8

compare 1
virtue 2
to 3
jade 4
defend (against) 5
selfishness 6
like 7
castle 8

"(One's) Virtue should
be compared to jade
as he defends against selfishness like
guarding a castle."

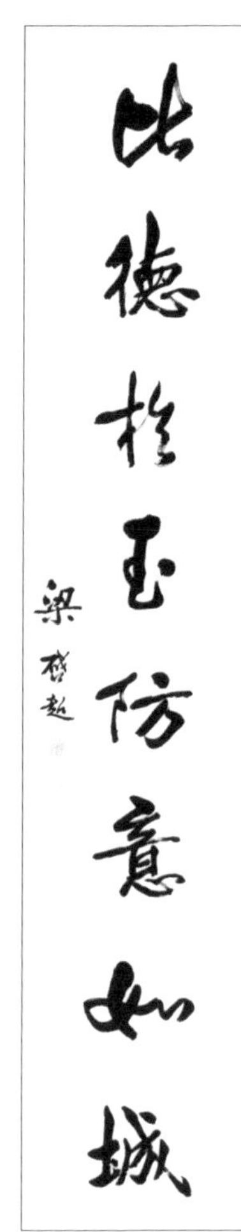

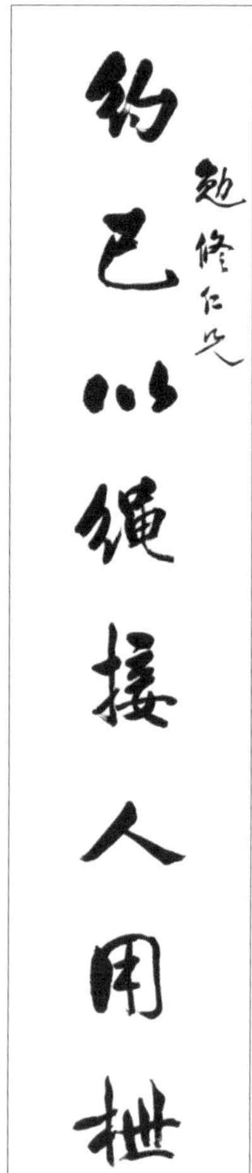

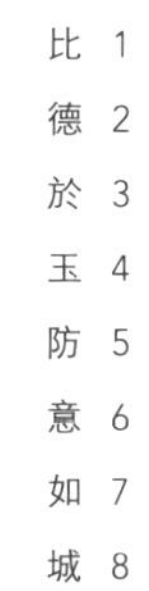

1 約
2 己
3 以
4 繩
5 接
6 人
7 用
8 枻

1 constrain
2 self
3 by
4 rope
5 treat
6 people
7 with
8 short oar

"(A respectable person) Constrains
oneself with discipline
but treats others with leniency."

10

LIANG Qichao 梁啟超 (1873–1929) | Couplet in Running Script | 20th century | Vertical scroll, ink on paper | Each L 188 x W 41 cm

HKU.Ca.1990.0952 a, b | Gift of Ms NG Shun Wah

幾	1		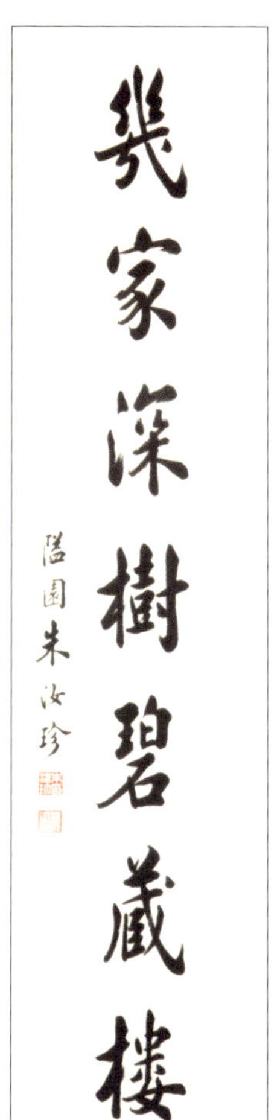	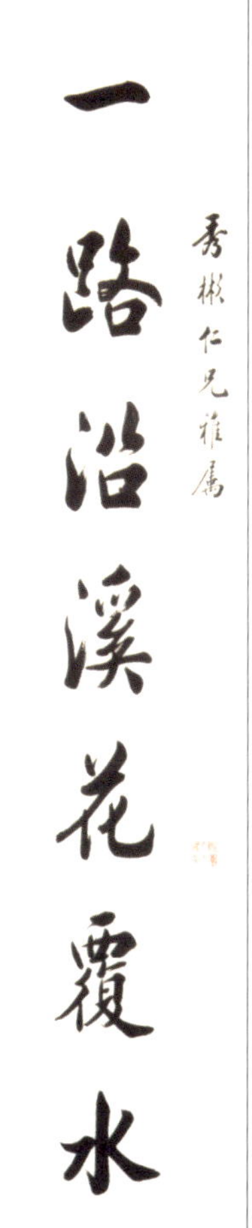		1	一
家	2					2	路
深	3					3	沿
樹	4					4	溪
碧	5					5	花
藏	6					6	覆
樓	7					7	水

several	1		1	one
huts	2		2	road
deep	3		3	along
tree	4		4	stream
green	5		5	flower
hide	6		6	cover
building	7		7	water

"Several dwellings hidden
in the green shade of trees."

"Flower petals drift
along the stream."

11

Couplet by YUAN Jiagu 袁嘉谷 (1872–1937) and Calligraphy in Regular Script by ZHU Ruzhen 朱汝珍 (1870–1942) | Early 20th century | Vertical scroll, ink on paper | Each L 132 x W 29 cm
HKU.Ca.1978.0644 a, b

卧 1
榻 2
清 3
風 4
滿 5
白 6
頭 7

bed 1
couch 2
clear 3
wind 4
full 5
white 6
head 7

"Wind fills the room,
caressing my white head."

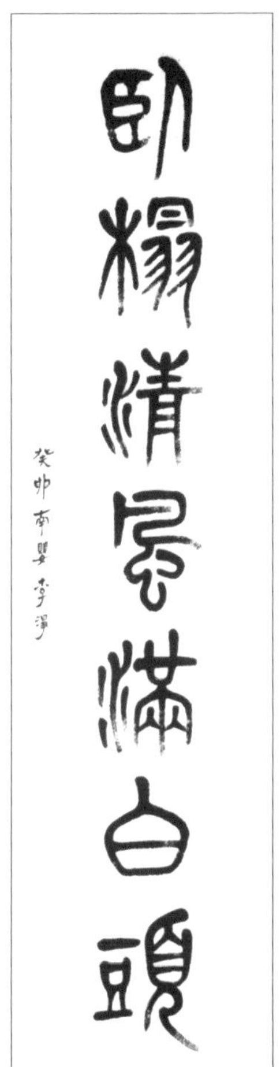

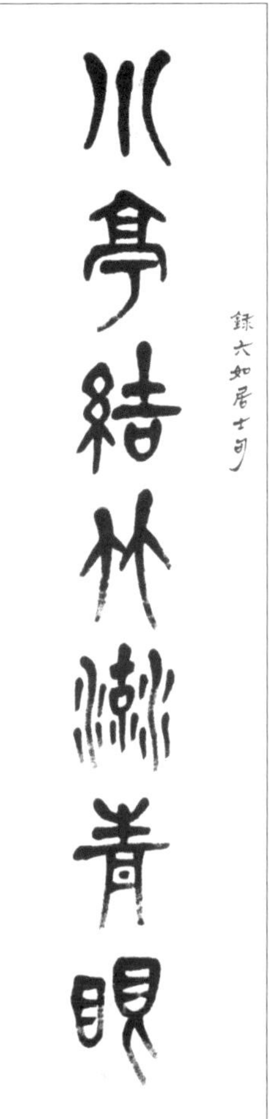

1 小
2 亭
3 結
4 竹
5 流
6 青
7 眼

1 little
2 pavilion
3 knot
4 bamboo
5 cover
6 green
7 sight

"In a small pavilion
bamboo knots flow into the eyes."

12

Couplet by TANG Yin 唐寅 (1470–1524) and Calligraphy by LI Jing 李淨 (*1972–) in Seal Script | 2023 | Vertical scroll, ink on paper | Each L 129.6 x W 31.2 cm

HKU Ca. 2024.2664 a, b | Gift of LI Jing

敦 1
純 2
守 3
素 4
獨 5
遺 6
世 7
榮 8

modest 1
pure 2
keep 3
frugality 4
alone 5
abandon 6
world 7
glory 8

"Adhering to purity and simplicity,
one leaves behind worldly glory."

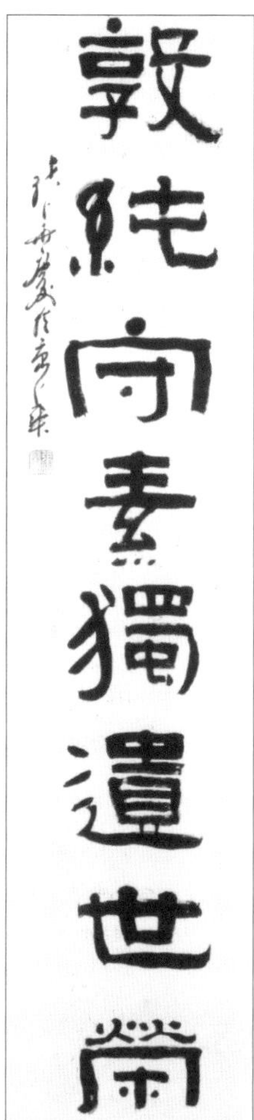

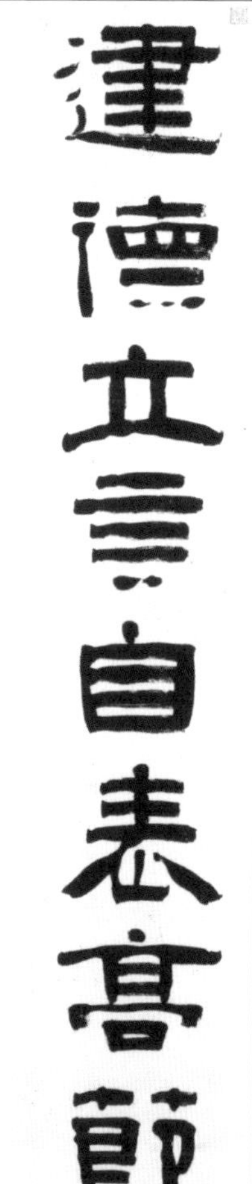

1 建
2 德
3 立
4 言
5 自
6 表
7 高
8 節

1 build
2 moral
3 establish
4 words
5 self
6 express
7 high
8 moral

"Virtuous deeds and words
show noble character."

13

ZHANG Huaqing 張華慶 (*1959–) | Calligraphy in Clerical Script | Late 20th/early 21st century | Vertical scroll, ink on paper | Each L 135.5 x W 30 cm

HKU.Ca.2015.2226 a, b | Gift of The Hong Kong Hard Pen Calligraphy Association

濃 1
霜 2
千 3
磵 4
老 5
松 6
心 7

heavy 1
frost 2
thousand 3
valleys 4
old 5
pine 6
heart 7

"My heart is as firm as
the pine tree in deep frost."

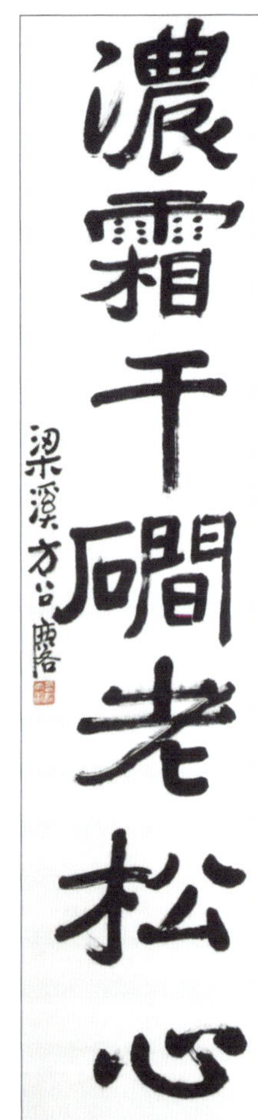

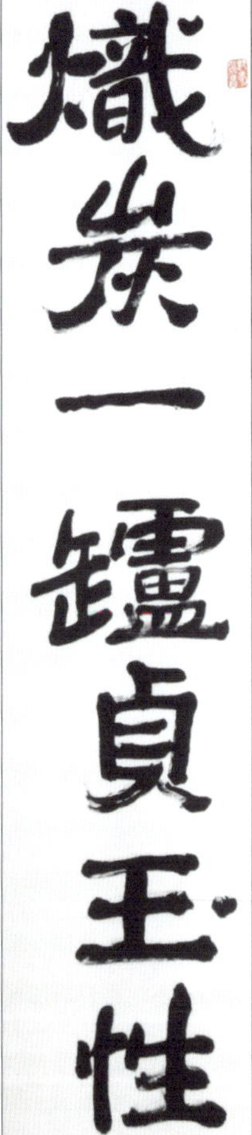

1 熾
2 炭
3 一
4 鑪
5 貞
6 玉
7 性

1 burning
2 charcoal
3 one
4 stove
5 pure
6 jade
7 character

"My spirit is as pure as
the stove's burning coal."

14
Couplet by HAN Wo 韓偓 (ca. 842 or 844–ca. 923) and Calligraphy in Clerical-running Script by FANG Zhaoling 方召麐 (1914–2006) | 1993 | Vertical scroll, ink on paper | Each L 133 x W 29 cm
HKU.Ca.1996.1234 a, b | Gift of FANG Zhaoling

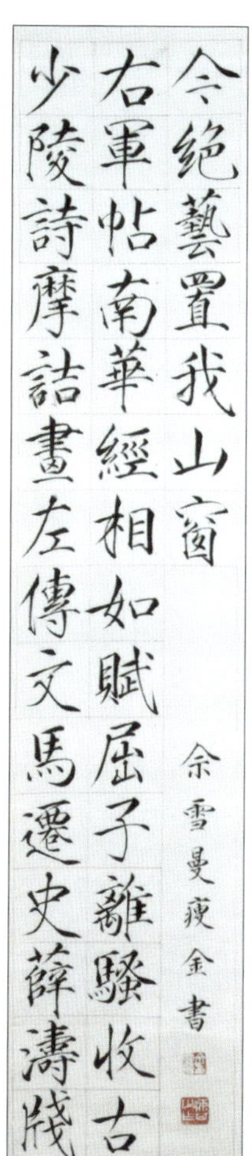

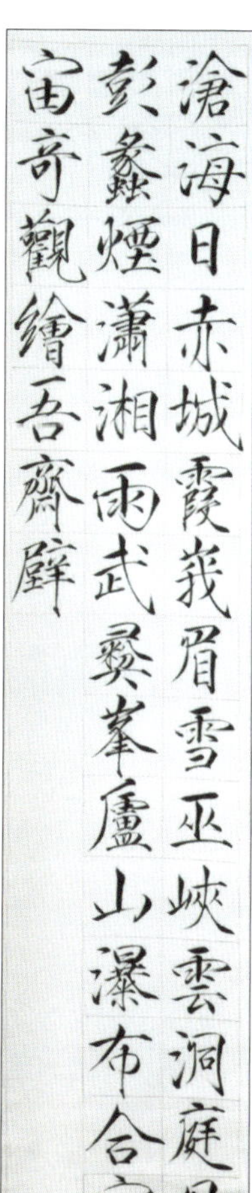

15

Couplet by DENG Shiru 鄧石如 (1743–1805) and Calligraphy in the Shoujin Style of Emperor Huizong of Song by SHE Xueman 佘雪曼 (1908–1993) | 20th century

Vertical scroll, ink on paper | Each L 159 x W 33 cm | HKU.Ca.1997.1262 a, b | Gift of Ms SHE Dingxiao

嘉 1
樹 2
來 3
鳴 4
禽 5

auspicious 1
tree 2
coming 3
singing 4
bird 5

"Singing birds
come to trees."

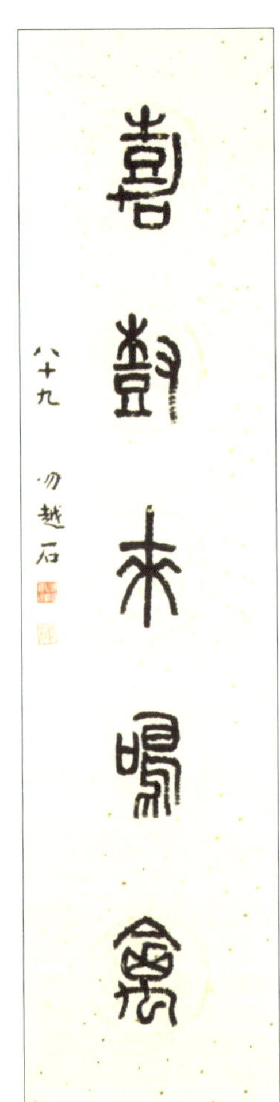

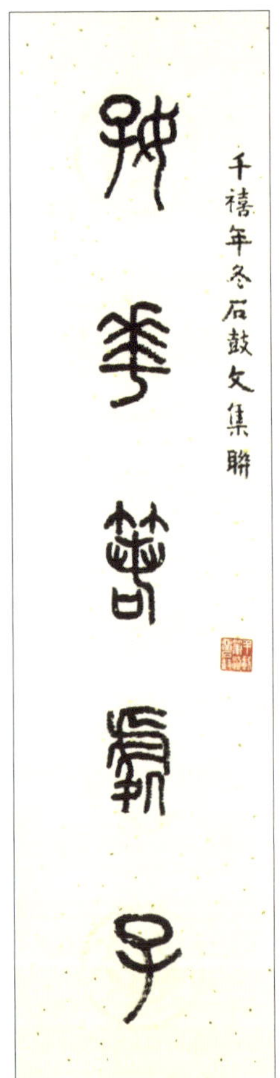

1 好
2 花
3 若
4 處
5 子

1 good
2 flower
3 resemble
4 virgin
5 lady

"Beautiful flowers
resemble elegant virgins."

16

YIK Yuet Sek 易越石 (1912–2007) | Couplet in Stone-Drum Script | 2000 | Vertical scroll, ink on paper | Each L 130.3 x W 33 cm

HKU.Ca.2001.1377 a, b | Gift of YI Yueshi

花 1
樹 2
及 3
嘉 4
時 5

flower 1
tree 2
come up to 3
happy 4
time 5

"Flowering trees bloom
with the joy of the season."

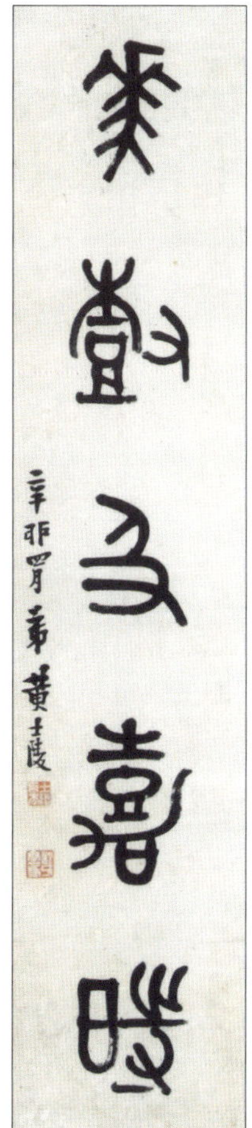

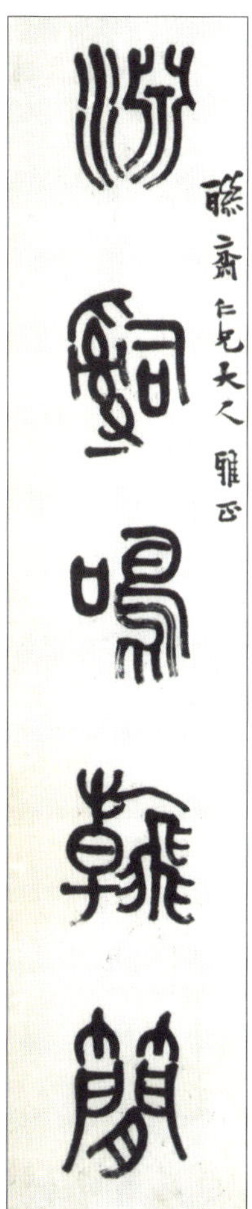

1 淵
2 辭
3 鳴
4 翰
5 簡

1 depth
2 language
3 sound
4 literati
5 bamboo slip

"The deep writing of literati sounds
like bamboo slips."

17
HUANG Shiling 黃士陵 (1849–1908) | Couplet in Seal Script | Late Qing dynasty (1644–1911) | Vertical scroll, ink on paper | Each L 91.8 x W 19.5 cm
HKU.Ca.2012.1974 a, b | Gift of TANG Cho Fung and LEUNG Wai Yee

花　1
孕　2
尌(樹)　3
身　4
濃　5

flower　1
procreate　2
tree　3
body　4
rich　5

"Flowers nourish luxuriant trees."

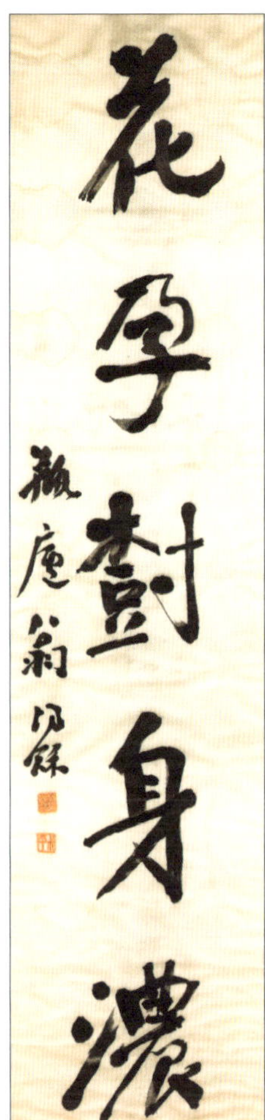

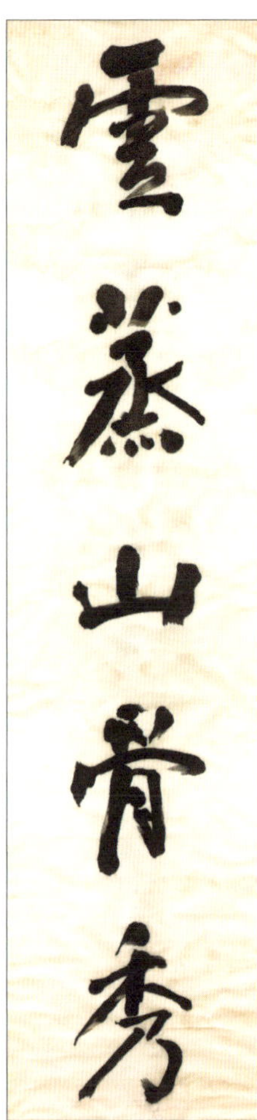

1　雲
2　蒸
3　山
4　骨
5　秀

1　cloud
2　steam
3　mountain
4　bone
5　beauty

"Steaming clouds that rise
from the hills illustrate the spirit and
resonance of graceful mountains."

18

Embroidered Calligraphic Panel Using a Couplet by WENG Tonghe 翁同龢 (1830–1904) | Late Qing dynasty (1644–1911) | Vertical scroll, silk | Each L 169 x W 41 cm

HKU.T.2008.1787 a, b | Gift of James W. C. HONG

龍 1
飛 2
鳳 3
舞 4
時 5

dragon 1

flies 2

phoenix 3

dances 4

time 5

"The dragon soars and
the phoenix dances."

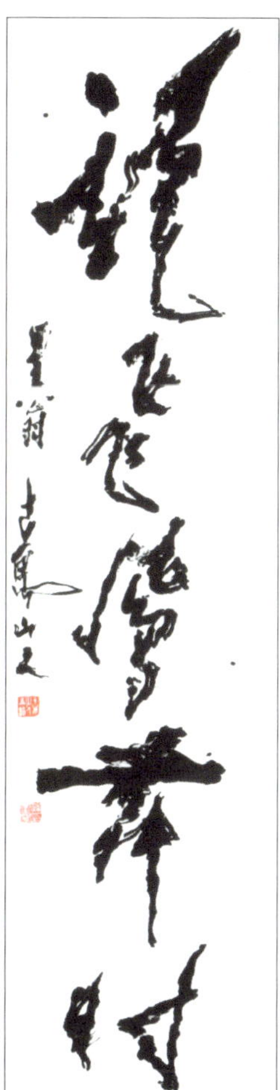

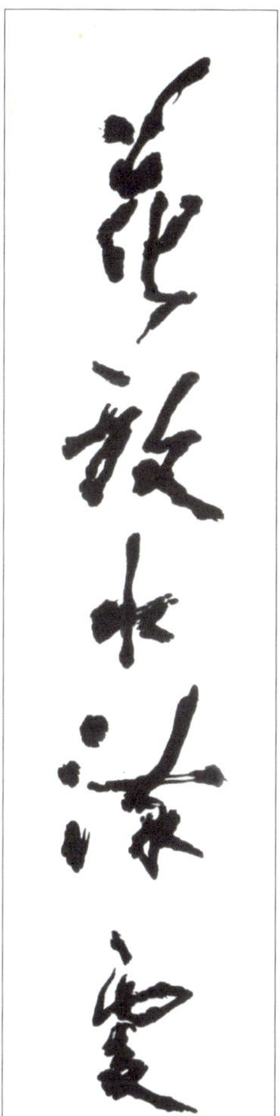

1 花
2 放
3 水
4 流
5 處

1 flower

2 blossoms

3 water

4 floating

5 place

"Flowers bloom
in floating water."

19

SUN Xingge 孫星閣 (1897–1996) | Couplet in Cursive Script | 20th century | Vertical scroll, ink on paper | Each L 137 x W 34 cm

HKU.Ca.2004.1516 a, b | Gift of Mr SEN Chungwun

松 1
柏 2
古 3
人 4
心 5

pine 1
cypress 2
ancient 3
people 4
heart 5

"Pines and cypresses are
the hearts of the ancients."

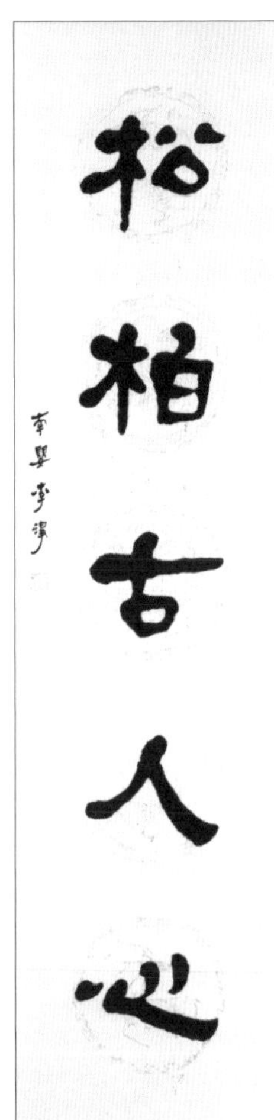

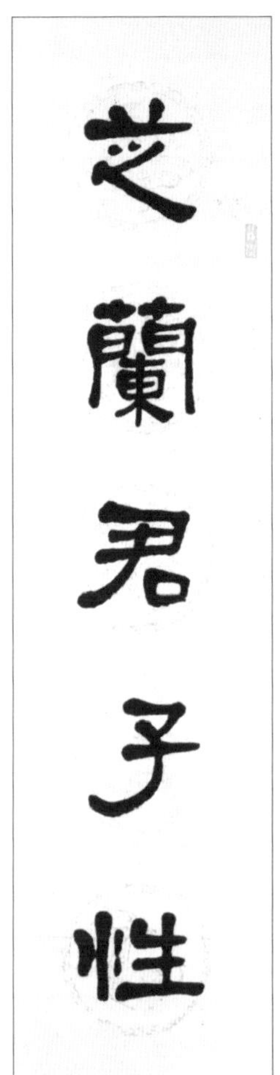

1 芝
2 蘭
3 君
4 子
5 性

1 irises
2 orchid
3 gentleman
4 son
5 character

"Irises and orchids are
the nature of the sages."

20

LI Jing 李淨 (*1972–) | Couplet by Anonymous Author and Calligraphy in Clerical Script by LI Jing | 2023 | Vertical scroll, ink on paper | Each L 134.7 x W 32.5 cm

HKU.Ca 2024.2665 a, b | Gift of LI Jing

江 1
山 2
萬 3
里 4
心 5

river 1
mountain 2
thousand 3
mile 4
heart 5

"Ten thousand miles of
rivers and mountains
in my heart."

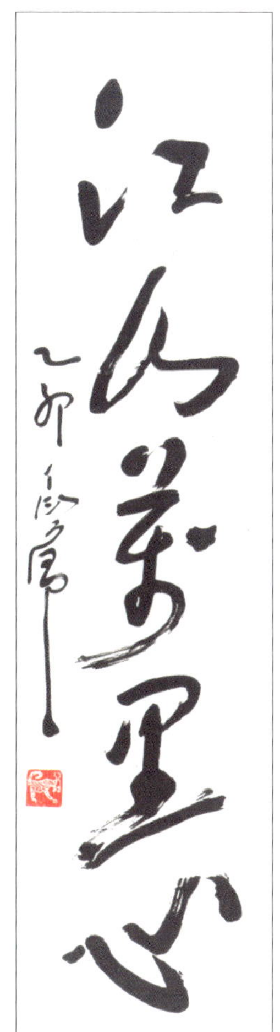
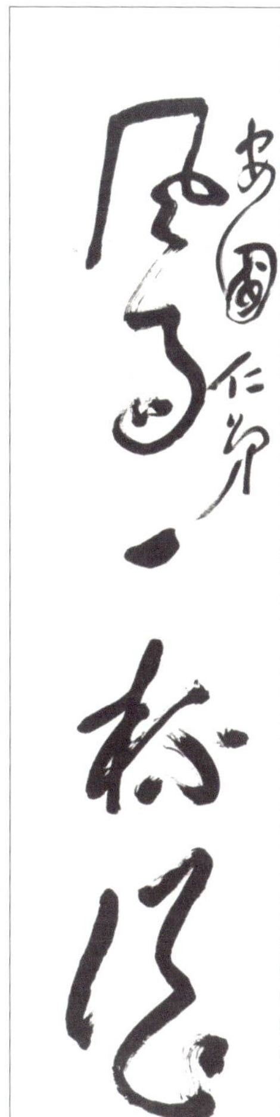

1 風
2 雨
3 一
4 杯
5 酒

1 wind
2 rain
3 one
4 cup
5 wine

"So much
wind and rain
in a cup of wine."

21

TING Yin Yung 丁衍庸 (1902–1978) | Couplet in Cursive Script | 1975 | Vertical scroll, ink on paper | Each L 137.2 x W 34.3 cm

HKU.Ca.2022.2579a, b | Gift of Mr NG On Kwok

孤 1
館 2
雨 3
留 4
人 5

lonely 1
inn 2
rain 3
halt 4
people 5

"The rain causes them
to halt in the lonely pavilion."

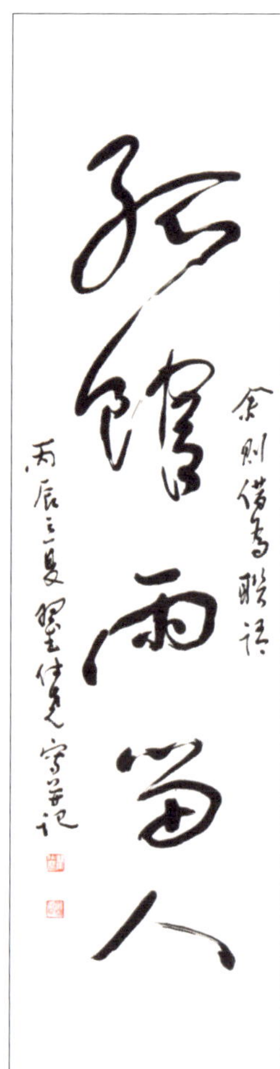

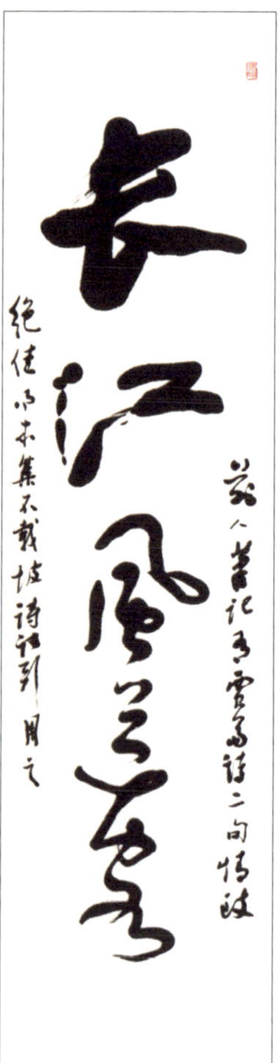

1 長
2 江
3 風
4 送
5 客

1 long
2 river
3 wind
4 send
5 guest

"The wind carries travellers
along the river."

22

Couplet by .JIA Dao 賈島 (779–843) and Calligraphy in Cursive Script by JAT See Yeu 翟仕堯 (1935–2009) | 1970s | Vertical scroll, ink on paper | Each L 152 x W 40.2 cm

HKU.Ca.1979.0797 a, b

龍 1
馬 2
精 3
神 4

dragon 1
horse 2
vigour 3
vitality 4

"The vigour of
a dragon and horse."

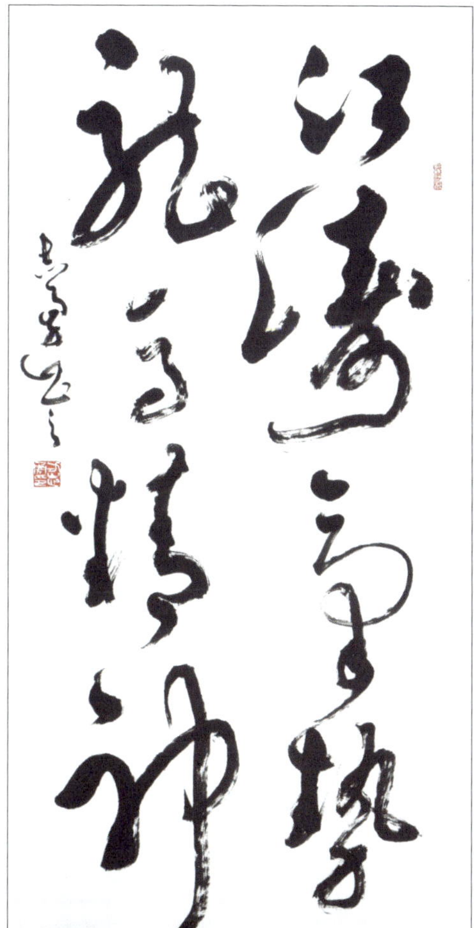

1 江
2 濤
4 氣
5 勢

1 river
2 wave
3 qi (spirit /manner)
4 strength (powerful aura)

"The spiritual strength of
a river and wave."

23

FANG Zhiyong 方志勇 (*1959–) | Couplet in Cursive Script | 21st century | Vertical scroll, ink on paper | L 142.5 x W 35.7 cm

HKU.Ca.2015.2227 | Gift of The Hong Kong Hard Pen Calligraphy Association

PAIR Balance

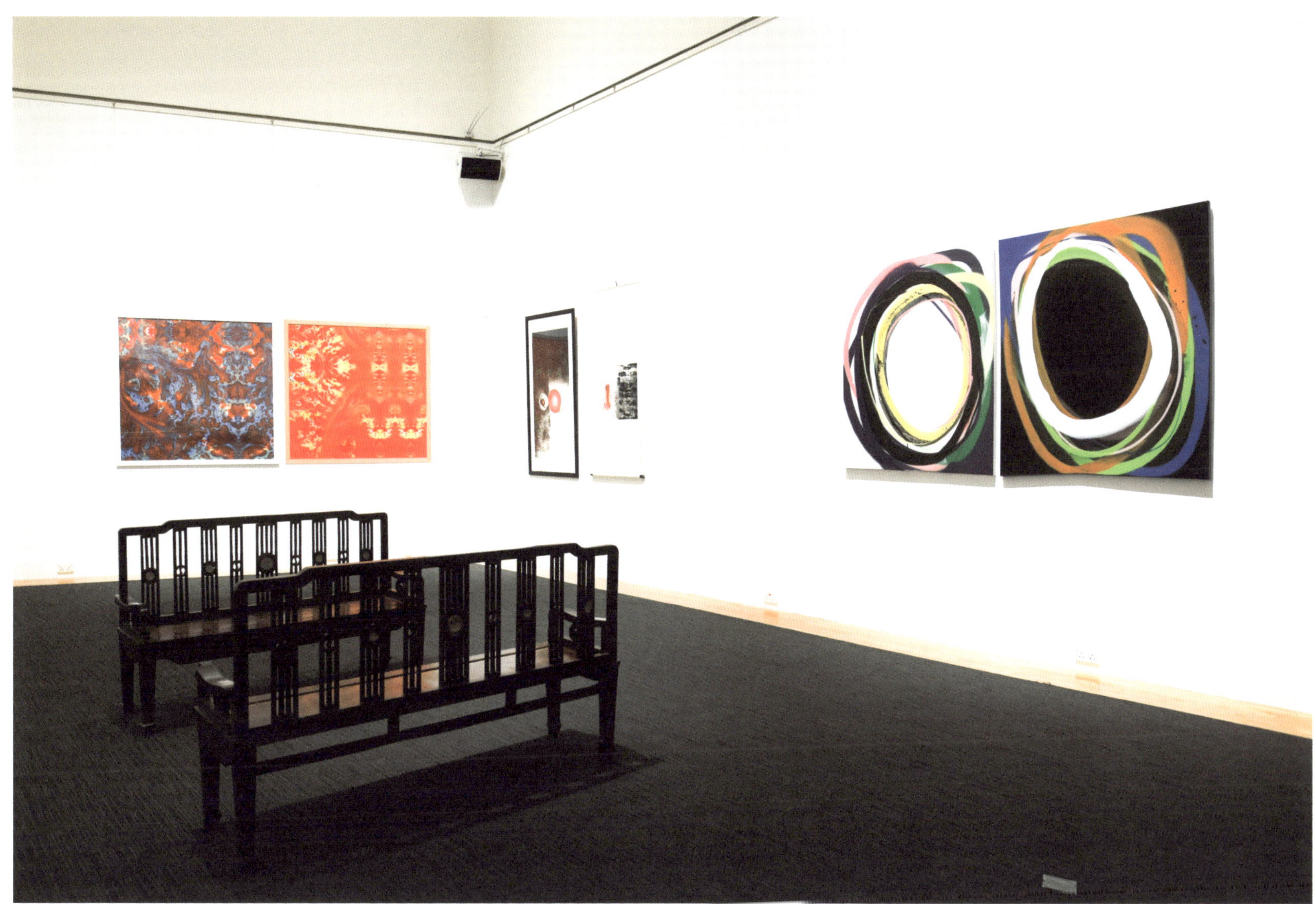

Introduction

The room COUPLET is designed as a reading room, while the second room entitled PAIR is conceived as a form of balanced three-dimensional space. The term PAIR denotes two things that can be similar or complementary. They can be persons, animals or objects, as well as motifs or ornaments. In art, the motif of the pair is used to connect like or unlike elements, to represent sequences in time or space and to enable serial storytelling. Symmetry is a crucial element that can be found in many objects of applied art and as part of ornaments (Gombrich 1984). Works of abstract art are also often based on the idea of balance and equilibrium. The works exhibited here are grouped as pairs and situated to face each other. This creates a balanced three-dimensional space.

Three of the four walls contain works of art arranged in pairs. The fourth wall has two pairs of figurative paintings grouped to the left and right of two central portraits. In the center are two benches from the late Qing dynasty and eight display cases with various artifacts from the UMAG collection. The aim is to juxtapose works of fine art with artifacts from the world of arts and crafts. These follow the main theme of the exhibition and were selected according to specific criteria.

Display Cases Number 1 and 2

The display cases number 1 and 2, placed next to each other, contain four very different types of artifacts that have one thing in common: two identical pieces form a single unit.

The bronze food serving vessel with string design, known as a Duì (弦紋敦), from the Warring States period (ca. 475–221 BCE) also served as an icon for the poster due to its unusually modern shape (fig. 39). The vessel, consisting of two symmetrical hemispheres, was used during ritual processes and festivals to commemorate ancestors.

The two hemispheres of the Duì are meant to contrast with the conjoined bowls (雙連碗) from the Majiayao culture (馬家窯文化) of the Neolithic period (fig. 40). The bowls are Banshan phase pottery, which is known for its curved geometric patterns and the use of black and red colors.

Opposed to the Duì is an impressively carved cinnabar lacquer box and cover in conjoined rhomboid form (剔紅雕漆錦地方勝式蓋盒) from the Qianling period (1736–1795) of the Qing dynasty (fig. 42).

The Neolithic conjoined container also has a counterpart—a rare example of two snuff bottles made of burr wood that have been fused to form a conjoined unit (fig. 41). Smoking tobacco was forbidden during the Qing dynasty but it was taken as a remedy in China, so the use of small quantities was permitted. Snuff and other medicines were carried in small, often attractively decorated bottles made of various materials.

Number 3

Display case number 3 contains bronze objects from several periods. Some of these are pairs that belong together in terms of their function. 28 of UMAG's collection of 979 Nestorian crosses—with motifs of swastikas, birds, floral patterns and radiating beams—appear in the center (fig. 43). The bronze Nestorian crosses were extremely popular in the Yuan dynasty (1272–1368) and originated from the Ordos region in northwest China. Based on four basic forms, the Nestorian crosses play with a variety of variations in which symmetrical and ornamental decoration takes center stage.

The Nestorian crosses are complemented by two bronze pairs of chariot fittings from the Spring and Autumn period (770–ca. 475 BCE), a pair of gilt bronze hinges from the Six Dynasties period (220–589) decorated with phoenixes and dragons (fig. 44) and a pair of bronze horse masks from the Western Zhou period (ca. 11th–771 BCE).

Number 4

The four bronze mirrors, two stoneware bowls and six porcelain vessels in display case number 4 all bear decorative depictions of phoenixes and dragons.

The bronze mirror (fig. 45) from the Warring States period (ca. 475–221 BCE), which has a decorative painting with four phoenixes and four dragons, is particularly noteworthy. While the phoenixes, recognizable by their bird-like heads and three tail feathers, form an inner circle; the four dragons are arranged in a circle on the exterior. The two opposing forces are separated by a convex-concave band that appears to be in constant motion.

The pair of dishes (fig. 46) from Jingdezhen, made in the Wanli period (1573–1620), also shows three phoenixes and three dragons in the center and around the edges (UMAG: *Objectifying 2017*, 76–77). However, while the phoenixes and dragons in the mirror are in a balanced equilibrium, here they appear to be chasing each other. The phoenix (female, passive) and dragon (male, active) embody the duality of Yin and Yang. Together they represent the unity of opposing forces and the striving for harmonious balance in all aspects of life.

Number 5

Juxtapositions of two forces can be perceived as a dialogue or confrontation. In case number 5, wooden architectural ornaments with various animals face each other to symbolize power relations. Regardless of whether they are mythical animals such as phoenix and qílín (fig. 47), dragons (fig. 48) or bats and birds, the composition of the animal pairs is largely mirrored and symmetrical, and based on a convex-concave composition criteria. This creates a balanced equilibrium of forces.

Numbers 6 and 7

Display cases 6 and 7 contain a selection of 20 of UMAG's collection of more than 1,600 paper cuttings. Silhouettes, the oldest and perhaps most popular folk art in China, range from simple motifs cut from a single sheet to compositions made from several sheets of colored paper.

Among these are examples designed according to symmetrical features, such as the Beijing opera masks of the characters from *Journey to the West* from Tianjin (figs. 55, 56), flower blossom patterns from Yueqing (fig. 51) and palace lanterns (fig. 52). The latter are true masterpieces of the art form due to their filigree nature. As they are presented at weddings, the lanterns contain numerous symbols such as the double happiness motif, as well as pairs of fish, cranes, mandarin ducks, butterflies and flowers.

The two paper cuts from Yuhuan with motifs in Wuxi, such as the Chinese garden pavilion (fig. 50) and the pond with goldfish stand out. In the former, the four pavilions are grouped like a wreath around a central tree motif; in the latter, the goldfish swim towards a central point.

The Baiyun Mountain (fig. 53) cutting was also created in Yuhuan, based on a series of paper cuts of landscape motifs from Guangzhou. This work showcases the intricate details and exemplifies the ancient craft's high level of perfection. Another group contains antithetical pairs that perfectly complement each other. These include the paper cutouts of dancing couples (fig. 54) from different Chinese ethnic groups made using the *yinyangke* technique, or couples with motifs from fauna and flora (fig. 49), also from Yangzhou.

Number 8

Finally, display case number 8 contains 10 terracotta or earthenware figures from various dynasties, all of which appear in pairs. It makes no difference whether they are guardians, servants (fig. 59) or bodhisattvas. Some of them look like a mirrored duplication, while others display variations in facial expression or posture. These subtle imperfections make the figures, which were originally painted, more human.

One exception is the mismatched pair of figures from the Han dynasty (206 BCE–220 CE). These figures depict a man and woman and their disparate proportions—the woman towers over the man by a head (figs. 57, 58). The attention to detail, such as the man's striking eyebrows and thinning beard, can still make us smile today.

The arrangement of the eight showcases follows the form of hexagram 49 from the *I Ching* (Yìjīng 易經) (see eight showcases on p. 87):

Display cases 1 to 4 = ☱ lake (Duì 兌)
Display cases 5 to 8 = ☲ fire (Lí 離)

This hexagram (Gé 革) consists of the two trigrams ☱ (Duì 兌) which means lake and ☲ (Lí 離) which means fire.

Lake is placed above Fire. Water hovering over the fire presents two contradictory forces; the water can extinguish the fire and the fire can vaporize the water. Their forces are directed against each other and characterize the impending transformation. Thus, hexagram 49 (Gé 革) stands for upheaval, change and metamorphosis. (Cleary 1992, chapter 49, 109–111). Richard Wilhelm speaks of "transformation". Change is necessary and also constant, so that the balance can constantly realign and find itself anew.

Hexagram 49 was chosen to match the theme of the exhibition and is intended to highlight that we are living in times of great change, and that major changes are in store for us in the future. As we are able to influence some of the causes we will also share in responsibility for the effects. We are at the mercy of other causes, and must find a way to adapt and deal with this change.

By arranging the display cases according to hexagram 49, the aim is not only to honor one of the oldest explanatory models for understanding our world, but also to emphasize the *I Ching's* contemporaneity. The objects arranged in the eight display cases should be viewed against the background of this constant change.

There are two wooden objects—a pair of doors and a pair of carved wooden panels with ornaments—on the wall in the extension of the axis of the showcases. These serve as a connecting element between the artifacts in the display cases and the works of fine art on the walls.

The two panels (fig. 29) contain groups of children playing, animals, vases of flowers and entwined plants, each with two of the eight Daoist Immortals appearing in the center. Despite the multiple details, both doors are designed as juxtapositions.

The pair of carved wooden panels (fig. 30) contains a number of surprises. The left-hand panel consists of numerous Chinese characters that promise luck, longevity and prosperity. The right-hand panel contains 20 symbols. If looking at the panels from the exterior and interior, these symbols remain unchanged. This means there is no duplication of the symbols, and that both views are completely equivalent.

In Hinduism, the symbol facing clockwise to the right (卐) is called a "swastika" and symbolizes Surya (sun), prosperity and happiness, while the symbol facing anti-clockwise to the left (卍) is called "sauvastika" and symbolizes the night or tantric aspects of the goddess Kali, the Hindu goddess associated with time, change, creation, power, destruction and death. Together, the "swastika" and "sauvastika" symbolize the constant change of the wheel of life (Wilson 2014).

The ornamental order of the two wooden artifacts is located axially on the opposite wall along with the diptych *Attractiveness 02* by Hong Kong artist **Victor LI Ki-kwok** 李其國 (*1951), created in 2002. This two-part large-format ink drawing (fig. 25) stands out from his œuvre, as he is better known for his wooden objects (UMAG: *Concepts in Wood*, 2004). There are 16 fields facing each other, each showing a rich formal language ranging from disc-like shapes to crescent moons, paisleys and arabesques. Each of the 32 fields has a different dynamic. Some are symmetrically structured, while others are highly condensed through overlapping circles or convex-concave forms.

In their diversity, the entire thing seems like mutations or metamorphoses of a uniform original that has long since dissolved, but still resonates echo-like in all its variations. The two wooden ornamental artifacts, which hang opposite this diptych, are a system of static order in view of the drawing's fleeting nature. In a way, the wooden works also show their respect for Victor LI Ki-kwok, who is regarded as one of Hong Kong's leading wood sculptors.

Immediately to the left is the two-part work *Déjà vu* (fig. 24) created in 2023 by the Hong Kong-based German artist **Tobias KLEIN** (*1979), whose artistic work is situated in the digital arts and crafts field of tension (Klein 2020). Two lenticular prints mounted in front of lightbox panels show a section of an abstract, digitally created structure that is reminiscent of a patch of forest. Although it is a two-part work, the motif actually consists of three distinct parts. The right-hand area of forest appears again in mirrored form on the left side. In between is another area of forest without a mirrored counterpart.

The fascination of looking at this highly complex artificial view of nature lies in the fact that it radiates a suggestive spatial effect, and that the slow movements of the lightbox panels, which are driven by motors, constantly jump back and forth between absolute sharpness and blurriness. Because the image can never be clearly defined as a whole, the artist is playing with the simultaneity of non-simultaneity and contrasting the chaos of the blur with the order of a clear spatial view.

As there are no concrete assignments to places or seasons, this image can be found in many places and at many times. It is therefore placeless and timeless, as if it could be a segment of nature that we vaguely recall. Something that we may have seen and experienced in childhood and that still remains in us as a fragment of the past.

However, memory transfigures details and the partial blurring of the motif reinforces this impression. We soften unpleasant memories or block them out completely. Whether what we see here is a deception, an illusion or a falsification of our memory remains an open question. We believe that we have experienced such an event. The effect is a simultaneous feeling of familiarity and uncertainty. In the lenticular works *Simulacra Naturans* (2017) and *Beyond Homeostasis* (2021), the artist experiments with the potential of perception held by our subconscious, which also explains the title of the work, *Déjà vu* (Kraemer 2022, 172–175).

The two digital paintings created by **Robert LETTNER** (1943–2012), done in collaboration with **Philipp STADLER** (*1975), hang across from KLEIN's *Déjà vu*, and likewise interact with the subconscious. The titles hint at this association: *The Water Garden in Neptune's House* (fig. 31) and *Nature Is Not a Catastrophe* (fig. 32).

These digital paintings from the series *Images of Magical Geometry* are based on organic drawings (Lettner 2017, 60; Kraemer 2018a; 2018b). The attraction lies in the fact that the free-flowing abstract and partially marbled forms contrast with symmetries created by reflections and multiplications that are reminiscent of Rorschach tests. It is surprising that multiple mirrored images can give rise to such complex structures. LETTNER speaks here of the "original psychogram," which is "no longer visible" but "omnipresent." When asked about these ornamental phenomena, LETTNER replied that every form seems familiar, but does not actually exist in its form as such (Lettner 2017, 39–45).

In his classic book *The Sense of Order*, Ernst H. Gombrich comments in the chapter "The Perception of Order" on the phenomenon of conceptualization in the face of abstract symmetrical forms, such as those that can arise from a Rorschach test, as follows:

> "The symmetrical configuration loses its accidental look and therefore invites us to search for a meaningful description. Maybe it is relevant here that so many objects in our environment exhibit symmetries. Nearly all organisms do and it is not surprising that butterflies or faces are frequently seen in these Rorschach blots. But maybe there is more to this tendency of projecting some overriding meaning into the symmetrical blot. Symmetry […] implies cohesion. […] Since it is unlikely to have come about by a mere accidental shuffling of shapes and colors, it must be classified as an object in its own right, and as such we must be able to give it a meaning and a name. What must interest us here is the fact that this process of identification, which is technically known as projection, invariably affects the way the blot is seen."
>
> Gombrich 1984, 157–158.

Symmetry also plays a decisive role in the phenomenon of recognizing abstract motifs in the context of a Rorschach test. The two digital paintings gain their tension from the co-existence between symmetrical order and asymmetrical chaos. These colorful works thus also address the interplay and invite transformation. With his series of *Paintings on Magical Geometry*, Robert LETTNER questions the significance of the auratic original as an original form and its effects in the form of digital reproductions, which can be infinitely duplicated from the same origin. In view of this digital painting, terms such as original and reproduction become obsolete (Kraemer 2018b).

This diptych is juxtaposed with a pair of paintings by two artists. The one on the right, *A Flower Is Not a Flower* (fig. 27), is by **LEUNG Kui-ting** 梁巨廷 (*1945). Originally from Guangzhou, the artist, who studied under Lui Shou-kwan and Wucius Wong, is known for his rich and experimental approaches within the New Ink Painting Movement. He was one of six artists who took part in the legendary exhibition *Art Now Hong Kong: Ink Painting I* at the City Museum and Art Gallery in 1971. LEUNG Kui-ting divides his creative work into an earlier phase, which he calls the "cause phase," and since 2000 into a later phase, the "effects phase" (see interview in: Lee 2001, Leung 2005). His landscape-format painting is divided into two sections and contains a light area on the left and a dark area on the right (UMAG: *Tradition* 2018, 222–223). While the darker half evokes memories of an expanse of water interspersed with plants and stones, and can be found in several of his landscape paintings, the lighter area on the left breaks with this illusion by aggressively placing a strongly contrasting red color in the lower third of the picture field. Together, the two different areas create a tension and yet appear balanced in relation to each other.

Irene CHOU's 周綠雲 (1924–2011) painting *Abstract Composition* (fig. 26) from the late 1970s stands as a form of antithesis to LEUNG Kui-ting. In the 1950s, she was trained in the traditional Lingnan School style. In the late 1960s abstract expressionism inspired CHOU to experiment with different techniques. Her teacher Lui Shou-kwan, one of the founders of the Hong Kong New Ink Movement, encouraged her to work more spontaneously. With her strong interest in experimenting with new styles, CHOU revolutionized ink painting and brought abstract motifs to the fore.

What at first glance appears to be a simple light and dark arrangement with two central circular shapes turns out, upon closer inspection, to be a highly complex composition made from a wealth of techniques. While the left half consists of short brushstrokes that the artist called "impact structural strokes," which intensify towards the top, the upper right consists of several layers of ink applied to both sides of the thin paper (UMAG: *Tradition* 2018, 174–175). When given time to unfold, the painting seems as if punctual, quasi-short-term events are meeting the incessant, slowly drifting stream of time. The two primary round shapes appear to represent our place within this continuously flowing time event, our impact. Like a cell surrounded by a membrane, the two structures present themselves as a diverging pair that belongs together. Remotely reminiscent of fertilized egg cells, Irene CHOU's composition achieves a balance. In the same way, CHOU's work stands in stark contrast to her counterpart by LEUNG Kui-ting and forms a harmonious counterbalance to the two digital paintings by Robert LETTNER.

Order as symmetry or chaos as asymmetry is not found exclusively in abstract or ornamental works of art. Symmetry and asymmetry can also be expressed through narratives. The northern wall of the room PAIR contains seven paintings by six artists that present themselves as a single unit whose message must be decoded, thus anticipating the REBUS theme in the next room.

On the right-hand side of the wall, the two paintings have been deliberately juxtaposed as an antithetical pair opposed to the abstract paintings by LEUNG Kui-ting and Irene CHOU. Like the latter, they do not form a harmonious dialogue, but rather a kind of irritating confrontation.

DUAN Jianwei 段建偉 (*1961) , who comes from Henan, is known for his "new rustic" painting style, in which his paintings focus on bucolic culture and the facial expressions of peasants (Duan 1999). In *Preparing a Meal* (fig. 35) a young woman is depicted holding a large bowl of meat in her hands in front of a rural backdrop along with six men in work clothes. The woman is also wearing work clothes and appears strangely unconcerned by what is happening behind her. We can assume that she is preparing a meal for the labourers, but ultimately it remains an open question. She appears to be a foreign body, like a daydreamer who is merely doing her job and is otherwise uninvolved.

The man in the painting *Computer Game* (fig. 36) by Chengdu-born XIN Haizhou 忻海洲 (*1966) also appears absent-minded and yet highly focused (Xin 2005). The exact game he is playing is left to the viewer's imagination. Surrounded by ten small colored avatars that are representations of him, this individual also has an understanding of space and time that separates him from his surroundings. This is a constant state of sensory overload—games, virtual worlds, and avatars. The importance of human contact often only becomes apparent with its failure, or by actually experiencing it in daily life

If he and the working woman were a couple, the specific conflicts would most likely be pre-programmed. The saying "The way to a man's heart is through his stomach" might not be enough to cure the absent partner of his addiction. Both artists thematize different levels of reality in which their protagonists move. If, in addition, their needs are too different and this cannot be communicated, the chances of a partnership developing that is equally balanced and of equal value are extremely slim.

On the left-hand side, two further paintings thematize the challenge of sexuality in a partnership. In the painting *Green Wine* (fig. 33) by POON Yeuk Fai 潘躍輝 (*1966) from 2009, a young couple stands close to each other. Looking directly at the viewer, the young man kisses his companion on the cheek. She is holding a champagne glass in her left hand. The young lady smiles, resting her right hand on her hip and coquettishly holding her left hand at the level of her companion's genitals. Her index finger is outstretched in a playful approach to sexuality by the Fujian-born artist; an exploration and clarification of boundaries. *Green Wine* refers to the young vintage, in our case a couple who are still discovering each other. At the beginning of a relationship, we are seldom aware that the causes for the ultimate success or failure of the partnership already exist in plain sight.

The 1992 painting *Elderly Couple* (fig. 34) by the Hebei-born artist **SONG Yonghong** 宋永紅 (*1966) offers an incredibly strong contrast to this young love. A participant in the '85 New Wave Movement, SONG is a representative of so-called "Cynical Realism," which touched on alienation in China in the 1990s (Song 2008). The motif shows an elderly couple standing in a room that is arranged like a stage. A curtain decorated with ornaments covers a window letting daylight into the room. On the left is a bed and on the right some envelopes and a booklet. In front is a small table with a lamp and two smaller works of art hang on the wall in the background. There are also some music cassettes on the floor. The couple are undressed. While she looks directly at the viewer and covers her shame with her two hands, he holds a pair of glasses in his left hand and reaches for her breast with his right. He gazes into the distance. Even though the couple are undressed, they are not naked and lack any erotic aura. Their sexuality has evaporated. The ritual that has been established over the decades has lost its meaning. The thrill is gone. Both have realized this at the same moment. The intimacy lies in the realization that their needs have changed. Sexual desire will no longer play a role here and in the future. Other needs will come to the fore and in order to find a new balance in their partnership, our couple must learn to grow old together.

Gahda (fig. 37) and her husband *Sayed* (fig. 38) have already passed through this phase of life. However, the expressive black-and-white photographic portraits of the Cairo-based couple were chosen for a different reason. In her series *Our House Is on Fire*, Iranian-born artist **Shirin NESHAT** (*1957) portrays people who lost loved ones in Egypt's military coup in 2013. *Gahda* and *Sayed* have lost their son and we can see the sorrow, grief and despair in their faces. We can also sense a gentleness and hope, reflecting an enduring partnership that offers a security and stability during uncertain times. Together they carry the grief and give each other hope.

In the interplay of forces with the surrounding pairs on the left and right, the two act as an equal force which has learned to understand fate as challenges that must be faced. Or to paraphrase TING Yin Yung's Couplet: "Ten thousand miles of rivers and mountains in 'our hearts'." (fig. 21).

The two-part painting *Untitled (Hong Kong)* (fig. 28) by **Adrian FALKNER** (*1979), created in Hong Kong in 2016, hangs in opposition to the timeless Egyptian couple. It is a rather unusual work for the Basel-born artist, whose roots lie in Street Art. This diptych marks a turning point, a transition in the artist's œuvre, which was to lead him from colorful, neo-informal painting to a linear abstraction greatly reduced in its symbolism (Kraemer 2013).

Lines of different widths create a central, egg-shaped form. The circles are eccentrically placed. The painting on the left, primed in white, has its center of gravity to the right of the canvas' middle; the black, on the other hand, is primed on the left. This results in a strong dynamic, a right spin in the left painting and a left spin in the right. The linear structures, each of which was sprayed onto the canvas in a single circular movement, resonate like an echo. It almost seems as if the circular structure is trying to settle itself in order to find its center. The two power centers move towards each other.

This impression is further reinforced by the fact that the supports of the two paintings do not form a rectangle, as the white on the left and the black on the right of the bottom are bent, almost as if the stretchers have been broken or warped due to improper storage. The canvases were actually purchased by the artist in this condition in May 2016 in Kowloon.

By juxtaposing the two curved shapes, FALKNER adds another strong counterpoint to the existing contrast of white and black. It is only through the interplay of contrasting forms of the stretchers, the strongly contrasting colors and their flowing linear forms, that this balance of forces emerges which is reminiscent of "Everything flows"—the Panta rhei of Heraclitus of Ephesus, and distantly reminiscent of Yin and Yang. And like the latter, the pair from FALKNER is dynamic. In a word, changing.

Form and destroy. Become and pass away. There is hardly a better way to describe change, where change refers to becoming without destroying the constant; change is a necessary condition.

This tension within the formal composition, which is felt to the point of bursting, and the balanced, yet almost daring balance of color scheme, allows the diptych to enter into a robust dialogue with the works around it. Thus, FALKNER's diptych closes the circle, which began with the installation of the eight display cases situated in accordance with hexagram 49 of the *I Ching*. West and East are now reconciled.

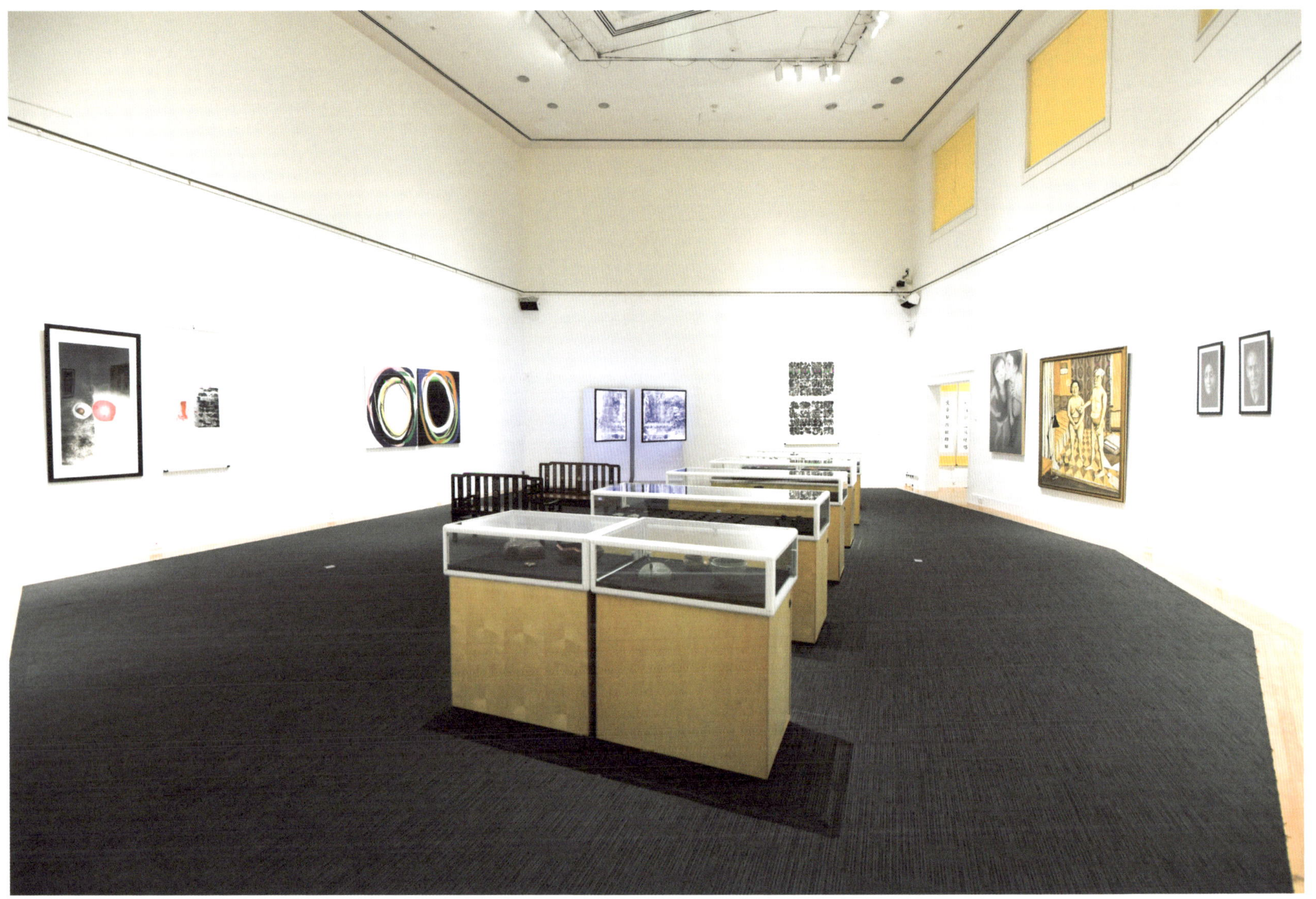

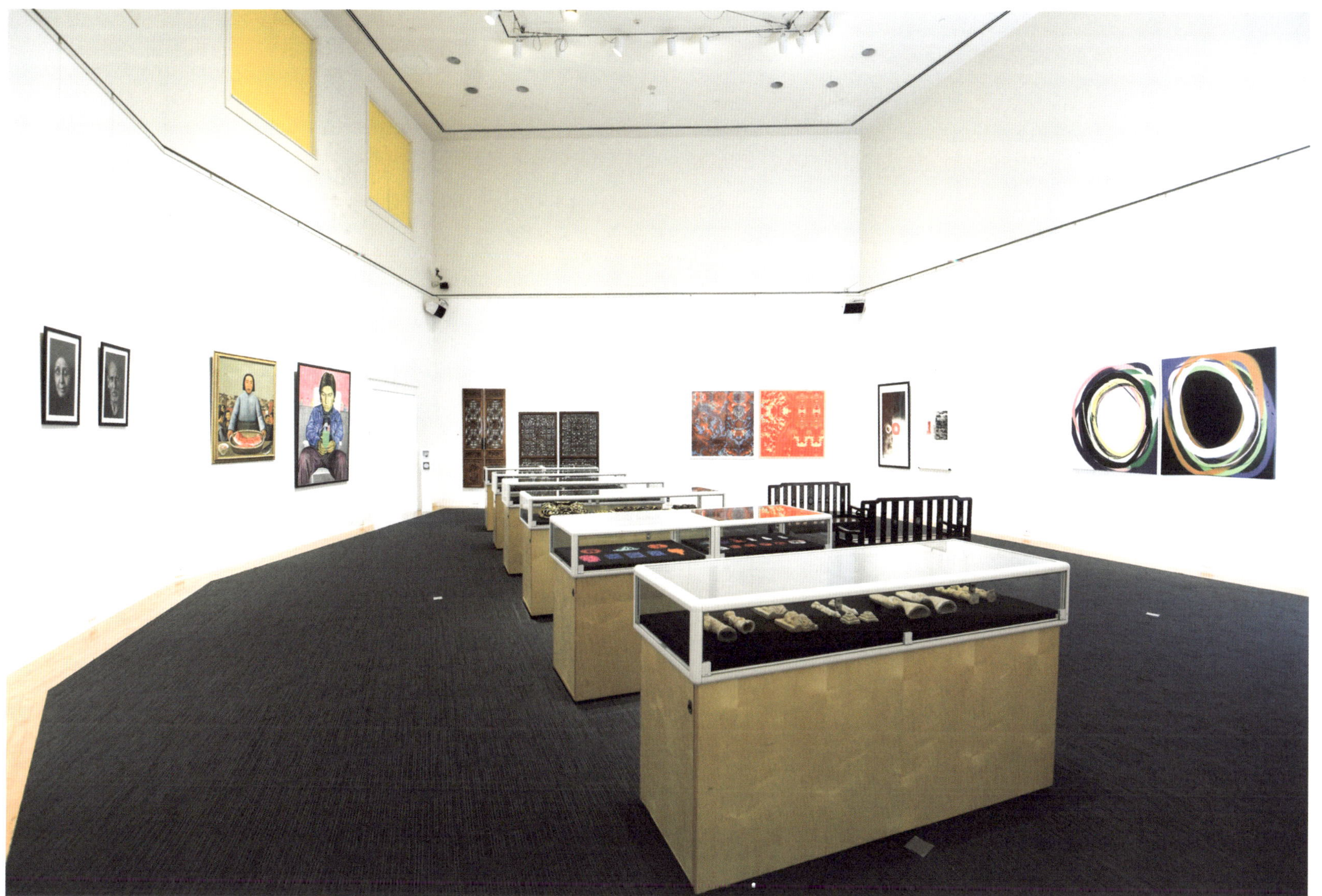

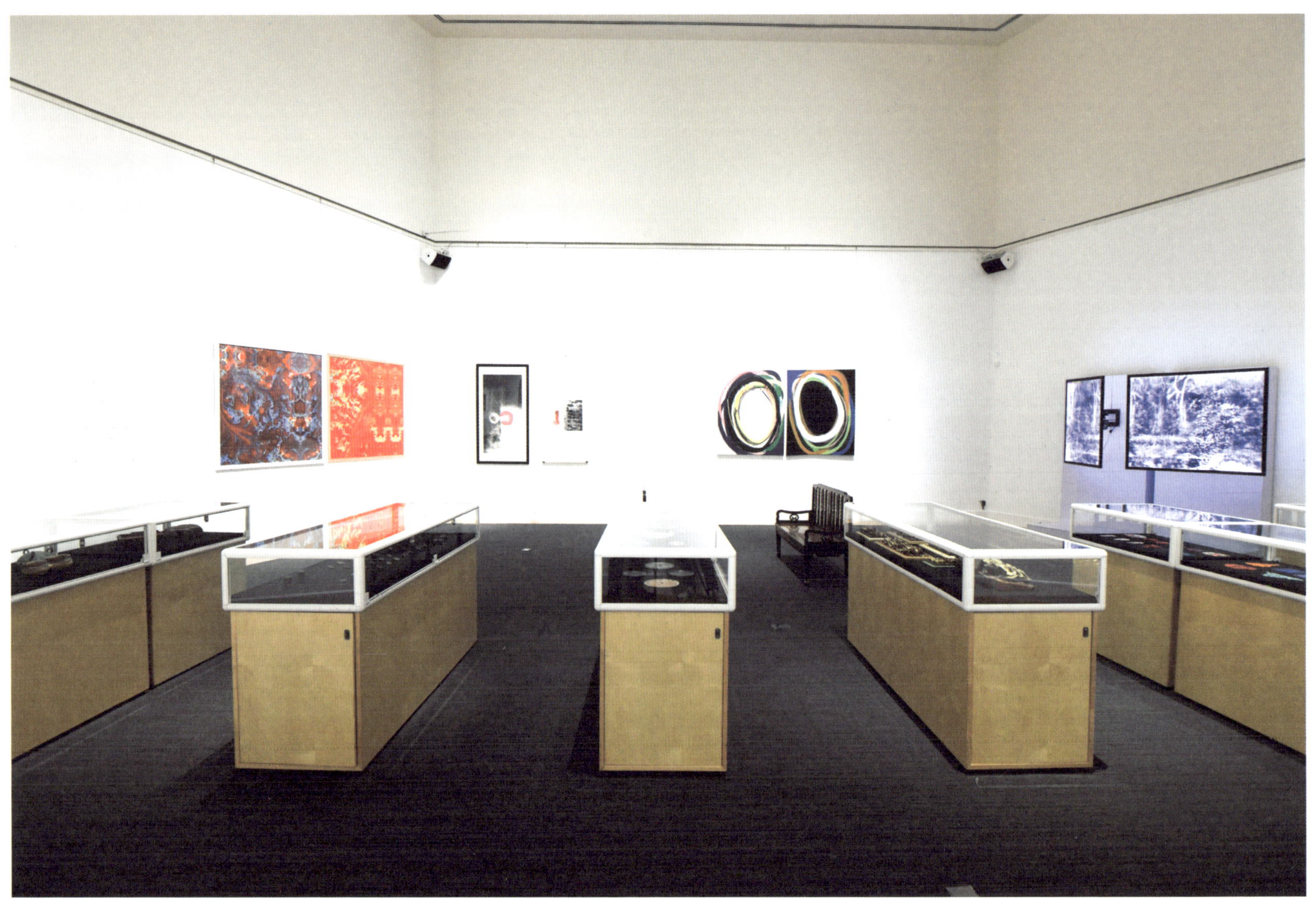

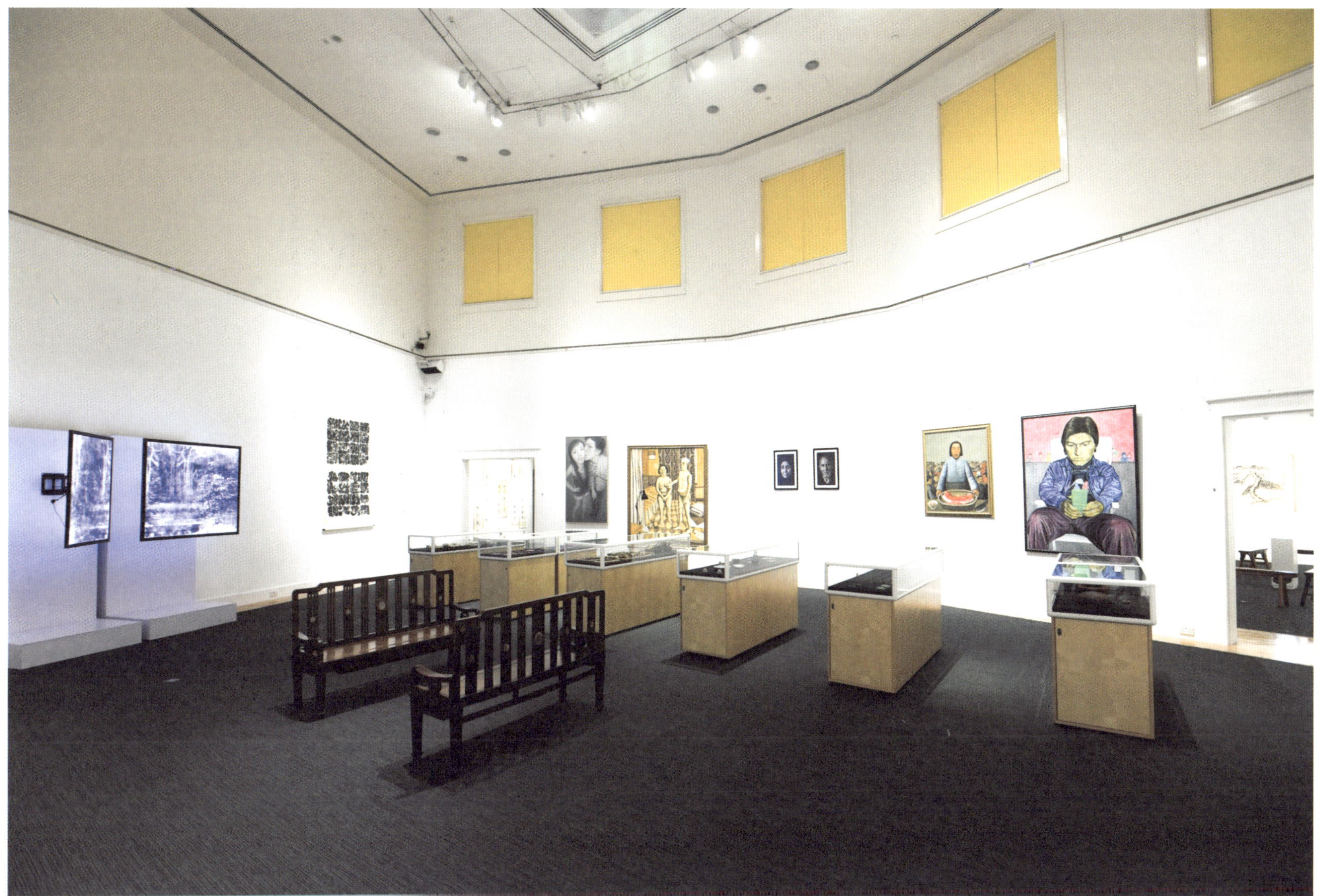

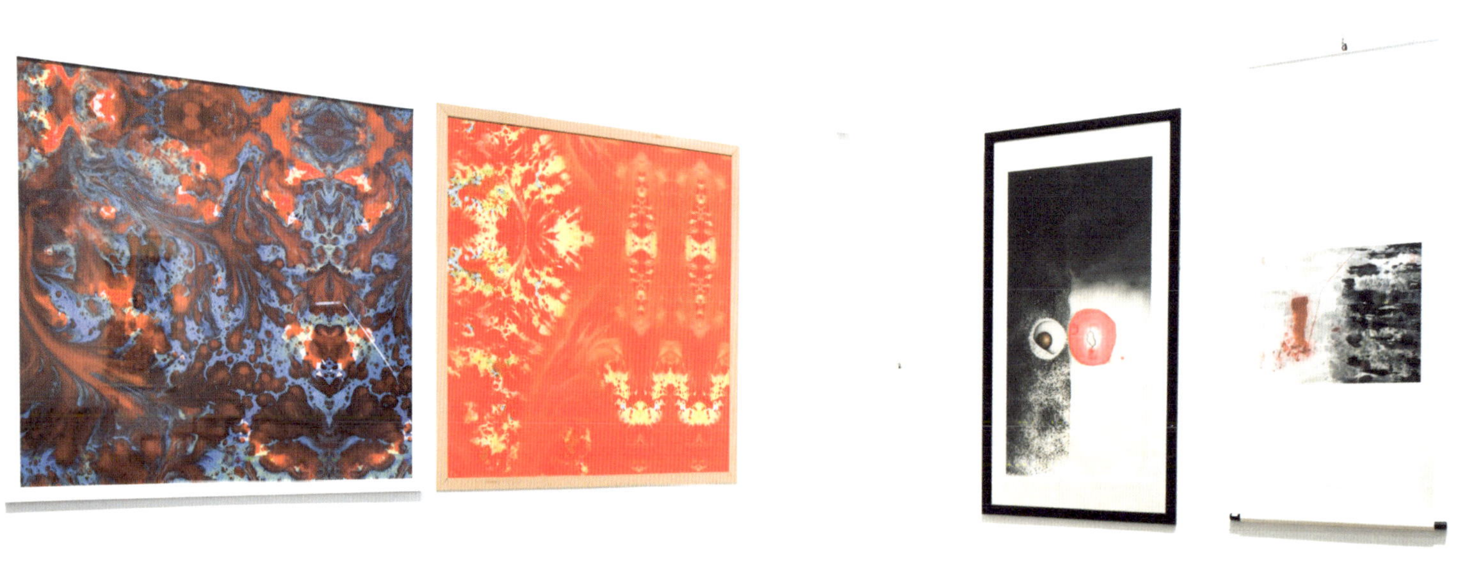

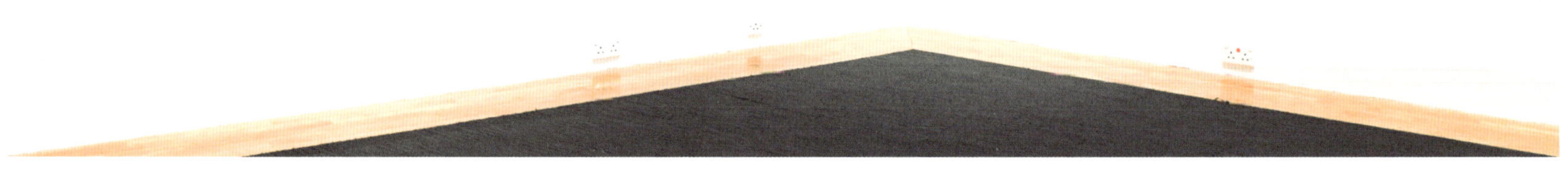

Robert LETTNER
Philipp STADLER

Robert LETTNER
Philipp STADLER

Irene CHOU
周綠雲

LEUNG Kui Ting
梁巨廷

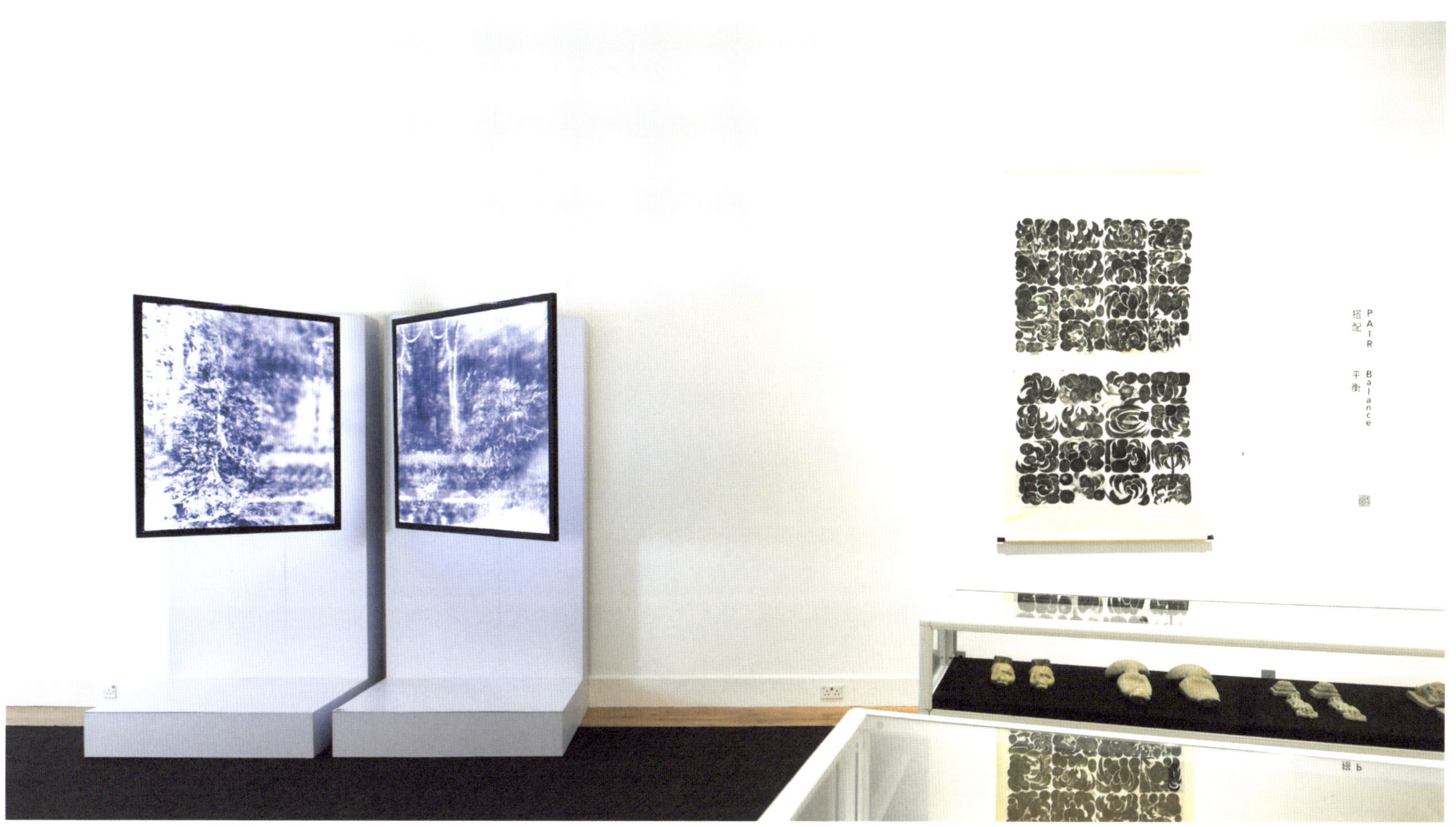

Tobias KLEIN

簡鳴謙

LI Ki Kwok Victor

李其國

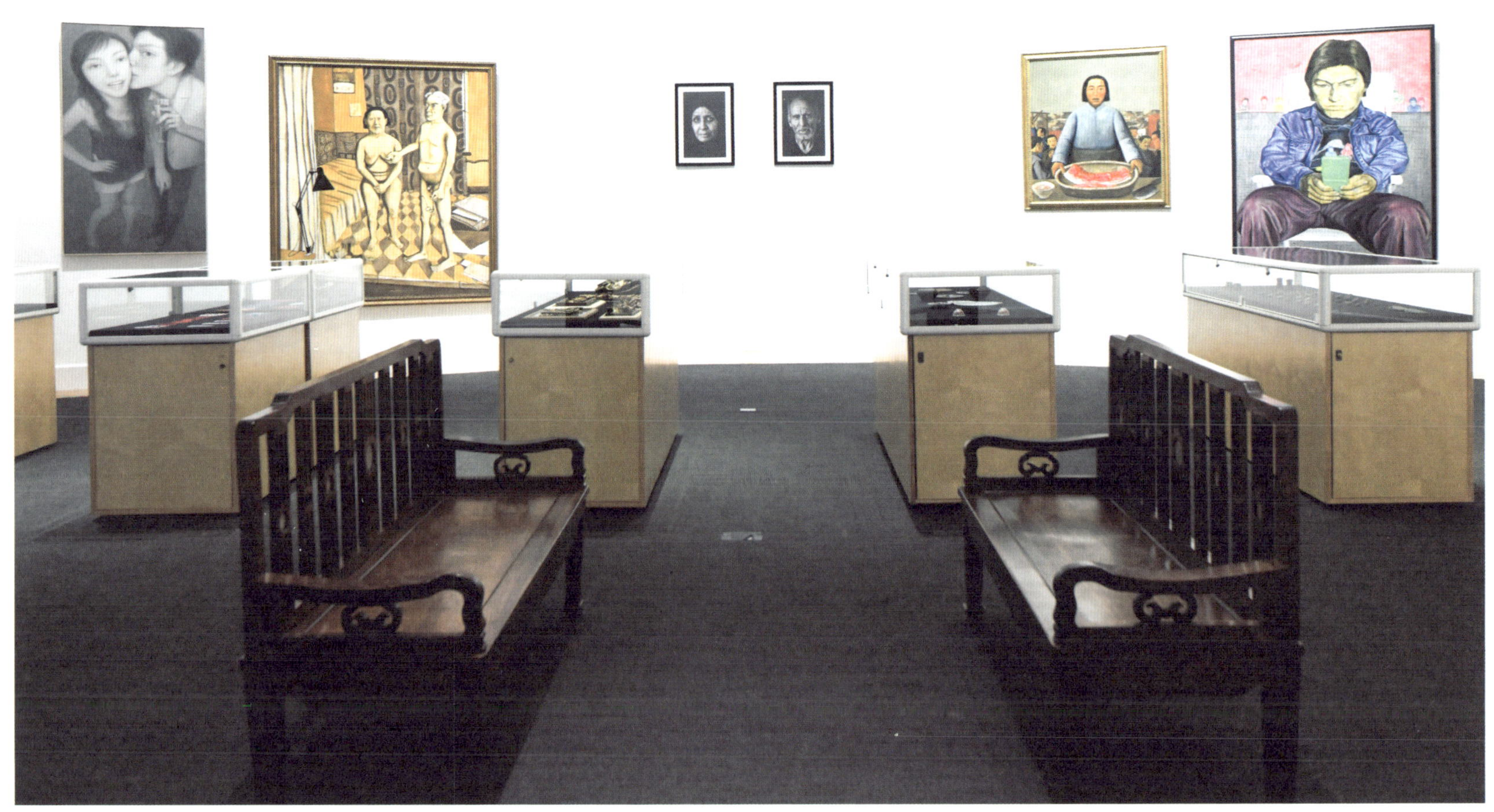

POON Yeuk Fai   SONG Yonghong   Shirin NESHAT   DUAN Jianwei   XIN Haizhou
潘躍輝   宋永紅   段建偉   忻海洲

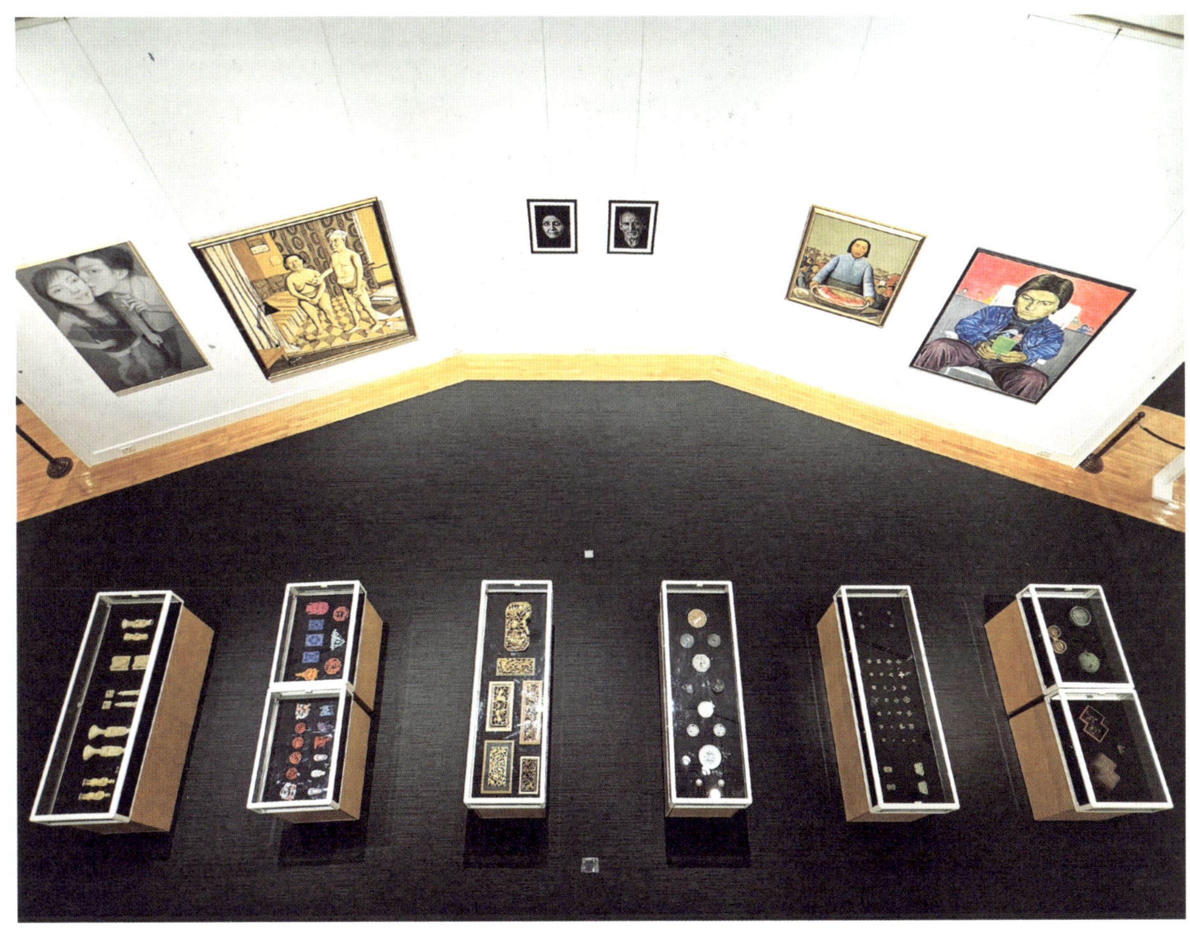

Eight showcases (from left to right):

Figures of earthenware (8), paper cuts (6, 7), wooden architectural ornaments (5), mirrors, bowls, vessels with phoenixes and dragons (4), bronze objects (3), two pieces form a single unit (1, 2).

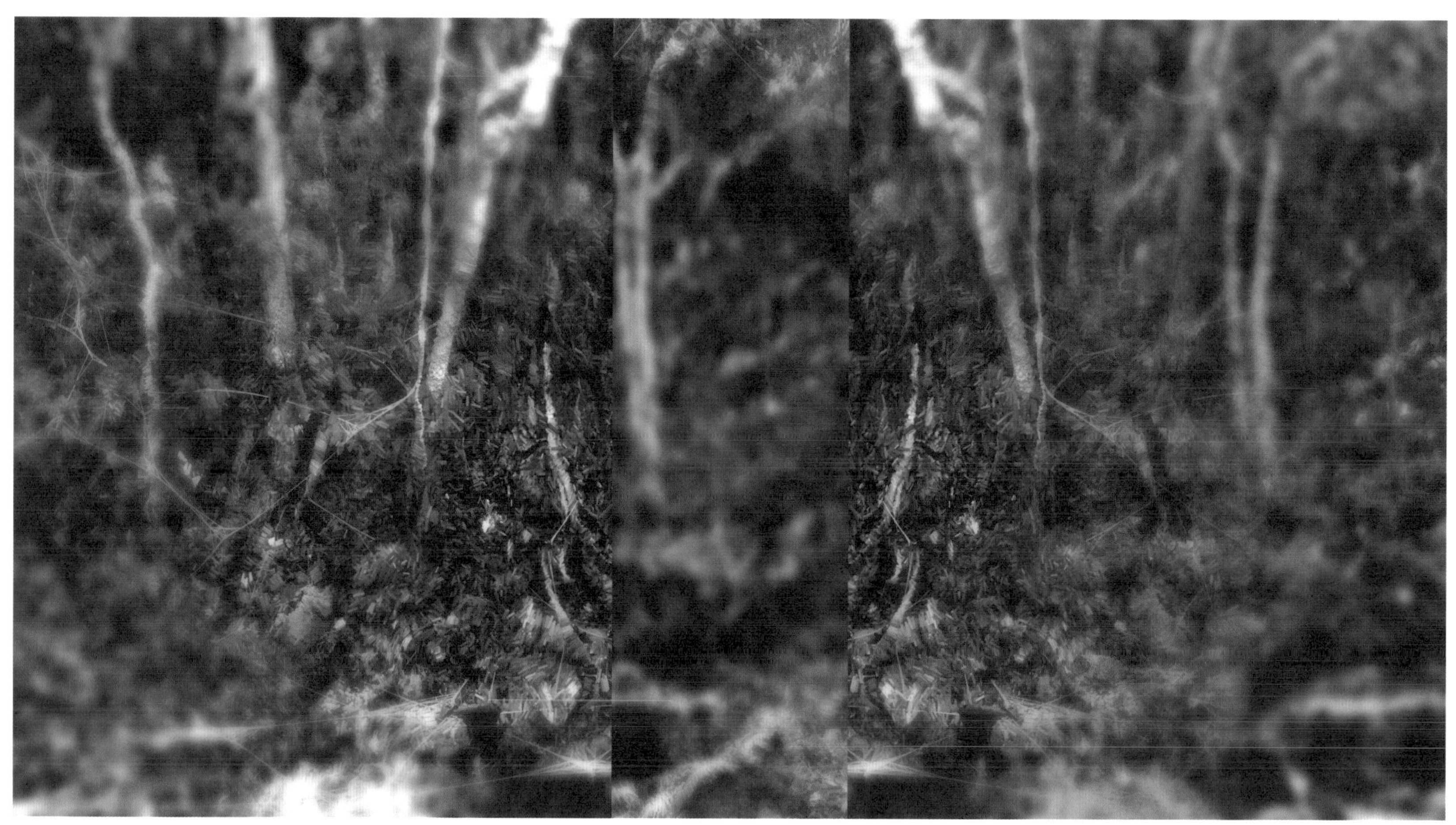

24 Tobias KLEIN 簡鳴謙

Déjà Vu | 2023

Kinetic installation with two independent pivoting lenticular prints

H 120 x W 140 x D 60 cm / H 120 x W 100 x D 60 cm

Collection of the artist

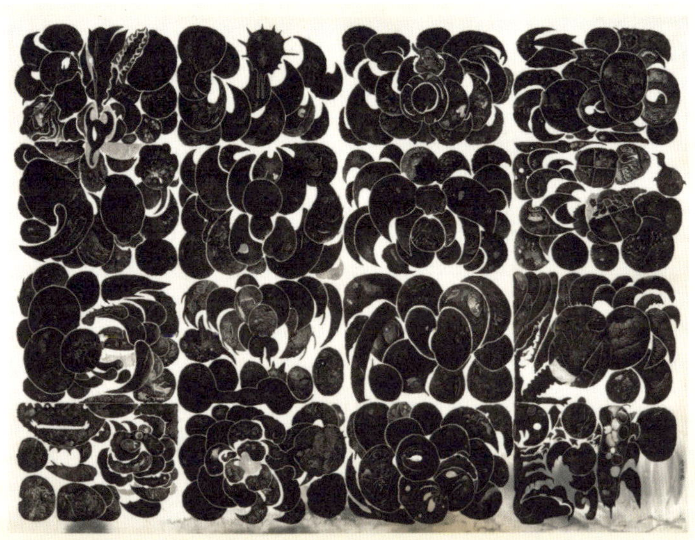

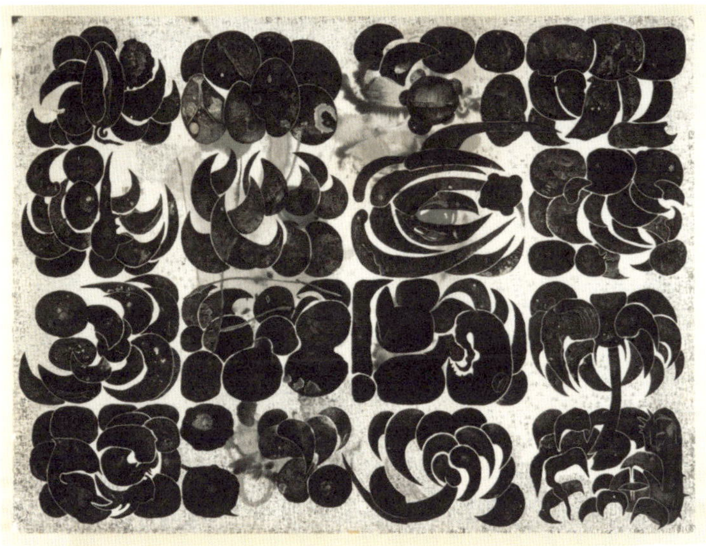

25 LI Ki Kwok, Victor 李其國
Attractiveness 02 《吸引力‧零二》 | 2002
Hanging scroll, diptych, ink on paper
L 199 x W 119.5 cm
HKU.P.2008.1715 | Gift of Professor KO W.M. Norman

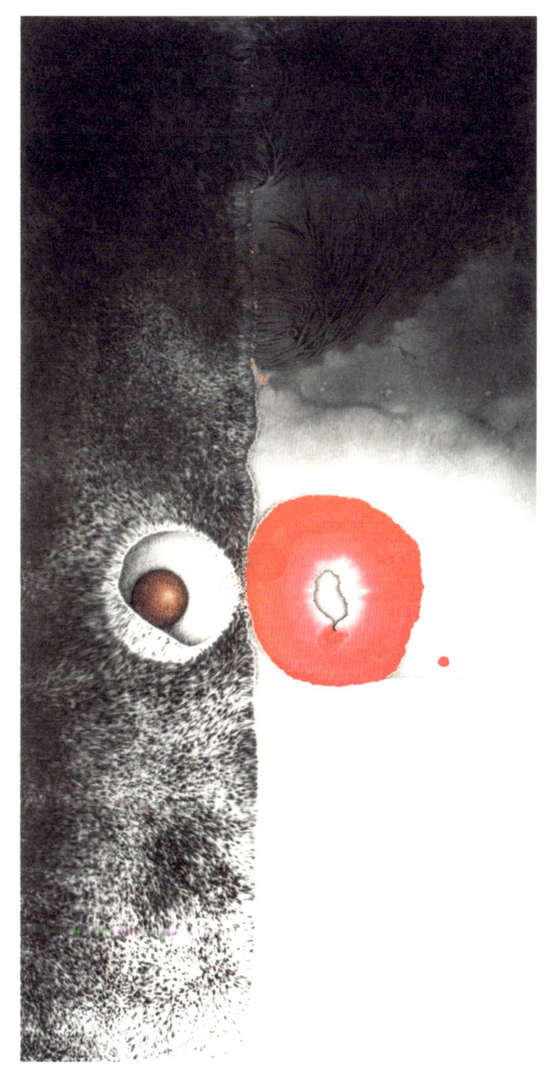

26 Irene CHOU 周綠雲

Abstract Composition 《抽象畫》 | 1980s

Vertical scroll, ink and color on paper | H 138.8 x W 69 cm

HKU.P.1986.1414

27 LEUNG Kui Ting 梁巨廷

A Flower Is Not a Flower 《花非花》 | 1996–2001

Hanging scroll, ink and color on paper | L 54 x W 63 cm

HKU.P.2008.1714 | Gift of Professor KO W.M. Norman

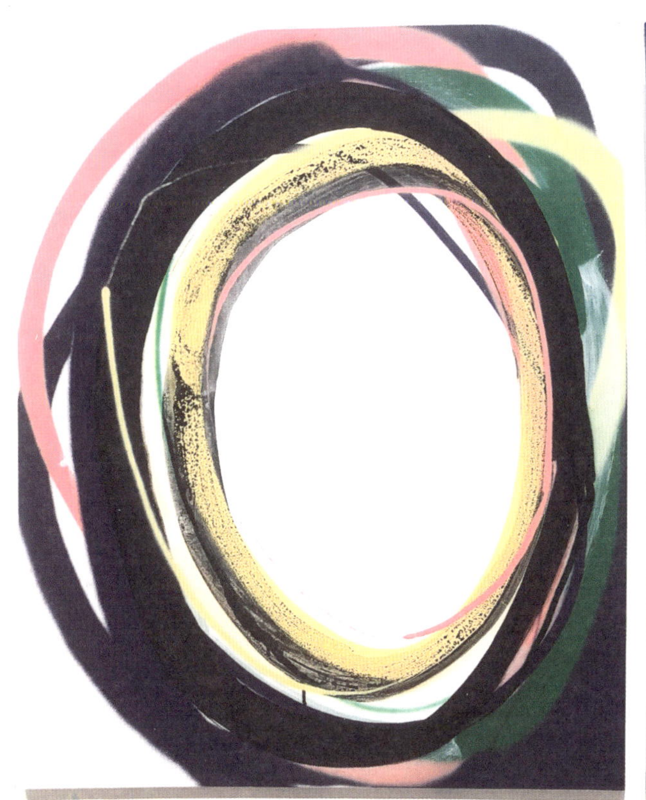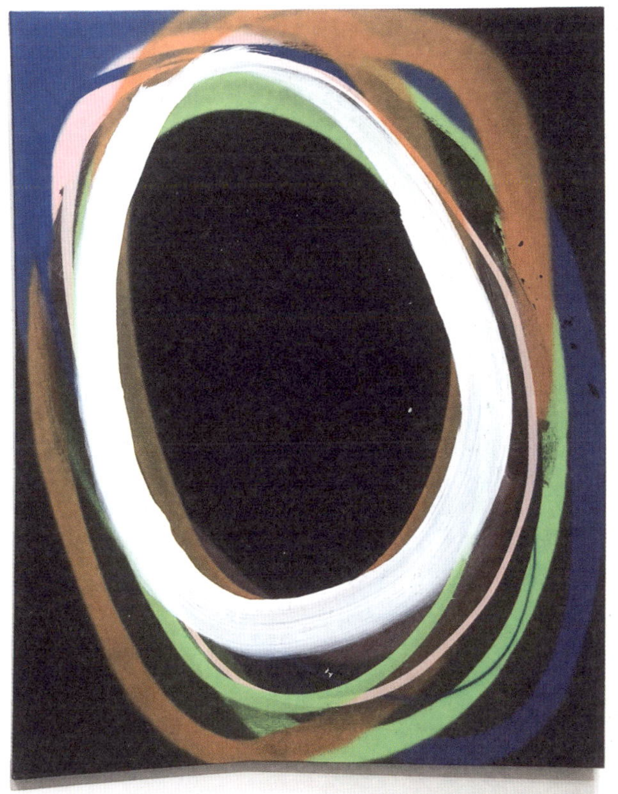

28 Adrian FALKNER
Untitled (Hong Kong) | 2016
Diptych, acrylic on canvas | H 151 x W 122 cm
Collection of the artist

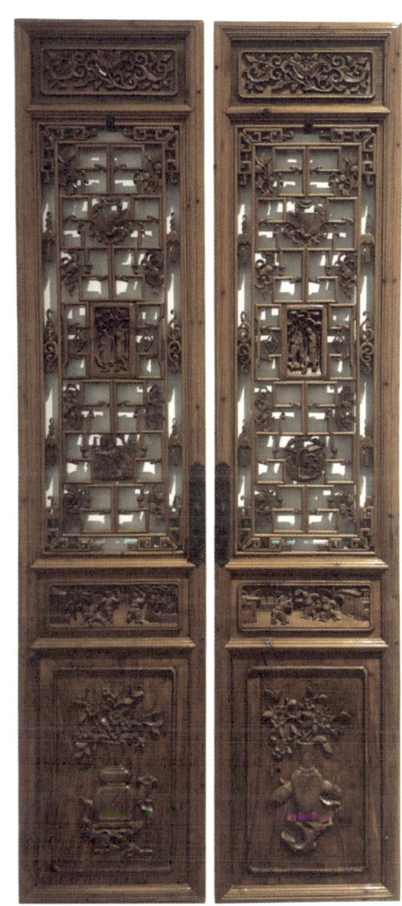

29 Pair of Wooden Doors with Daoist Immortals
Early 20th century
Wood | Each H 226 x W 49 x D 4.5 cm
HKU.W.2000.1360 a, b

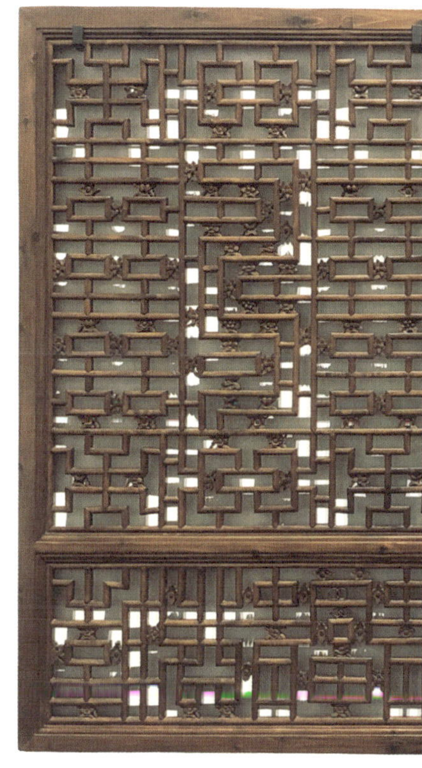

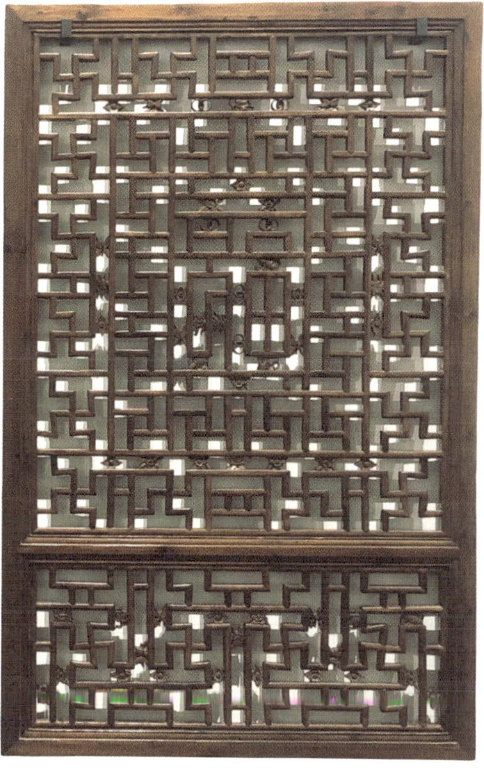

30 Pair of Carved Wooden Panels with Ornaments (Swastika)
Early 20th century
Wood | Each H 144 x W 92 x D 5 cm
HKU.W.2024.2658 a, b

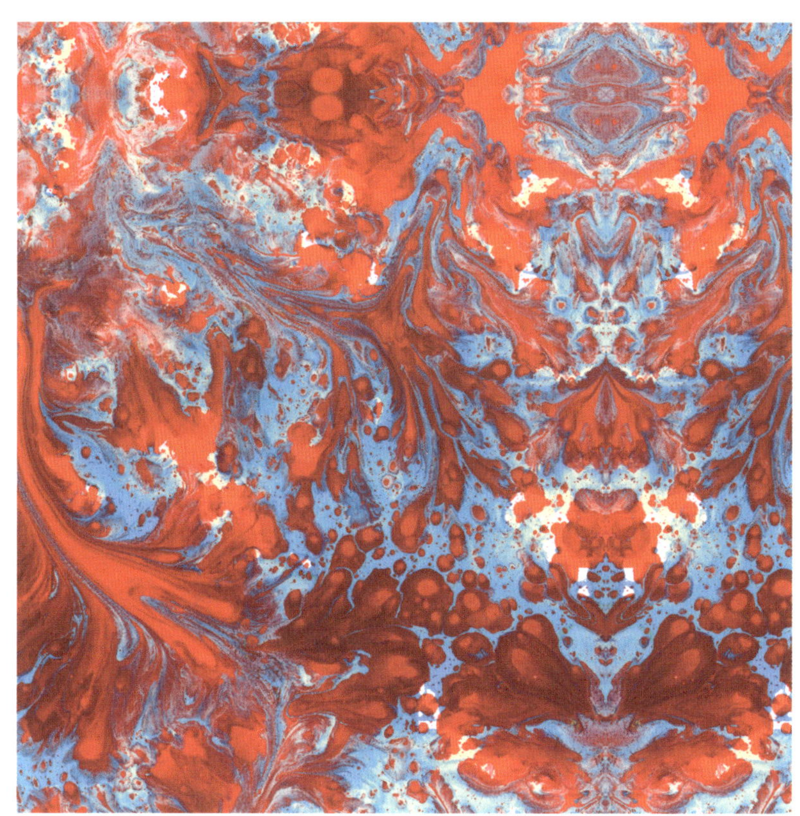 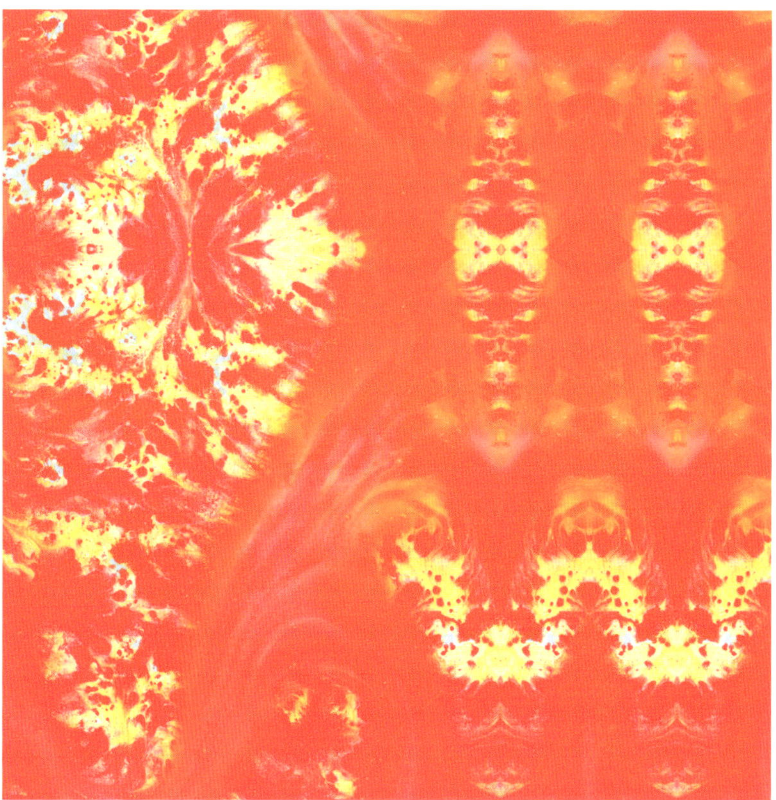

31 | 32 Robert LETTNER and Philipp STADLER

The Water Garden in Neptune's House | Nature Is Not a Catastrophe | 2017 (2003)
Inkprint on paper | Each H 150 x W 150 cm
Private collection, Hong Kong

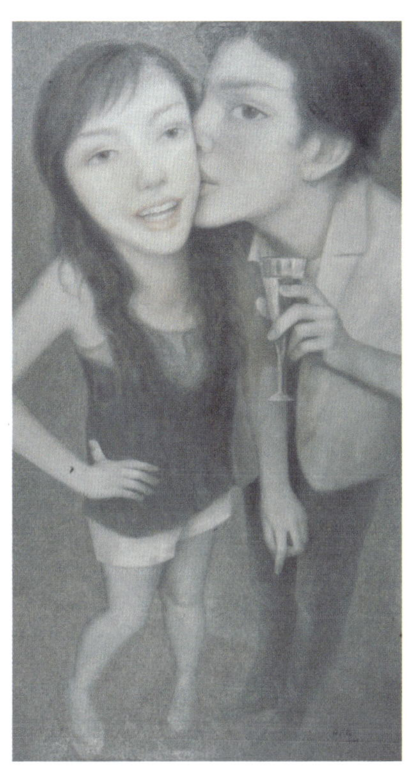

33 POON Yeuk Fai 潘躍輝
Green Wine 《青酒》 | 2009
Oil on canvas | H 183 x W 109 cm
HKU.P.2011.1890

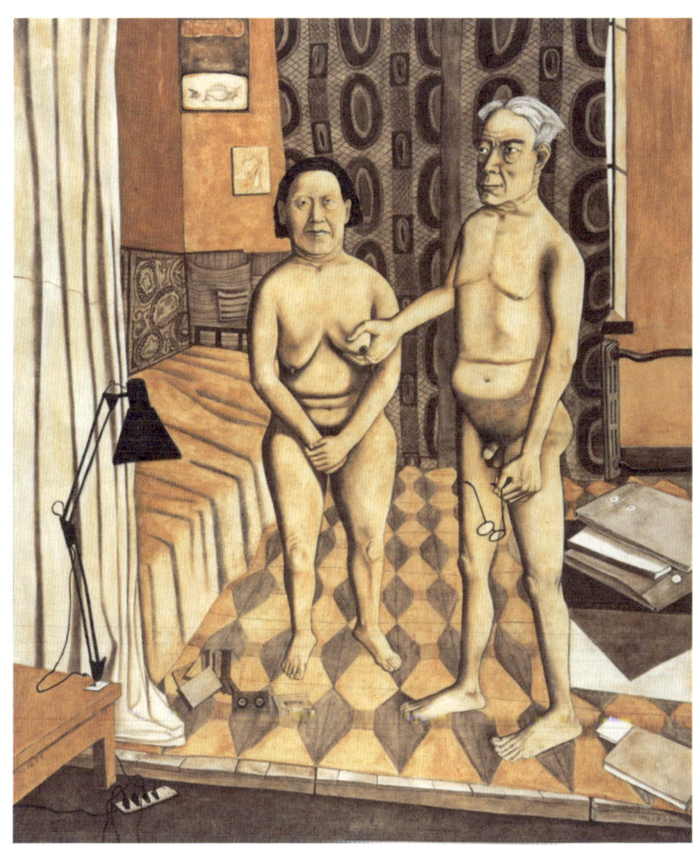

34 SONG Yonghong 宋永紅
Elderly Couple 《老年夫妻》 | 1992
Oil on canvas | H 198 x W 169 cm
HKU.P.1994.1034

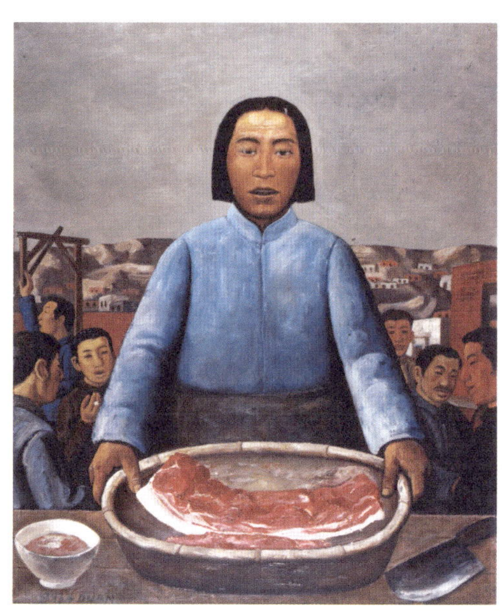

35 DUAN Jianwei 段建偉
Preparing a Meal 《做飯》 | 1993
Oil on canvas | H 110 x W 106 cm
HKU.P.1994.1037

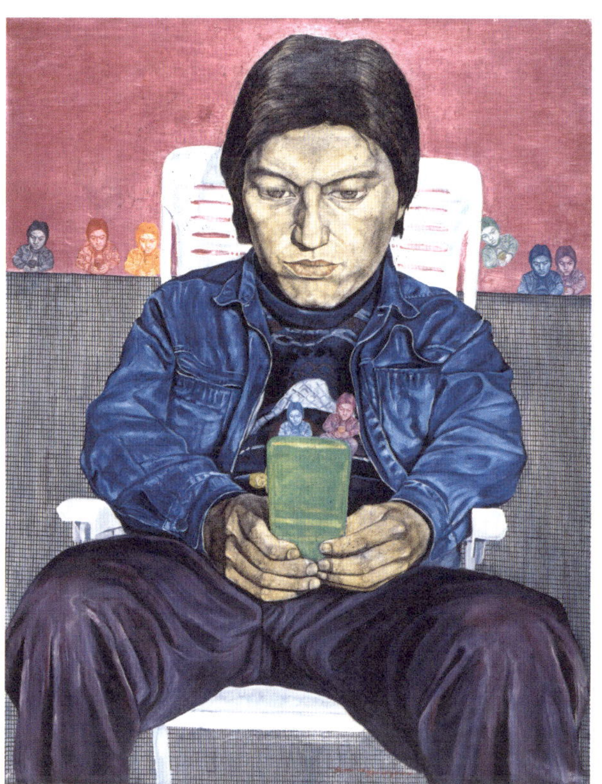

36 XIN Haizhou 忻海洲
Computer Game 《遊戲機的遊戲》 | 1993
Oil on canvas | H 180 x W 140 cm
HKU.P.1994.1036

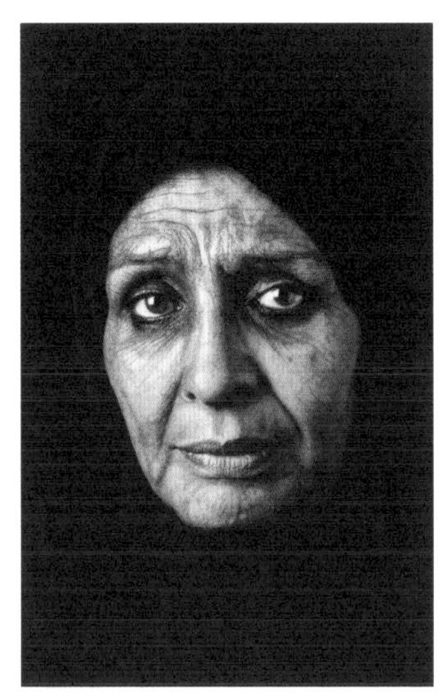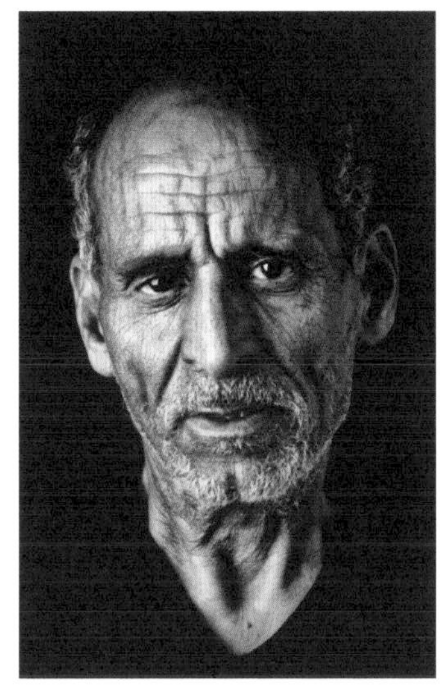

37 | 38 Shirin NESHAT
Ghada | Sayed (from the series *Our House Is on Fire*) | 2013
35/50, Digital C-print and ink | Each H 66 x W 44.5 cm
HKU.Pr.2022.2612 | HKU.Pr.2022.2611
Donation from Robert Rauschenberg Foundation

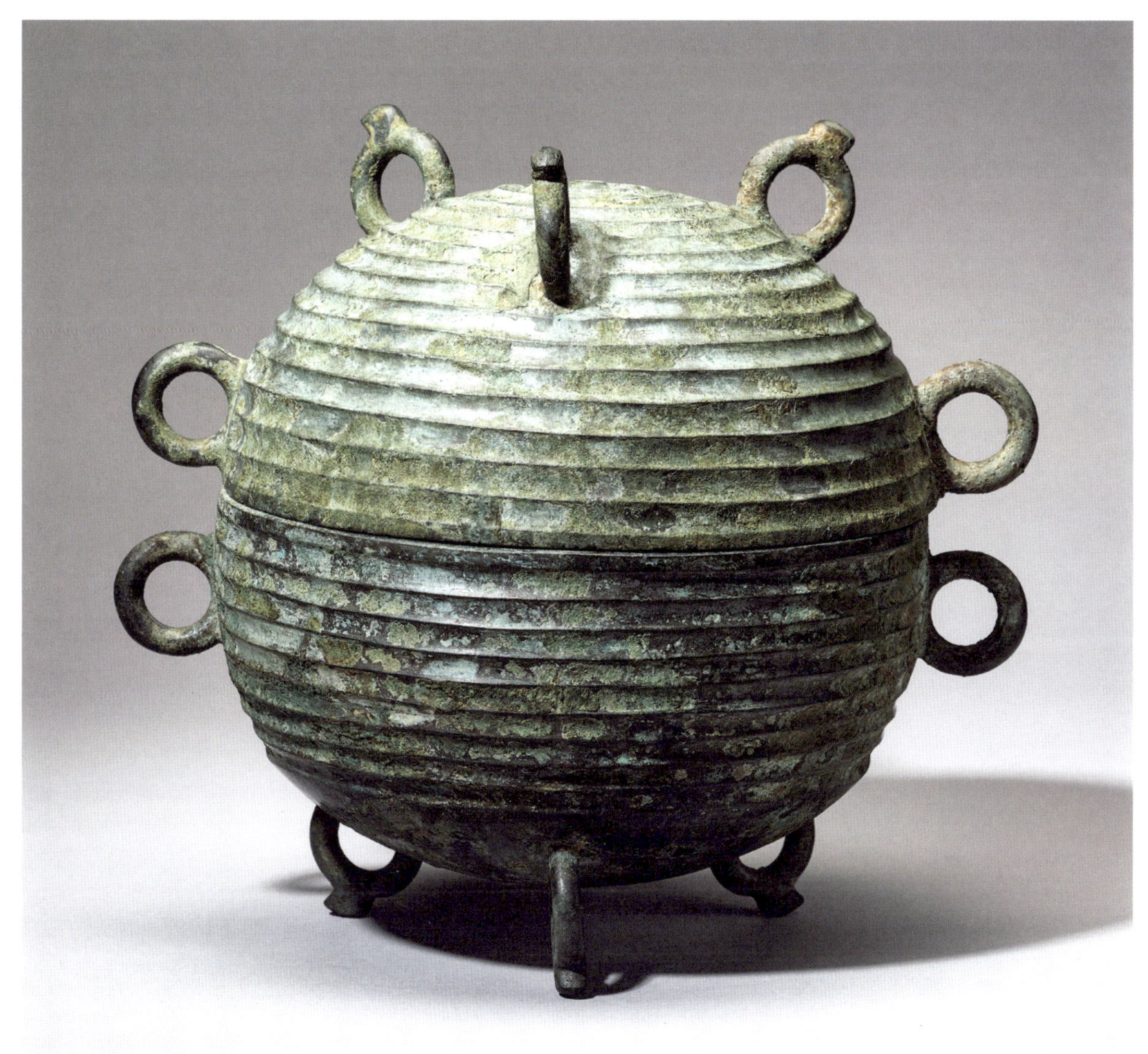

39 Duì (Food Container) with String Design
Warring States period (ca. 475–221 BCE)
Bronze | H 21.7 x W 24.4 x Ø 18.6 cm
HKU.B.1955.0173 a, b

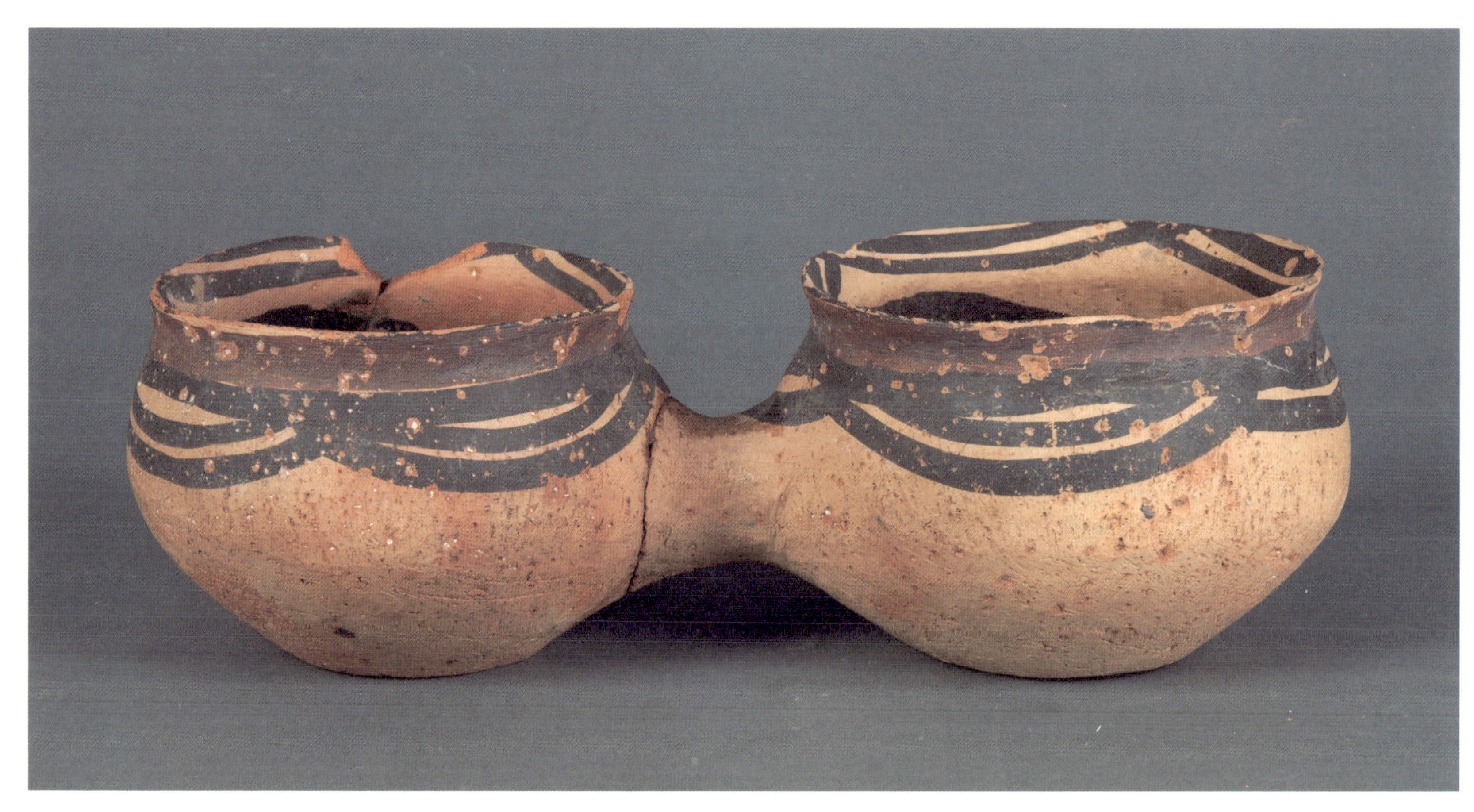

40 Conjoined Bowls
Neolithic, Majiayao culture, Banshan (ca. 2650–2350 BCE)
Earthenware with pigment | H 8 x W 26.6 cm
HKU.C.1986.0882

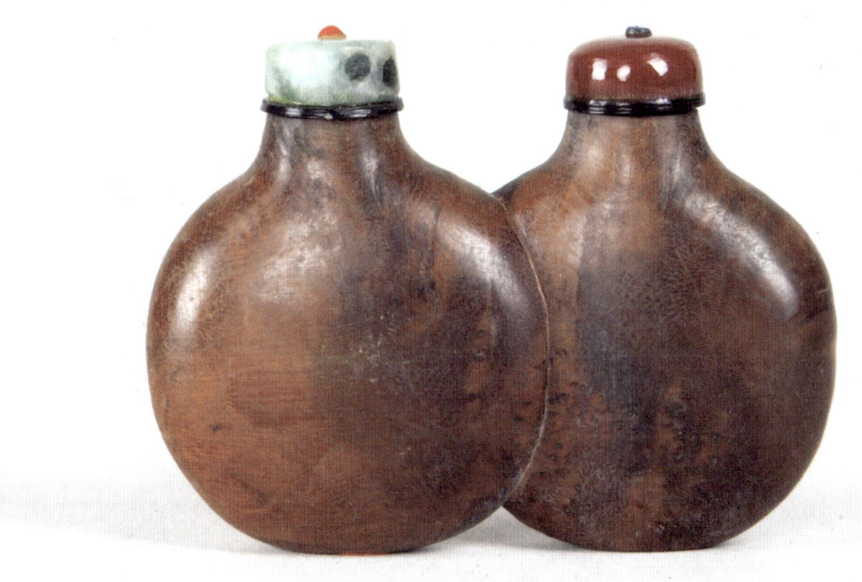

41 Snuff Bottles
Late Qing dynasty (1644–1911)
Burr wood | H 5.8 x W 7.8 x D 1.9 cm
HKU.M.1993.0994.38 | Gift of Mr Yeung Iat-che

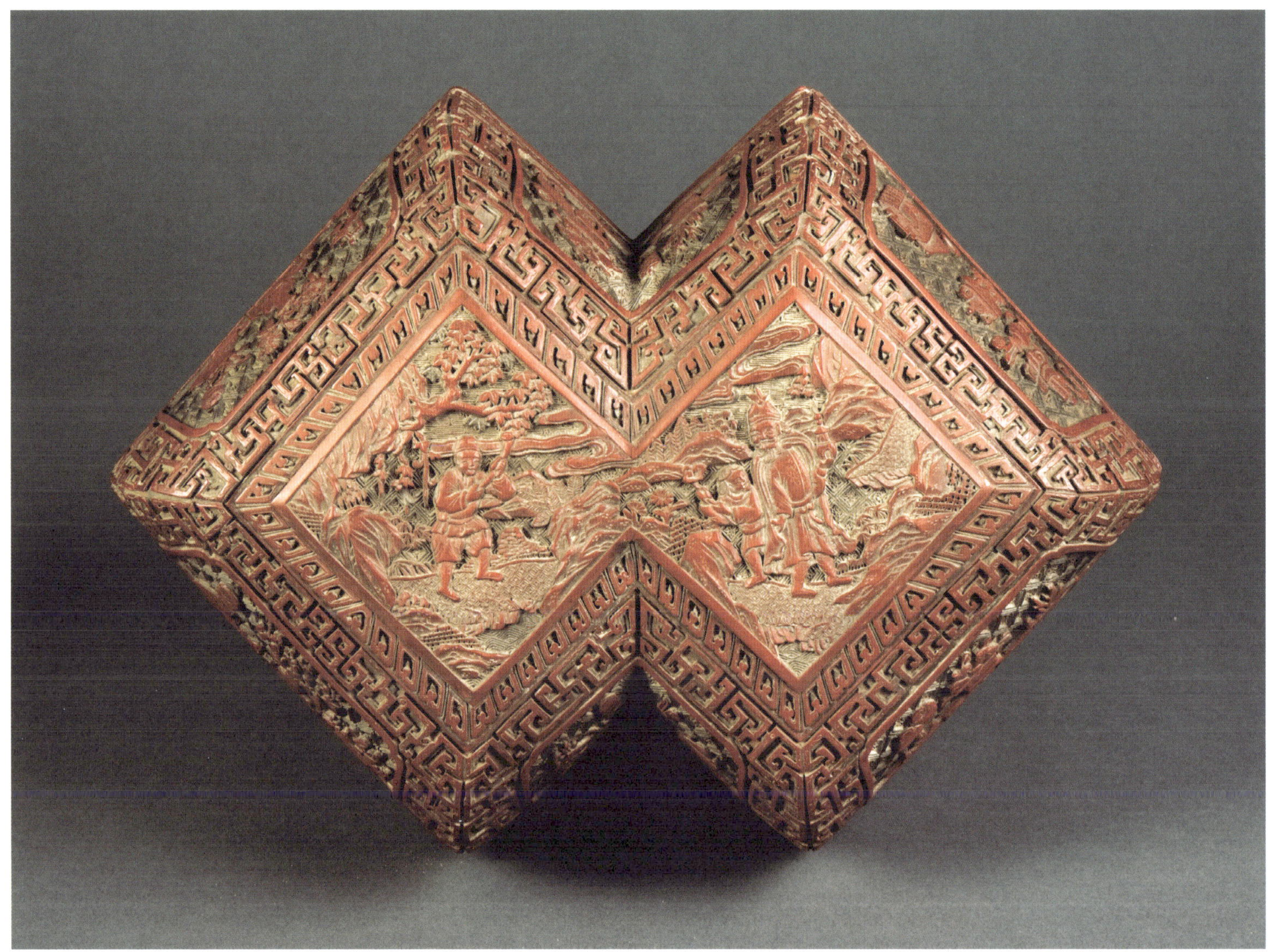

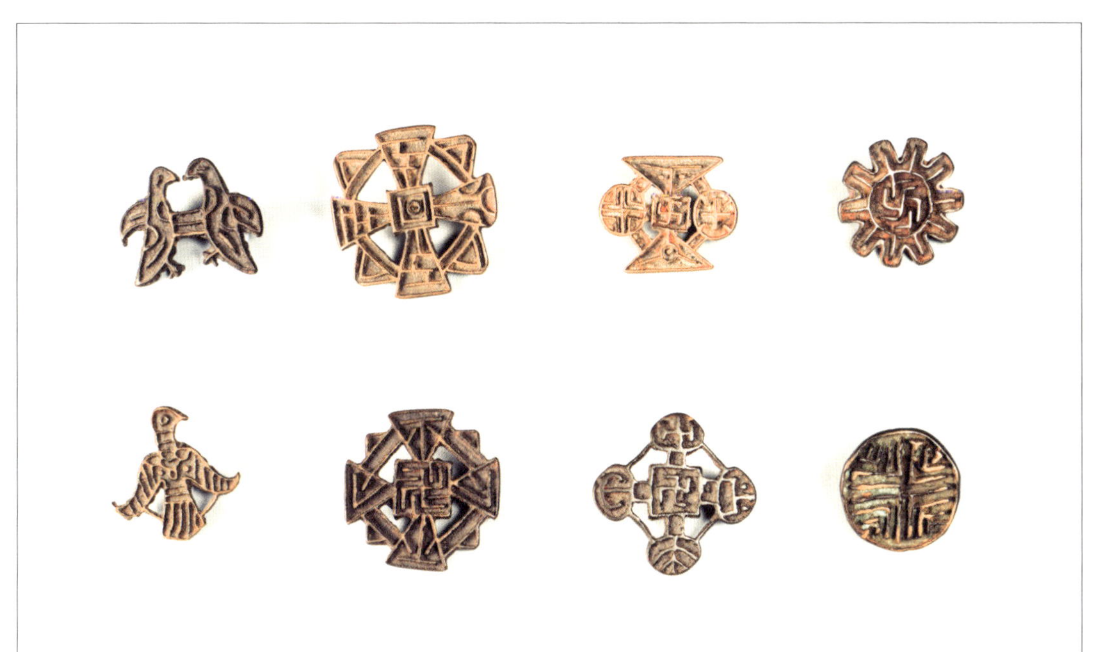

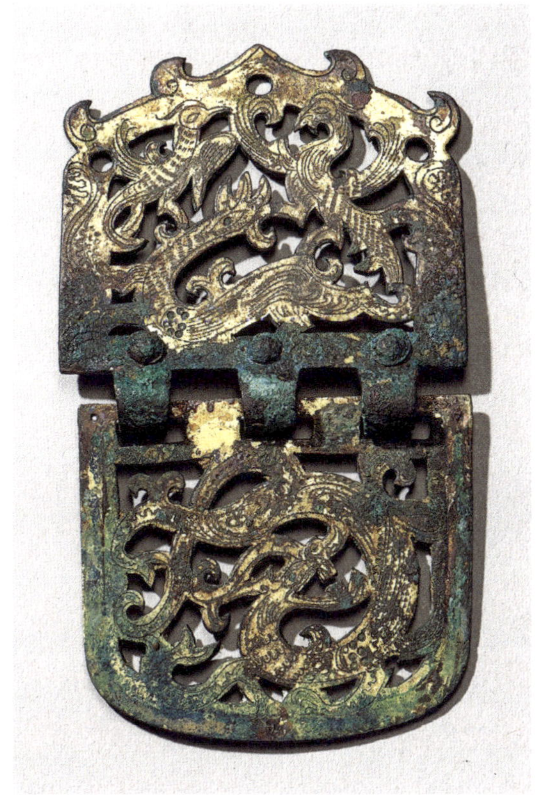

< 42 Carved Cinnabar Lacquer Box and
Cover in Conjoined Rhomboid Form
Qing dynasty, Qianlong period (1736–1795)
Red lacquer, carved decorations | H 17.3 x W 31 x D 23 cm
HKU.L.1971.0457 a, b

43 Selection of UMAG's Collection of 979 Nestorian Crosses
Ordos region, Northwest China | Yuan dynasty (1272–1368)
Bronze, Various dimensions
HKU.B.1961.0243 | Gift of Lee Hysan Estate Company
(Formerly FA Nixon Collection)

44 Gilt Bronze Hinge with Phoenixes and Dragons
Six Dynasties period (220–589 CE)
Gilt bronze
H 8 x W 4.7 cm | H 8 x W 4.5 cm
HKU.B.1983.0865 b

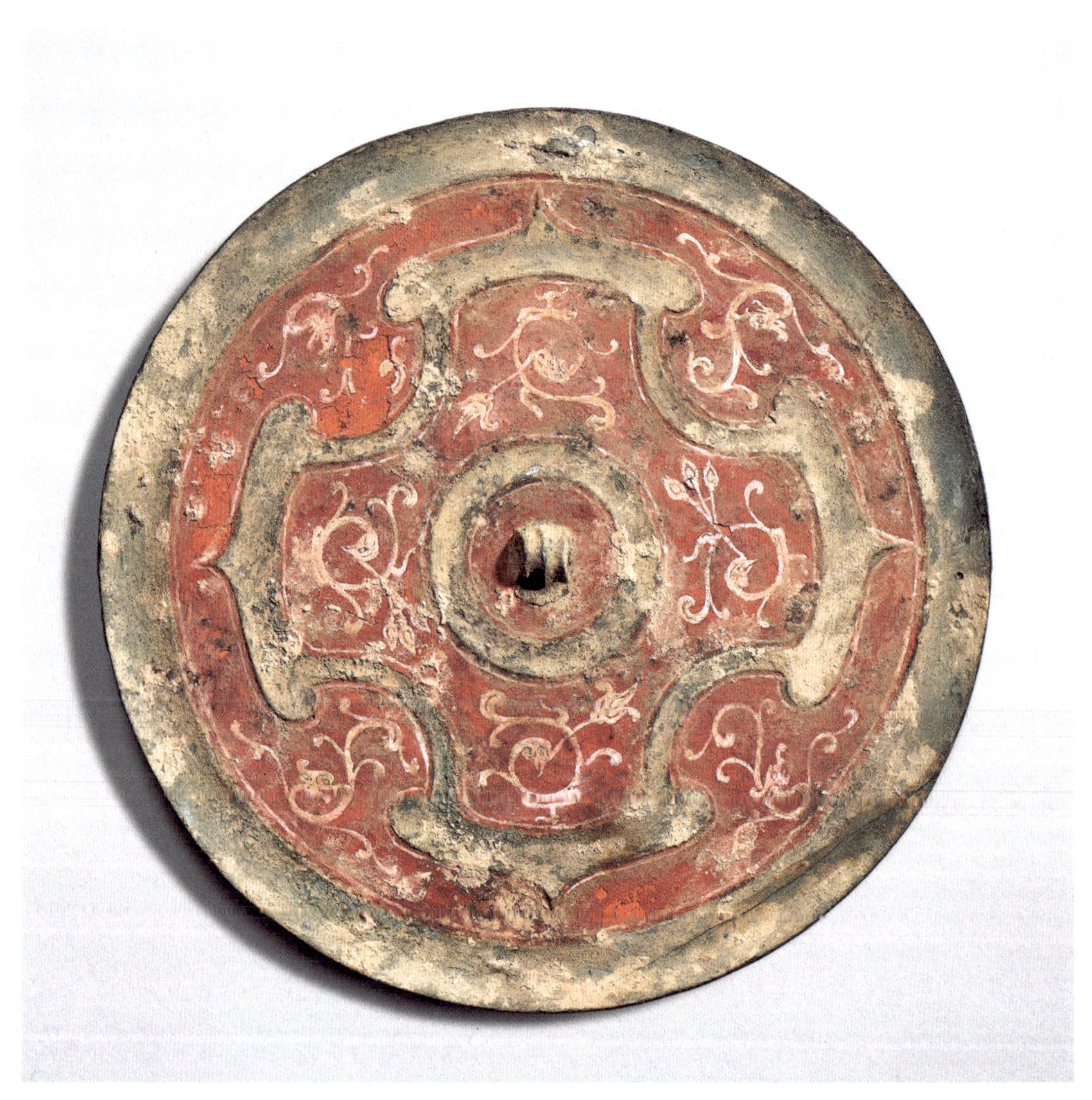

45 Bronze Mirror with Painted Decoration of Dragons and
Phoenixes | Warring States period (ca. 475–221 BCE)
Bronze | H 0.4 x Ø 19 cm
HKU.B.1955.0154 | Gift of .J Keswick

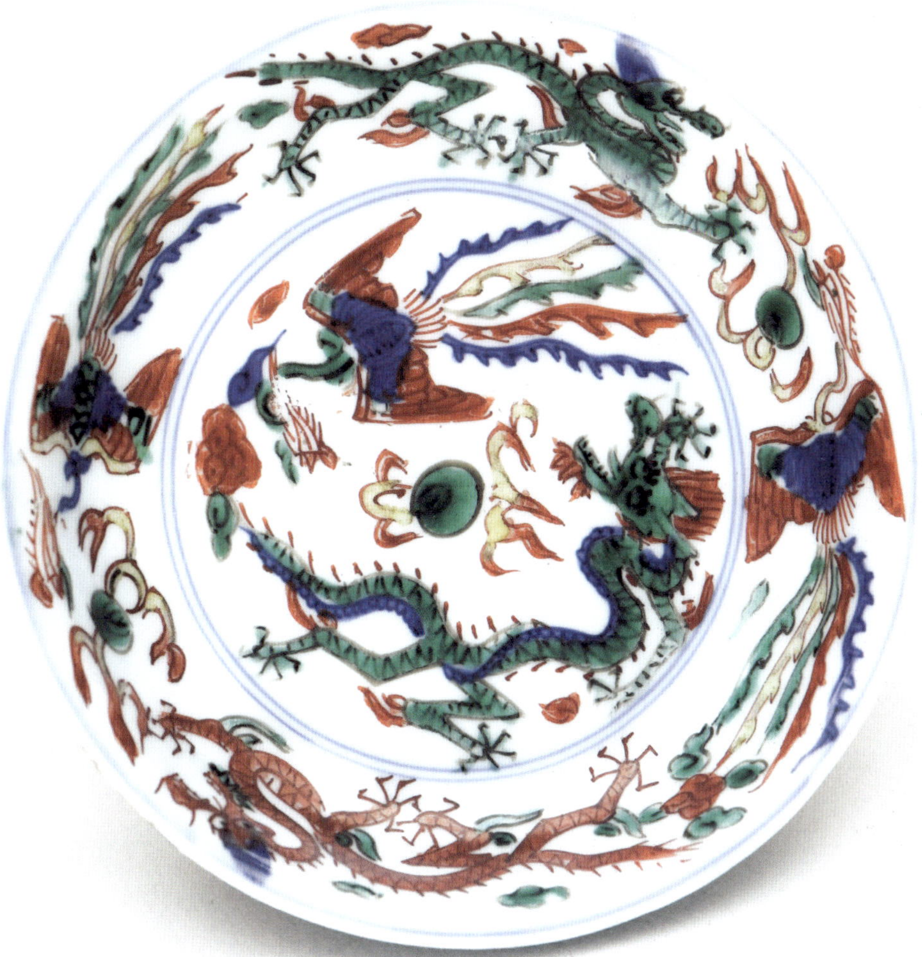

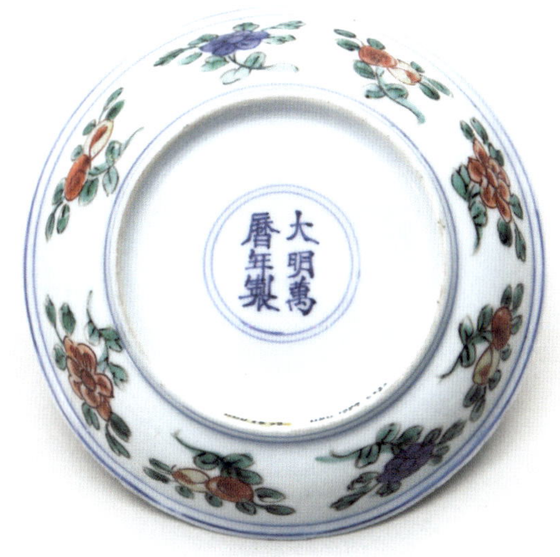

46 Dish with Dragons and Phoenixes
Ming dynasty, Wanli period (1573–1620)
Jingdezhen, Jiangxi province
Porcelain with underglaze blue and overglaze enamels
H 2.2 x Ø 11 cm | HKU.C.1959.0232

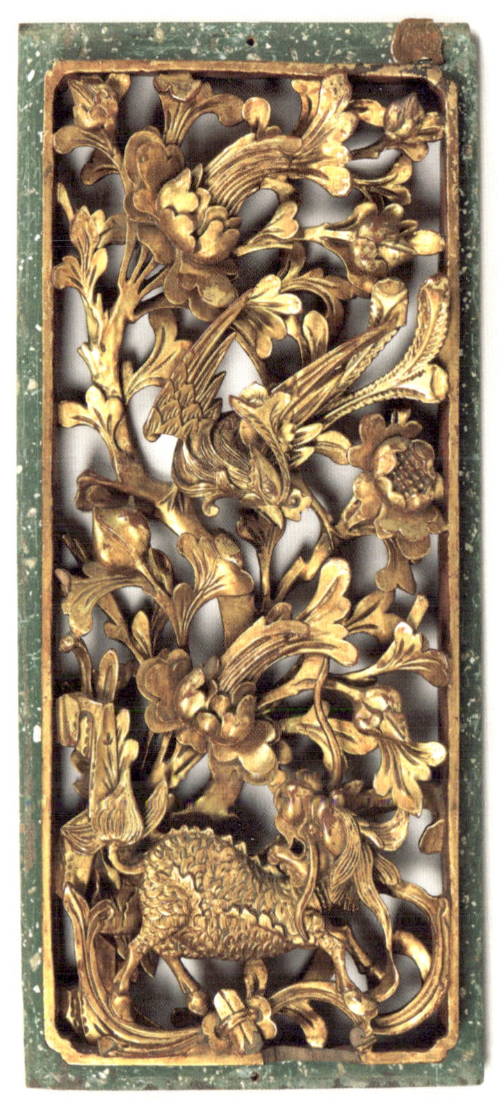

47 Gilt Wood Carving with Phoenix and Qílín
Early 20th century | Wood with gilding | H 37 x W 16.5 cm
HKU.W.1995.1057.11

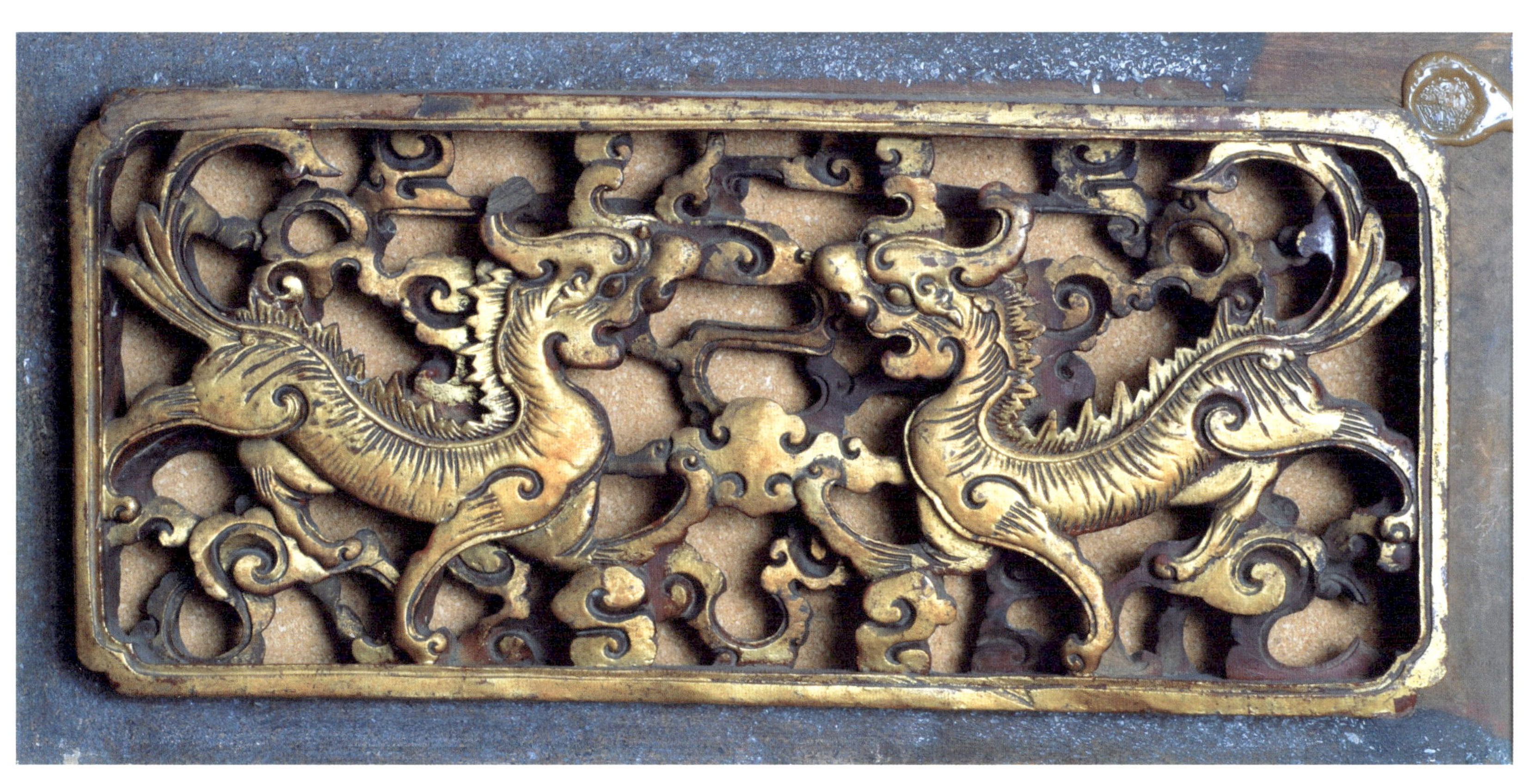

48 Gilt Wood Carving with Two Dragons
Early 20th century | Wood with gilding | H 20 x W 41 cm
HKU.W.1995.1057.4

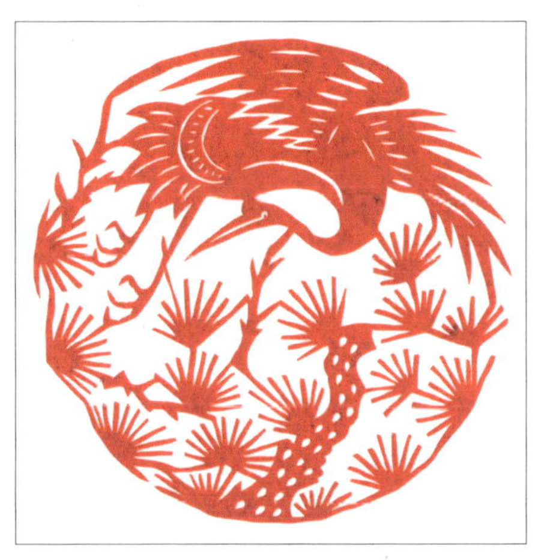

49 Papercut with Crane and Palm Tree Pattern
Yangzhou, Jiangsu province | 20th century
Paper, single color | H 12 x W 11 cm
HKU.Pc.1976.2477.577

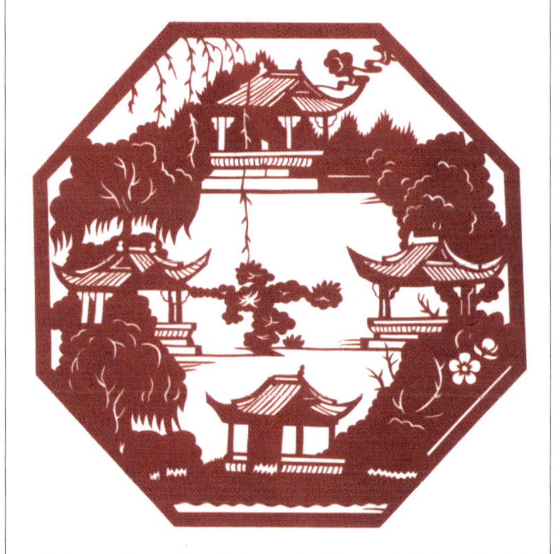

50 Papercut of a Chinese Garden Pavilion in Wuxi
Yuhuan, Zhejiang province | 20th century
Paper, single color | H 18 x W 18 cm
HKU.Pc.1976.2477.154

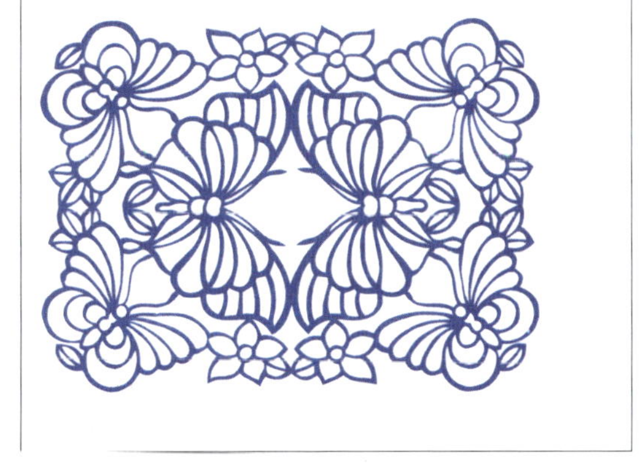

51 Papercut with Symmetrical Butterfly Pattern
Yueqing, Zhejiang province | 20th century
Paper, single color | H 13 x W 18 cm
HKU.Pc.1976.2477.804

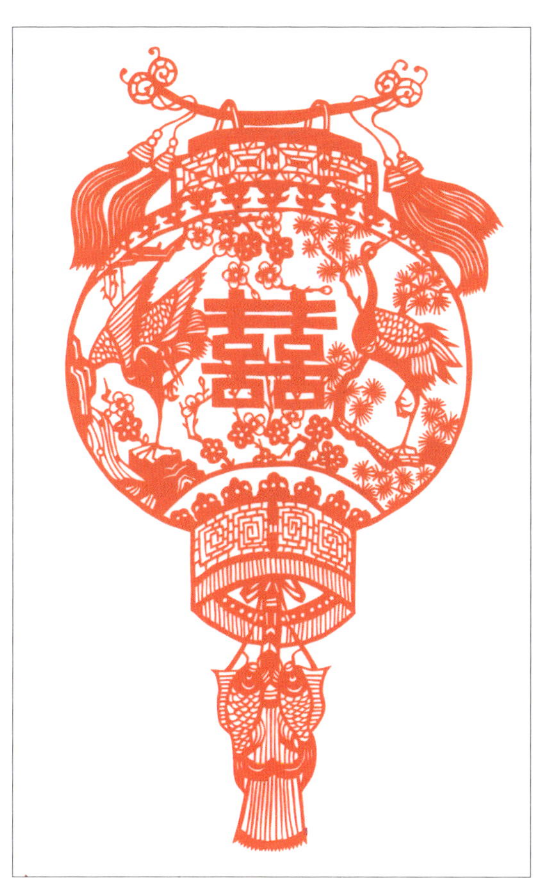

52 Palace Lantern with Double Happiness Motif for Marriage, a Pair of Fish and two Cranes | 20th century
Paper, single color | H 24 x W 15 cm
HKU.Pc.1976.2477.1158

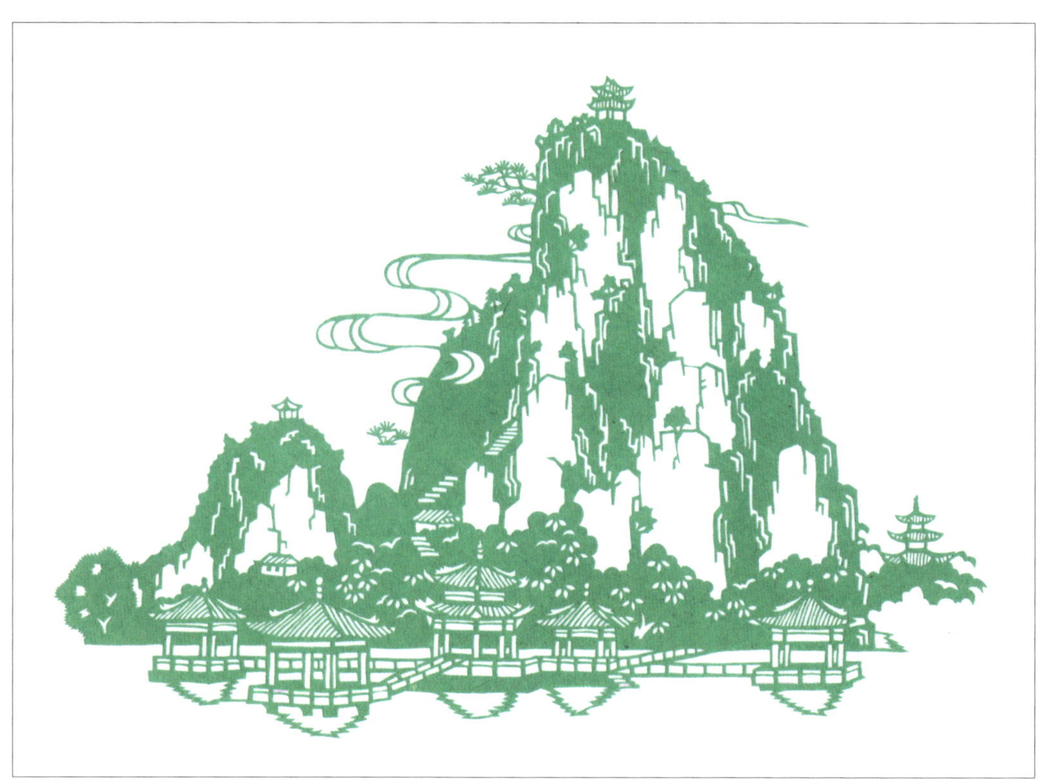

53 Baiyun Mountain, Guangzhou Scenery
Yuhuan, Zhejiang province | 20th century
Paper, single color, *yinyangke* technique | H 18 x W 24 cm
HKU.Pc.1976.2477.233

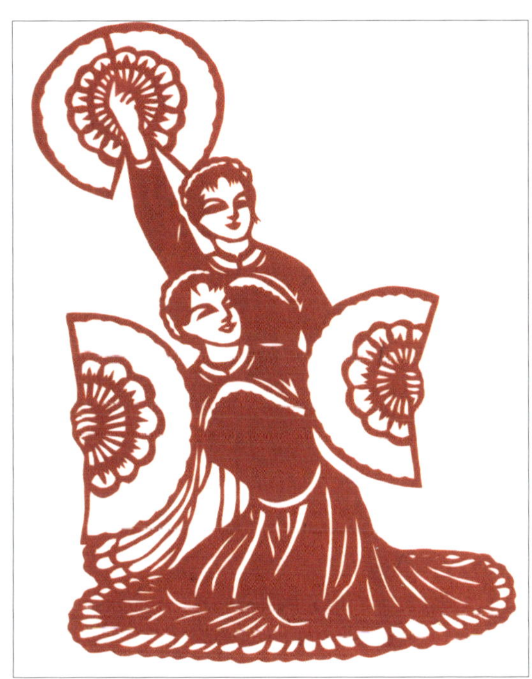

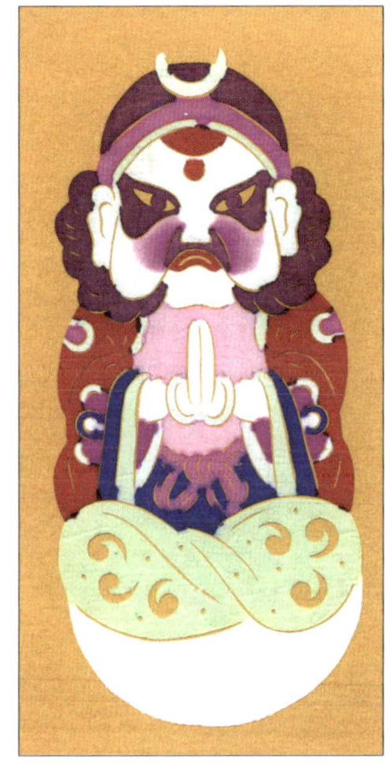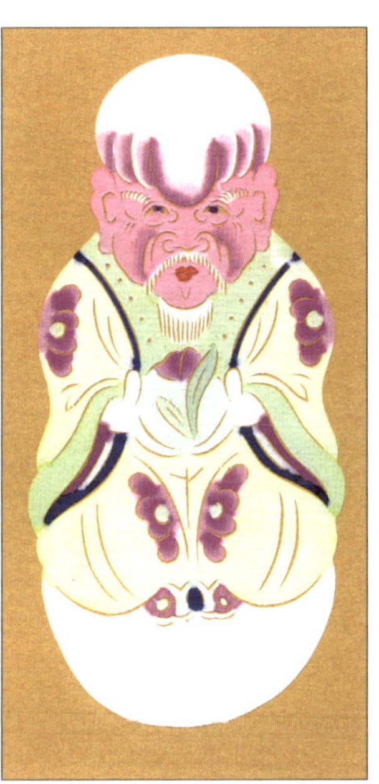

54 Two Female Dancers of the Yi Ethnic Group
Performing a Fan Dance (Shanwu)
Yangzhou, Jiangsu province | 20th century
Paper, single color, *yinyangke* technique | H 17 x W 12 cm
HKU.Pc.1976.2477.59

55 | 56 Papercuts with Beijing Opera Mask
Sha Wujing | Shoulao God of Longevity
Tianjin | 20th century | Paper, multi-colored papercuts
painted with a brush (dianse jianzhi) | Each H 14 x W 9 cm
HKU.Pc.1976.2477.34

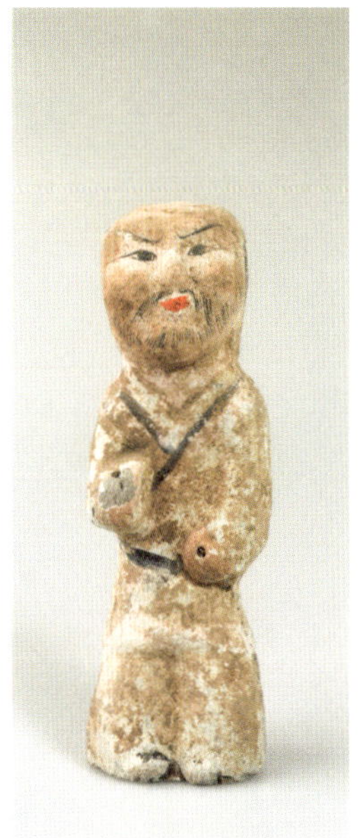
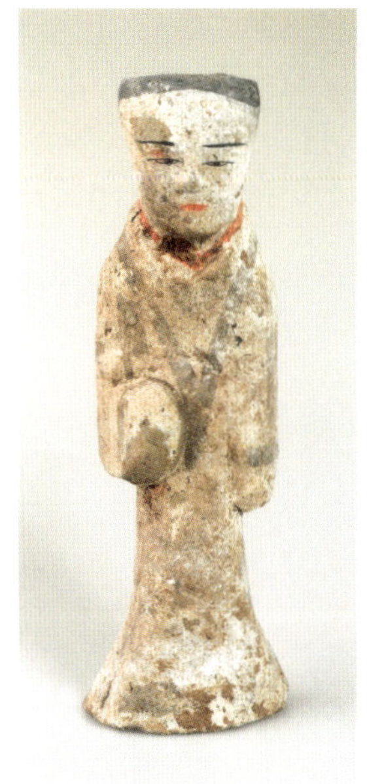
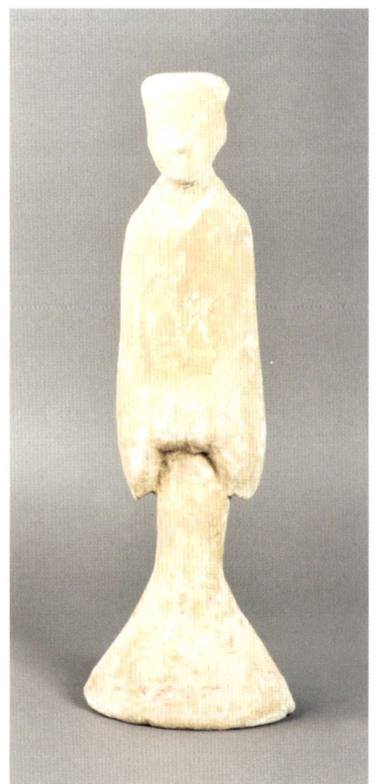
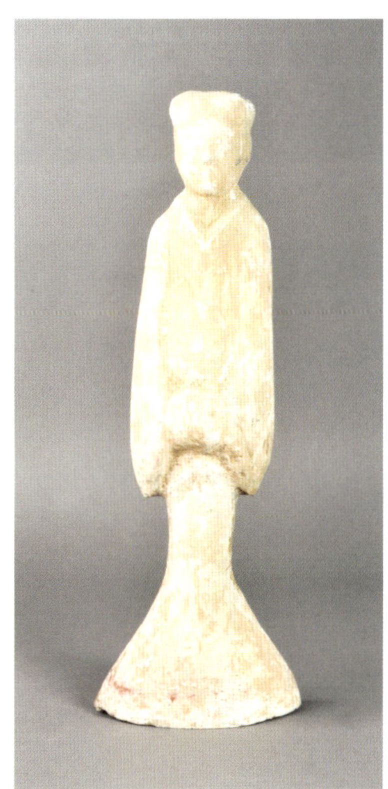

57 | 58 Pair of Figures
Han dynasty (206 BCE–220 CE)
Earthenware with pigment | H 21 cm | H 28 cm
HKU.C.1997.1108 b, a | Gift of Ms LI Lai-wa (Wilford Antique Co.)

59 Pair of Female Figures
Han dynasty (206 BCE–220 CE)
Earthenware | H 38.2 x W 13 cm | H 38.2 x W 13.2 cm
HKU.C.1991.0968 a, b | Gift of Charles Lee

REBUS Mystery

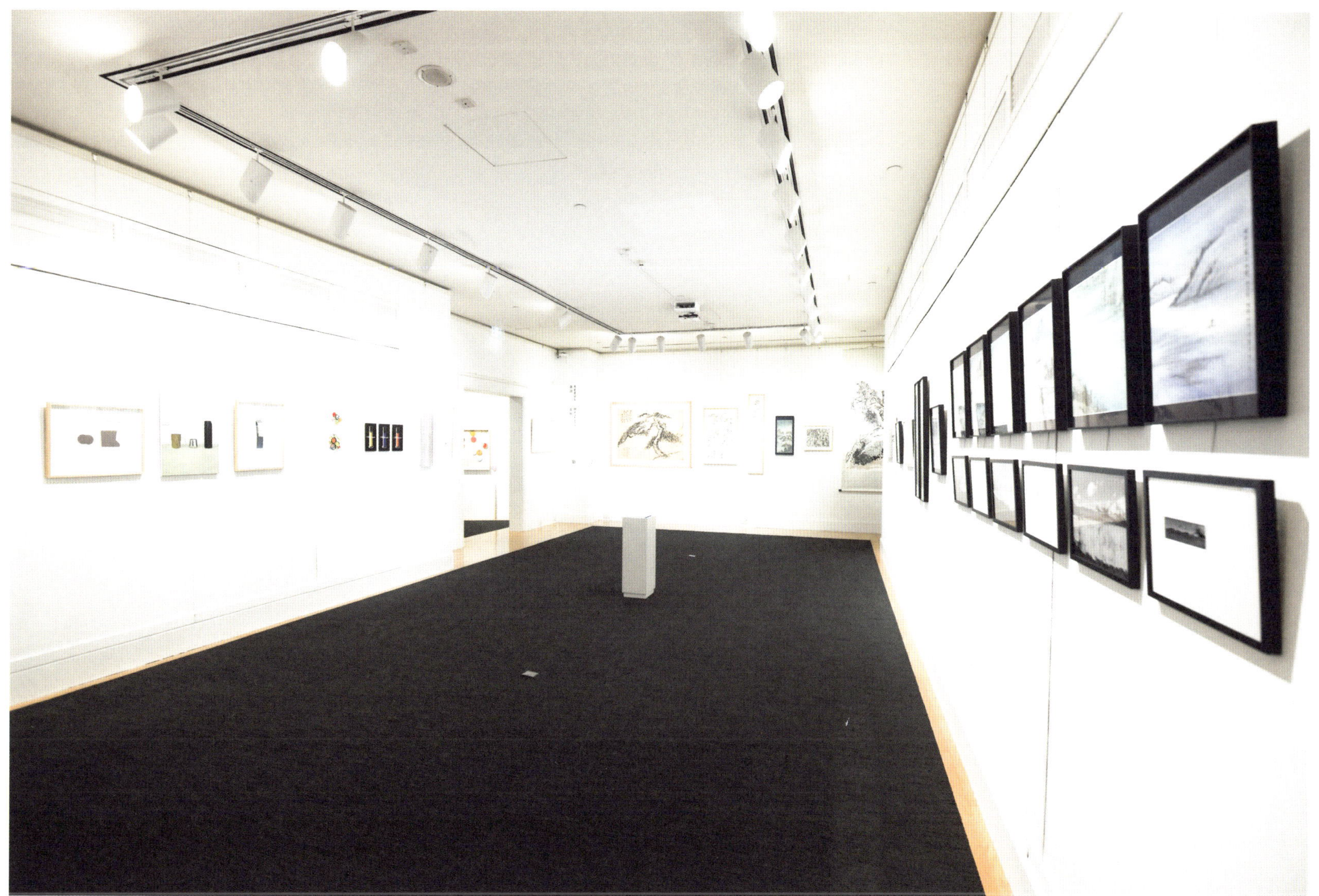

What happens when causal relationships are called into question and the symmetry seems out of balance?—when two artworks suddenly appear in a completely new light due to an unexpected connection?

REBUS, the third section of the exhibition, allows for a playful and thought-provoking approach to the artworks. Their arrangement brings them into a new relationship with each other; an unexpected constellation. Each of the four walls contains a thematically related group. The connections between individual works are not immediately obvious and have to be deciphered. The four themes to be explored are as follows:

Connected
The Sum and Its Parts
6 Ways to Live a Life
On Heaven and Earth – The Void in Between

The challenge is to decode what connects the various artworks. These can be relationships and dependencies between humans and the environment and nature ("Connected"), or recognizing the individual components from which works of art are created ("The Sum and Its Parts"). Or possibly about overarching themes of understanding our world and the philosophy of landscape in art ("On Heaven and Earth – The Void in Between")

and what paths we take to live, explore and understand our lives ("6 Ways to Live a Life").

Information on each artwork can be called up using a QR code, and the texts contain clues in the form of questions or brief statements that can help visitors decipher the individual artworks and themes. The arrangement of works in the space and their dialogical or confrontational relationship also conceal clues that must be explored.

One could say, that REBUS is in the tradition of the exhibition *L'Angelus de Daumier*, which the Belgian artist Marcel Broodthaers developed in Paris in 1975. In his last exhibition, the artist invited visitors to embark on new adventures by deciphering his last major work *La Salle Blanche* (Stoll 2018). In this way, decoding the secrets in REBUS is intended to help explain the complex interplay of cause and effect in an unconventional manner.

Connected

The sadness of the trees in the paintings *Snow and Tree Trunk* and *Snow and Tree Trunks-2* 樹幹殘雪 (figs. 60, 63) by **LIAO Zenping** 廖震平 (*1982) (Kraemer 2018c); the silence of the abandoned *Escalator at The Landmark* taken on 1 July 1996; and the emptiness sensed between architectural vessels at *Cheung Kong Center* on 14 November 1997 in the two black-and-white photographs of **David CLARKE** 祈大衛 (*1954) together present an interplay of nature and architecture. The loneliness of the individual is made visible. By juxtaposing the works of LIAO Zenping and David CLARKE, nature and architecture are thematized and the individual's feeling of loneliness and powerlessness is displayed.

The two objects by **Debe SHAM** 岑愷怡 (*1988 Hong Kong) make us aware that we are all part of a larger and more fragile whole. In her object *Still Flying* from the 2022 *Clothespin Doll Series* 衣夾公仔系列, three brass figures move like marionettes tied to thin ropes (fig. 64). No one can leave the cage. And in her wall object *Clothespin Doll 02* from 2022, two brass figures work to keep their balance on a seesaw (fig. 65). Nature, architecture and humanity are interconnected in a construction built on extremely fragile ground. "Connected" to everything, we need to be aware of this interconnectedness as individual actions have consequences for all.

The Sum and Its Parts

What are the defining features of an artwork? The individual artworks on this wall are each works in their own right. Considered together, they function as a system that defines the most crucial of artistic concepts. In "The Sum and Its Parts," artworks interact with the precise components that artists use to create their works.

The Viennese artist **Herbert STAREK** (*1954) created numerous geometric abstractions in the 1990s, and increasingly radicalized his visual language through the use of thesis, antithesis and synthesis. A key work is *HATTAH* (fig. 66) from 1994—a two-part work consisting of a square screen print on black plexiglas and a vinyl album (Starek 2002, 48–51). The first side of the album contains a crescendo that repeats at regular intervals, while the other side contains a decrescendo. In total, there are four equally valid ways of reading and listening. Thesis and antithesis cancel each other out; the supposed opposites disappear. *HATTAH* is vaguely reminiscent of Kazimir Malevich's 1913 paintings of a black square, a black circle on a white background and a cross. The archetypes of abstraction, formed by the square and circle, are intensified by the permanently recurring sound so as to become symbols of perfection, balance and harmony; the ornament becomes rhythm in space.

Immediately next to this is a group of three works that all interact with various forms of composition. In the drawing *Dos Amigos* (fig. 67) by Swiss artist **Beat FELLER** (*1955) from 2008, the two friends—circle and square—are transformed (Kraemer 2015, 96–97). The former duplicates and reproduces itself and the latter transforms into an abstract form.

LIAO Zenping's *Still Life-4* (fig. 68) from 2019 shows an unusually daring composition of three objects that are strictly aligned with each other (Liao 2022, 57). They contradict the canon of interlocking objects commonly seen in still life paintings. The Taiwanese artist follows the rules that generally apply to still lifes ad absurdum. Through this type of unusual juxtaposition, LIAO's painting of "unmoving existence" ("stil leven"), as these works were known in the Netherlands from 1650 onwards, leads to the realization that all three objects appear to be of equal value. They know their place and, more importantly, their essence and the essence of others, which they respect. These insights can reveal themselves as a form of harmonious coexistence out of respect and humility. When this happens, a serenity often sets in that is based on the certainty that everything has its place. LIAO's still lifes are philosophical interpretations of the inner relationship of those visible things that hold our world together on both the outside and inside.

The collage *Dimensiones* (fig. 69) from 2010, also created by **Beat FELLER**, embraces the juxtaposition of reality and abstraction (Kraemer 2015, 113, 141). Above a monochrome black rectangle is placed the motif of an upside-down column from a book that is tilted slightly to the left. This combination is extremely rare, as artists generally prefer naturalistic motifs (column) or abstract motifs (black rectangle). Thus, reality and abstraction meet and play with our imagination and sense of illusion.

The two-part work *Small Windows* (figs. 70, 71) from 2013 is from a series of glass works for which the German artist **Christoph DAHLHAUSEN** (*1960) has used differently sized and colored filters made for cameras (Dahlhausen 2021, 125–132, Dahlhausen 2017). Placed at a sufficient distance from the wall and illuminated by a light source, the result is a rich interplay of soft shades of color.

While the upper work is a balanced composition with six filters placed around a central filter, the lower work has twelve small filters grouped around three larger filters in red, blue and yellow. The lower work appears disordered compared to the upper, so that chaos and order are shown through the compositional arrangement, which brings *Small Windows* closer to the digital Rorschach tests of Robert LETTNER and Philipp STADLER (figs. 31, 32).

DAHLHAUSEN also uses this interchange of order and chaos in his expansive installation *New Ways to Colour the Wall*, which is located in the adjoining room (fig. 104), by first intervening in the order of the room with his 60 colored magnetic discs and then by asking the viewer to change the tone in the room by moving the discs.

The colors of this world are contained in the three primary colors of yellow, red and blue, and the non-colors of white and black. In *Alchemia*, three silk screen prints on aluminum (figs. 72, 73, 74) from 1999, by **Herbert STAREK**, depict test tubes floating in front of a black pictorial space, approximately 70% of which are filled with primary colors (Starek 2002, 75). "Alchemia" is written in white on the center of each of the three test tubes. Any color can be made from the three primary colors in the form of secondary colors and the refracted tertiary colors by adding white to control the level of brightness (Itten 1973). However, mixing all three primary colors does not produce pure black, as is often mistakenly assumed.

The juxtaposition of yellow, blue and red creates a grey, a so-called achromatic color, depending on the amount of white added. This is represented by myriad yellow, red and blue pixel like dots in the C-print on aluminum entitled *Bardos* from 1999 (Dahlhausen 2021, 118–123). This work (fig. 91) was also created by **Christoph DAHLHAUSEN**, who has long worked with light and color. *Bardos* is actually the result of a photographic process. Grey has an intermediate value that symbolizes restraint, the middle and neutrality, and thus in a way also represents the middle way between the extremes of white and black.

In the last two works on this wall by Scottish artist **Ian Hamilton FINLAY** (1925 Nassau, Bahamas–2006 Edinburgh, Scotland), which he made together with **John FURNIVAL**, text and image are illustrated. The two silkscreens labeled *Poem/Print No. 11 Xmas Star* from 1969 (fig. 75) and *Poem/Print No. 14 Xmas Rose* from 1970 (fig. 76) were placed in the exhibition so that they can hang to the left and right of a passageway through which one can see from the third room REBUS into the first room COUPLET (Finlay 1997, 24; 29).

The axial link between poems by Ian Hamilton FINLAY and the couplet (fig. 21) by TING Yin Yung was a deliberate choice. This couplet also tells of a journey, using the words "river, mountain, thousand, mile, heart" in the tail. By reading the words and imagining the rivers and mountains that must be overcome, we fill them with our lived experience and borrow images from our memory. So if the words "river, mountain" evoke the images of the challenges we have to overcome on our journey through life, then a fishing boat can also be understood as a symbol of this journey. All these symbols have a strong poetic power and refer to René Magritte. The relationship between an object, its name and its representation was explored by Magritte in 1929, in his painting *The Treachery of Images*, better known as *This is not a pipe*, and in his essay *Une poétique des mots et des images* (Magritte 1981, 71–73).

In "The Sum and Its Parts" genres or different techniques are displayed, including painting, drawing, photography, collage, and printmaking, along with objects (like glass and audio) and serial image sequences.

Naturalism, abstraction and conceptual approaches appear in the form of still lifes, ornaments, typography, color fields and minimalist language. Light and color are thematized, along with reality and illusion, order and chaos, geometric archetypes, semantic meanings, transformations and alienation.

Each of these individual building blocks are used when artists compose their works. The interplay of individual elements offers far more than the individual parts on their own. Or in the words of Hans Sedlmayr, who wrote in his 1958 publication *Art and Truth*: "When we are dealing with real entities, the whole has to be understood from all the parts, all the parts from the whole." (Sedlmayr 1958, 103).

6 Ways to Live a Life

Six ink drawings on paper were selected for this wall in the REBUS room. Each drawing depicts pine trees. In Chinese culture, the motif of the pine tree is regarded as a symbol of longevity, immortality and endurance (Eberhard 1981, 153–154; Welch 2008, 36–37). This is partly due to the fact that pine trees can live for hundreds of years and survive under inhospitable conditions on barren soils. Are these characteristics and meanings also expressed in the artistic representation of the pine tree? And how is this expressed? The visitor is challenged to read different approaches to life based on the artworks.

In **LIU Haisu**'s 劉海粟 (1896–1994) large-format ink drawing *The Lone Pine at Huangshan Mountain* 黃山孤松圖 from 1935, homage is paid to a pine tree with two strong branches and a stunted top (fig. 77). It almost seems as if the vital energy in the branches has been completely absorbed and at the end of the path there is hardly any strength left at the top of the tree, and it now appears powerless.

SHUM Kwan Yi 沈君怡 (*1995 Hong Kong) created two ink drawings for the exhibition in 2023 under the title *The Comic Strip of Tree* 樹木連環圖, both of which use sequences familiar from comics or manga. The larger drawing (fig. 78) involves detailed planning. Life is divided into sequences, which are then worked on section by section. However, individual branches that go beyond the framework indicate that life cannot be planned in its entirety; they contain unforeseen events. These strokes of fate are difficult to predict. The second, longer ink drawing (fig. 79) shows a development that seems to progress from an empty state of nothingness to the fullness of life. In nine chapters, knowledge, power, experience and consumer goods are accumulated step by step. What fills up can empty out again, so that in the end spiritual values are more important than material things.

In the colorful drawing *Liang Qiu Tan Poetic Painting* 梁秋潭詩意圖 by **LI Jing** 李淨 (*1972 Minnan, Fujian) from 2023, three neighboring pine trees stand powerfully in the center of the picture like three brothers (fig. 84). The rock in front finds its counterpart in the mountains behind, which mark the horizon. The tree branches imitate the outline of the mountains. The three pines are the connecting element between all others. The blue and green tones create an all-encompassing harmony. All areas of the painting merge. LI Jing has aptly added a line of poetry by Liang Qiu Tan 梁秋潭: "A newly risen stream is lost in the foreground. The green hills are everywhere."

The Viennese artist **Robert LETTNER**, who spent months in a small village in Lower Austria during his convalescence, draws a network of touching branches in *Pines* (fig. 81) from 2010 (Lettner 2017, 31; Kraemer 2018a). In Asia, the needles appearing in pairs also stand for the joyful togetherness of marriage. Despite the incredible density, the drawing nevertheless appears strangely light, as if the artist had recalled these lines from the

Hagakure: "Matters of great importance should be treated lightly. Matters of little importance should be treated seriously." (Tsunetomo 2002, chap. 1). The seriousness with which the artist approached his ink drawing can be seen in the process of its creation. First he sketched in pencil, outlined the outer lines of the pencil strokes with a fine liner and then finally filled them in. The process of creating a single drawing sometimes took weeks and had a strong meditative power due to the constant repetition.

With her *Pine of Longevity* 長壽 from 1956, **FANG Zhaoling** 方召麐 (1914–2006) presents us with a powerful tree that leans from the foreground to the center of the picture (fig. 82). Though the trunk is strong, some branches are dead and there are dense patches of needles. This tree has experienced a great deal and yet it appears sublime. The fact that it has not grown straight shows it has had to fight adversity time and again. As an image, it signals defying the blows of fate and making your own path.

Life can only be planned to a limited extent. What has happened cannot be undone. But occasionally we get the chance to look at what has happened from a different perspective and make alternate decisions. The six pine trees and their implied readings symbolize the diversity of our lives. By bringing together and arranging the six pine trees, they invite the viewer to reflect on their own life path. The fact that the viewer can recognize the potential of the pine trees to become a medium for determining their own position shifts the image's original message. As a result of this perception and the associated realization, artworks with pine trees will now be seen by the viewer in a different light.

On Heaven and Earth – The Void in Between
Artworks on this wall focus on the relationship between heaven and earth, along with the role that humans play in this relationship. The focus is on concepts that visualize the relationship between heaven and earth—above and below, here and now, emptiness and abundance, Yin and Yang. The first six works form a unit and are intended as opposing pairs.

The calligraphy *Mountain and Rivers* (山川) by **FUNG Yee Lick Eric** 馮以力 (*1985 Hong Kong), created in 2022, serves as an extension of an axis that begins in the first room with the Couplet (fig. 21) by **TING Yin Yung** and continues through to **LI Jing's** painting *Wang Changling's Poetic Painting* 王昌齡詩意圖 (fig. 84). All three works mentioned here thematize mountains and rivers differently. While TING Yin Yung and Eric FUNG do this through words that visualize the meaning of the words in calligraphy, LI Jing uses the motif of a waterfall and a line of poetry by the Tang dynasty poet Wáng Chānglíng 王昌齡 (698–756): "The valley is quiet with the sound of an autumn spring. The rock is deep and green." These lines describe the sound of a spring and thus the duration of the gushing water. By connecting the water falling vertically from above with the horizontal spray in the form of a cross, LI Jing emphasizes that mountain, water and air are one. In a way, he follows a line from the *Sansui Kyō* (山水經): "Mountains are mountains, waters are waters." (Shōbōgenzō, 2023). These lines from the work of the Sōtō Zen monk Eihei Dogen 永平道元 (1200–1253), also known as the *Mountain and Waters Sutra*, call for mountains and waters to be thoroughly investigated, for then they can become sages and wise men. LI Jing has achieved a strong connection between the mountain and river, with its waterfall plunging from nothingness into nothingness. The vertical is juxtaposed with a horizontal void.

Eric FUNG, on the other hand, skillfully uses the white of the surrounding space. Here, too, water falls down and forms a strong symbiosis with the mountain. Rivers and mountains need each other and become one; they are not perceived as fixed elements, yet they embody the dynamic law of continuous change between two poles. The idea of change is also expressed in finding the middle way between extremes, or in the shifting times between day and night or the seasons. Time and space are also the theme of the juxtaposition of several works by the artists LI Jing and Eric FUNG. Although there are no visible similarities at first glance, the title *Not Coming, Not Going* 不來不去 opens the key to understanding both works. The term "Not Coming Not Going" comes from the *Mūlamadhyamaka-kārikā* of the Buddhist philosopher Monk Nāgārjuna; the terms denote his idea of the emptiness of emptiness (Nāgārjuna 2014).

In this context, it is interesting to take a closer look at the way in which **Eric FUNG** approaches his kind of modern calligraphy. In contrast to the calligraphy used in traditional couplets, the artist retains the styles of the lettering but alters them by super-imposing them. He breaks down and reduces other characters so that they become mere lines in the spatial surface, as in the work *Becoming*. FUNG sees the entire surface of the picture as an arena. Thus, the signs in *Mountains and Rivers* appear like blurred shapes that flow downwards like water, but nevertheless contain the rock of the mountain through the firmness of the line. In the expressively placed signs of *Not Coming, Not Going* 不來不去 (fig. 85), the empty space between the two parts of the picture has the same function as the emptiness of the hub of a wagon wheel surrounded by thirty spokes or the emptiness of the inside of a flute (*Tao Te*

Ching, chapter 5; 11). Thus, this two-part work, which is reminiscent of a couplet, also denotes an in-between space, i.e. the space between two points, two places or two times, as well as the space between day and night. In combination with the two-part painting by LI Jing, it denotes the fine zone of transition—which can hardly be defined precisely—existing between day and night, life and death, Heaven and Earth.

The counterpart to *Not Coming, Not Going* 不來不去 is a diptych by **LI Jing**, which consists of two landscapes created in 2018, one at night and one during the day (figs. 86, 87). The artist has also added two poems to these diametrically opposed landscapes which show a group of trees in front of a rock face in portrait format at different times.

The night depiction entitled *Inspired by Venerable Fa Cheng's Poems* 法成禪師詩意圖 (fig. 86) quotes a poem by Shì Fǎchéng 釋法成 (1071–1128), also known as Pan, who was a Zen monk of the Cao Dong Sect in the Song dynasty: "The clear light contains the blue of the sky, and the round toad is white. The clear light above and below contains the virtual turquoise, for which the round toad is white."

This contrasts with the painting *Inspired by Venerable Miao Lun's Poems* 妙倫禪師詩意圖 (fig. 87), which depicts the day. It contains the following lines of great poetry by Zen master Miào Lún 妙倫

(1201–1261) from the Yangqi School of the Linji Sect: "At the point where the bridge breaks and the stream returns, three or four peach blossoms suddenly flow out."

The lines of poetry accompanying the paintings, which LI Jing describes as inspiration, are to be understood as commentaries. The text aims to enrich the viewer's understanding of the pictorial work by juxtaposing the text with the motif, encouraging a broader interpretation. In this respect, the interplay of image and text can be compared to a couplet's head and tail.

In the center of this group of six works is *Becoming* (化) from 2022 by Eric FUNG and next to it a simple *Zen Circle* (圓禪) drawn in 2010 by the Vietnamese Zen Master **THÍCH Nhất Hạnh** (釋一行禪師 (926 Huế, Vietnam–2022 Từ Hiếu Pagoda, Huế, Vietnam). In *Becoming* a red stamp floats in the empty space between characters. We search for the meaning of our existence in the brief span of time between beginning and end. So while *Becoming* playfully shows the process of becoming and finding one's own vocation and the path to it, the *Zen Circle* in its perfection reflects the result of this search (Thích 2010, 18–19). A simple circle painted in one fluid motion shows the state of mind at the moment of its creation. This circle, called Ensō in Japanese, symbolizes emptiness, enlightenment, strength, elegance and the universe. Or according to Laozi: "Great fullness seems empty, yet it cannot be exhausted." (*Tao Te Ching*, 45).

Opposite the *Zen Circle*, the light object created in 2020 by **Joseph LEUNG, Mong Sum** 梁望琛 (*1995 Hong Kong) is located in the middle of the room on a marble plinth. Two lightbulbs from the opposite sides of the spectrum appear to float in a translucent plexiglas box. One warm and yellowish, the other cold and rather bluish. Both colors are equally important to each other. The two light bulbs, one with warm light and one with cold, are strongly opposed manifestations that are reminiscent of the sun and moon or day and night. Through these two colors, the light object refers to LI Jing's diptych of landscapes in day and night. Viewed from the side, it looks like the blue embraces the yellow or the yellow surrounds the blue. Neither can exist without the other; both are involved in a mutually energetic exchange. They are two individually strong forces that still need each other. Almost like a Yin and Yang of light.

Cause and effect are mutually dependent. Can one exist without the other? The two here also stands for Yin and Yang, for which change is a primary attribute. The light object by Joseph LEUNG is placed in the center of the REBUS room and forms an axis with the *Zen Circle* by THÍCH Nhất Hạnh and *Bardos* by Christoph DAHLHAUSEN. This constellation of three works takes up a passage from the *Tao Te Ching*. In Chapter 42 (Legge 1891; Wilhelm 2003) from the *Tao Te Ching*, the Tao of Origin, also known as the Supreme Void, generates a form of unity as shown in the Zen Circle. "The Tao produced One. One produced Two." This duality, symbolized by the concepts of Yin and Yang and shown in LEUNG's lightbox, embodies continuous change.

Through the interaction of these two forces and the active emptiness within them, which is needed for change to occur, a trinity is generated, ultimately giving rise to all things. "Two produced Three; Three produced All Things."

All things are represented by the myriad yellow, blue and red dots in DAHLHAUSEN's *Bardos*. The central role of LEUNG's light object becomes even clearer as you continue reading Chapter 42 of the *Tao Te Ching*: "All things have the dark Yin behind them and strive for the light Yang, and the flowing force gives them harmony." (Wilhelm 2003, chapter 42). In a sense, these works of art are the tenets of the *Tao Te Ching* in action.

In the second part of the wall along with the motto "On Heaven and Earth – The Void in Between," two groups of works face each other. Below, the six-part group *La Geria I, II, III* from 2003, each consisting of three pairs of black-and-white photographs by the German photographer **Peter SCHLÖR** (*1964). In his series *La Geria*, the artist considers space, spatial depth, time and movement (figs. 92, 94, 96, 98, 100, 102). One of the areas he depicts in *La Geria* is an area located on Lanzarote (Canary Islands, Spain), known for the distinctiveness of its volcanic landscape. There is a larger shot and a small section of the same subject, almost like an echo (Schlör 2006, 96–99).

We appear to see the same motif three times, but always a slightly different detail. The camera has moved. Nevertheless, the white house pictured in the distance with the palm tree and hill behind seems unchanged in size. SCHLÖR knows the classic rules for depicting landscapes and actively manipulates them. His shots have an extremely close foreground, with almost no middle ground, which is primarily defined by the wall on the right and an extremely distant background.

To structure the space, SCHLÖR deftly manipulates density and emptiness simultaneously, though in a manner distinct from that of LI Jing. Fullness meets emptiness. As the counterpart of fullness, the void opens up possibilities for change. By changing the perspective in the space of the landscape, we learn to become flexible in our perceptions. We open ourselves up to the rich possibilities that arise in the interplay between heaven, earth and human beings, and experience the basic idea that underlies the *Tao Te Ching*.

These photographs are juxtaposed with six colored ink drawings in the style of a classical Chinese landscape painting by **LI Jing**. Created in 2023, LI Jing has given these works lines of poetry and invites us to explore them through observation and text (figs. 93, 95, 97, 99, 101, 103).

From the famous Tang dynasty poet Qián Qǐ 錢起 (710–782), also known as Zhongwen, is the following line for a work in delicate green tones: "Who knows that beyond the white clouds is a green radish in spring."

In another work in which a group of five pine trees stand in the foreground on the shore of a lake, these lines by Huáng Qīnglǎo 黃清老 (1290–1348), also called Mr. Woodcutting Water have been written: "Pines sit in the eternal sun. My mind is at ease with the clouds."

And from the little-known Zen Master Língyún Zhìqín 靈雲志勤, also known as Master Sacred Cloud, are fitting lines about a mountain range surrounded by fog: "The green mountain is immovable. The floating clouds come and go as they please."

The idea of emptiness can be explained using a leaf in delicate shades of blue. Since the whitish mist made of water between the lake and the mountain imitates the shape of the mountain, it forms an ideal connection between the mountains and water. A poem is attached: "White birds and smoke. Autumn water in the sky." These lines are from Hóngzhì Zhèngjué 宏智正覺 (1091–1157), a Chinese Zen Buddhist monk who wrote several influential texts including the *Book of Equanimity*, a collection of 100 koans.

As the river flows between two rocky banks, you can practically hear the sound of the cold flowing water. "The cold mountains turn pale and faded. The autumn water gurgles." Wáng Wéi 王維 (699–759) was a renowned Chinese poet, painter and musician in the Tang dynasty. While apparently none of his paintings have survived, around 400 of his poems remain. Most of the poems focus on nature.

In the final picture in this series, the reference to Peter SCHLÖR's motif is achieved in an almost masterful way. The small white house with a palm tree corresponds to the boat with a mast that floats gently on the river. "The boat returns, empty of fish but full of moonlight." Chuánzǐ Dé Chéng 船子德誠 (820–858), also known as The Boatman Monk, was popular as a subject and is depicted in many paintings.

What exactly is the concept of emptiness in Chinese painting? As François Cheng has explained in his excellent book *Empty and Full. The Language of Chinese Painting*, the void offers a crucial feature for understanding, for this is viewed in Chinese philosophy and art as being an active element that forms an arena in which change can take place (Cheng 1994). The void introduces the moment of reversibility and openness into a given system, thus making it possible to overcome the rules. It is only through the void that the possibility arises for people to perceive what is depicted in the painting as being a recurring cycle to be understood holistically.

This aspect becomes visible in LI Jing's masterfully created paintings. His graceful and inspiring landscapes seem like individual life cycles taking place between heaven and earth. The distant view and close-ups of Peter SCHLÖR's series *La Geria* contrast with the Eastern landscape painting's perception of the void and the Western dichotomy of abundance and reduction.

LI Jing's landscape paintings correspond to LIAO Zenping's tree studies and the black-and-white photographs of Peter SCHLÖR find their counterpart in the photographs of David CLARKE. Works on opposite walls correspond to each other. The circle is closed. Connected.

LI Jing 李淨

This is the Way—Opening the Door to Chinese Painting and Calligraphy

Let me begin the following remarks, which are the personal experiences I have gained over the years, with a story about Sū Dōngpō 蘇東坡 (1037–1101) and Zen Master Fó Yìn 佛印禪師 (1032–1098).

Sū Dōngpō and the Zen Master were good friends who often debated the tenets of Zen. Sū Dōngpō was a great writer, but Fó Yìn had a far better understanding of Zen philosophy. On one occasion, the two were meditating in the Zen Hall, and as they came out of their silent meditation, Dōngpō realized that he was sitting in an extremely solemn looking posture. He asked Fó Yìn, "What do you think I look like in this pose? Fó Yìn replied, "The Buddha." And then Fó Yìn asked, "What about me?" Dōngpō replied, "Like a pile of cow dung." Fó Yìn smiled. Dōngpō believed he had gained the verbal advantage and went home feeling superior.

When Dōngpō's younger sister Sū Xiǎomèi saw her brother she asked why he looked so pleased. He told her about the encounter with Fó Yìn. After hearing the story, Sū Xiǎomèi frowned and said, "Brother, you have lost." Dōngpō was puzzled and asked why. She replied, "The Zen master has Buddha in his heart, and sees the Buddha in all beings. But you looked at the Zen Master as if he were a piece of cow dung, which shows that there is still a great distance between your two practices!"

I begin with this story because it is crucial to remember the importance of mindset; the importance of viewing an exhibition with a different frame of mind. Do you go to an exhibition to seek knowledge with an open mind, or merely to take a quick look? Naturally, the end results will differ.

When one visits an exhibition, it is important to understand the curatorial concept. Only after understanding the curator's intent can one truly understand the relationship between the works. When considering the introductory text for COUPLET PAIR REBUS, we come to find that the idea behind this exhibition is derived from the "Gé" (革) hexagram in the *I Ching* (易經) which is the 49th hexagram. The "Gé" hexagram is composed of the symbol "—" for the Yang lines and " – – " for the Yin lines. Six Yin and Yang symbols form the "Gé" trigram. It consists of the two trigrams "Duì" (兌) and "Lí" (離). Its inner (lower) trigram is ☲ (Lí 離) radiance, which means fire (火), and its outer (upper) trigram is ☱ (Duì 兌) open, which means (澤) zephyr or water. The "Gé" hexagram is also known as "Zephyr-Fire-Geo," which can be translated as "Good luck lies in change and renewal."

This is the gene of Chinese Taoist thought. The Tao gives birth to one, one to two, two to three and three to everything (*Tao Te Ching*, 道德經, chapter 42). In this way, the non-polarity or nothingness, also known as "Wújí" (無極) generates the grand polarity or the supreme ultimate named "Tàijí" (太極), and "—" and "– –" give rise to the four signs, the eight trigrams and the 64 hexagrams of the *I Ching*.

This idea of the contrast between Yin and Yang has influenced the whole of Chinese philosophy, culture and art. Therefore, to understand traditional Chinese culture, one must start from the contrast between Yin and Yang. Under the influence of Yin and Yang, the theoretical system of painting and calligraphy has developed a theory of form and spirit, with form as Yang and spirit as Yin, which is also the key to understanding and appreciating Chinese painting and calligraphy.

But why is form Yang and spirit Yin? That which is visible is Yang and the invisible is Yin. However, the contrast between Yin and Yang is relative, and their relationship changes in different environments.

"In the wonderful art of calligraphy, the aura is most important, followed by the quality of form, and the one who has both will inherit the essence of the ancient masters."

This is the theory of calligraphy by Wáng Sēngqián 王僧虔 (425–485) from the Southern dynasty. In this context, the original meaning of "shao" is to inherit

In the Chinese art of painting and calligraphy, there has long been a theory suggesting that these two art forms share a common origin in ancient times. Wáng's perspective can also be applied to painting.

Aura may sound abstract and elusive. However, when personified it is equivalent to a person's temperament. How does one judge a person's temperament? Through appearance, speech and behavior. There is an old Chinese saying that "one's appearance is affected by the mind." Fortune tellers use appearance and demeanor to judge a person's character and to predict his or her fortune. In the same way, the aura of a painting or calligraphy is realized by its form, and to understand aura one must first understand form.

I summarize the manifestation of form into four elements: brushwork, modeling, composition and color, which are arranged in order from smallest to largest, from partial to the whole.

Brushwork: The use of brushes to accomplish different strokes.

Modeling: The combination of different strokes to create different objects.

Composition: Arranging different objects into an overall effect according to certain rules.

Color: Adding color effects to the artwork. Black, white and grey are also considered color tones.

When an artist finishes the conceptualization process and begins to paint, the order of creation is generally: brushwork > modeling > composition > color.

When the visitor appreciates a work of calligraphy or painting, he or she often will first be attracted by the work's color. Next they will notice the compositional momentum, then the various modeled components and finally the texture of each brushstroke.

If an artwork can withstand these four steps of scrutiny, it will cause an individual to pause and appreciate the work.

Now, let's look at Chinese painting and calligraphy from a visitor's point of view by focusing on the works in the exhibition.

The first thing that catches the eye is the colors of the works. I am not referring to the twelve rings of colors, hue, brightness and purity, but to the contrasting relationship of colors in terms of a different perception of color.

My painting *Inspired by Venerable Fa Cheng's Poems* 法成禪師詩意圖 (fig. 86) is rendered in greyish-blue tones. In the misty moonlight, the distant mountains are reflecting snow, giving the impression that it is a chilly night, and therefore the colors in this work express a sense of "cold." In contrast, my painting *Inspired by Venerable*

Miao Lun's Poems 妙倫禪師詩意圖 (fig. 87) depicts the sun setting in the west, the remaining sun's rays enveloping the mountains, rivers and earth in a golden hue that is "warm."

The painting *Immortal in Splashed Ink* 潑墨仙人圖 by Liáng Kǎi 梁楷 (ca.1140–1210) of the Southern Song dynasty is currently held in the National Palace Museum in Taipei. The artist has used a significant amount of water to produce various effects through blurred ink, showcasing the effect of a splashed ink painting made in a single stroke. Because the painting is so watery in appearance, I call this effect "wet."

Among the painters of the late Ming and early Qing dynasties, Chéng Suì 程邃 (1605–1691), a representative of the Huizhou School, excelled in painting with withered brushstrokes. His master-piece *Secluded Dwelling in a Bamboo Forest* 深竹幽居, collected by the Anhui Provincial Muse-um, is a masterpiece in which the brushstrokes are withered, yet each layer is distinct and the shades of light and darkness are wholly appropri-ate, while the work incorporates a large number of flecks of white, which I refer to as "dry."

Wild Goose and Autumn Lotus 秋荷野鳧圖, now in the National Palace Museum in Taipei, is an anonymous Song dynasty work. In the painting, there is a wild goose and weeds, and it is cold and quiet, portraying an emaciated and silent "withered" mood.

Also held in the National Palace Museum in Taipei is *New Year's Day* 歲朝圖 by Zhào Chāng 趙昌 (fl. 10th century) from the Northern Song dynasty. The painting was made on the first day of the first month of the lunar year and was a high-quality New Year's painting prepared by the court. Due to the arrival of spring, the various flowers in the picture are lush and extremely dec-orative. I refer to this aesthetic as "glorious."

These six artworks represent the six contrasting relationships of "cold, warm, wet, dry, withered and glorious." Categorized from the perspective of Yin and Yang, "cold, wet, and withered" are seen as Yin, while "warm, dry and glorious" are Yang.

The next point of discussion is the contrasting relationships of composition.

From the painting *Inspired by Zen Master Zhiqin's Poems* 志勤禪師詩意圖 (fig. 97)—"The green mountains are immovable, the white clouds come and go as they please"—we can feel that the mountains and rivers have come to a standstill. The white clouds appear to have com-pletely stopped moving, and there is nothing but utter silence in heaven and earth. I refer to this mood as "static."

Lù Yǎnshào's 陸儼少 (1909–1993) *The Great River in Autumn* 大江秋易盛圖 expresses a different kind of emotion. In this painting, the waves of the Xiajiang River surge in while the trees along the shore brace against the wind. The entire picture is full of movement. This mood is "dynamic."

In my painting *Inspired by Qian Qi's Poems* 錢起詩意圖 (fig. 93), both the direction of the rocks and the trees converge towards the painting's center, echoing each other, as if some invisible vein is stringing them together—"gathered."

A river with two banks is a common composition in literati paintings. The painting *Inspired by Wang Wei's Poems* 王維詩意圖 (fig. 101) adopts this composition, but the difference is that there are no large trees or boulders in the painting. The most active element is a gurgling autumn stream, with the scenery on both sides of the river occupying only one corner each, strewn along the upper and lower edges of the painting, or "scattered."

"The boat is empty and the moon is bright." From this inscription of my painting *Inspired by Zen Master De Cheng's Poems* (德誠禪師詩意圖)

(fig. 103), we can see that the boat is the focus of the painting, though it is accomplished with the least amount of ink and brushwork; whereas the distant mountains, forests and reeds, which contain the most ink and brushwork, are a backdrop. This is a technique of "supporting the primary with the subordinate," which I refer to as "secondary."

The inscription on my work *Wang Changling's Poetic Painting* 王昌齡詩意圖 (fig. 84) reads "the valley is quiet, the springs sound in autumn, the rocks are deep and the green mist lingers." This indicates that the work's focus is on the autumn spring and green mist, which are presented in the middle of the painting in the form of a cross, so that the theme is immediately clear. I call this kind of mood "primary."

These six compositional relationships—dynamic, static, gathered, scattered, primary and secondary—are categorized by the contrast of Yin and Yang. Static, gathered and secondary are Yin, while dynamic, scattered and primary are Yang.

In the stylistic contrasts that follow, the shapes of the rocks and trees are analyzed.

In **LIU Haisu**'s 劉海粟 painting *The Lone Pine at Huangshan Mountain* 黃山孤松圖 (fig. 77), we sense that the pine tree is under tremendous

pressure. Despite its bent and curved trunk, it remains resilient, growing upwards with determination. This artwork expresses an unwavering will to overcome adversity. The shape of the pine tree is made up of curved lines. I call this expressive technique "curved."

Hóngrén 弘仁 (1610–1664), one of the four great monks of the late Ming and early Qing dynasties, was an important figure in the Xin'an School of painting. Because of his straightforward, aloof, quiet and patient manner, he used straight lines and light ink to express his cold, simple and elegant state of mind. In the painting *Willow after Rain* 雨餘柳色圖, which is held in the Shanghai Museum, we can see an example of Hóngrén's extensive use of straight lines, a technique I call "straight."

The ink drawing *The Comic Strip of Tree I* 樹木連環圖I (fig. 78) by **SHUM Kwan Yi** 沈君怡 (*1995) is divided into forty-two sections, one of which is cut into three smaller sections. This is a relatively new way of composing a painting, in which each section is an independent work, and then when all of the sections are connected, they form a larger single painting. This is like a comic strip, where each page is pieced together to form a story. I call this style "disconnected."

In **Robert LETTNER**'s (1943–2012) ink drawing *Pines* (fig. 81) from 2010, the work shows only the pine needles and almost all of the strokes in the picture are linked. I call this treatment "connected."

Another work by **SHUM Kwan Yi**, *The Comic Strip of Tree II* 樹木連環圖II (fig. 79) is presented in the form of a scroll divided into nine squares. The first square at the bottom is divided into nine smaller squares, the second square is divided into eight smaller squares, and so on. The ninth square at the top then becomes a separate section. The forty-five small squares depict a partial detail of another pine tree, forming nine large blocks that are then synthesized into a complete work. I call this method, which focuses on the small features, "detailed."

FANG Zhaoling's 方召麐 (1914–2006) painting *Pine of Longevity* 長壽 (fig. 82), shows an old pine tree occupying the focal point of the artwork. The trunk of the tree is tilted in a way that divides the painting in two. In the lower-left corner, daffodils and rocks are depicted, balancing the strong presence of the pine tree as well as the soft elements of the daffodils. This composition reflects the traditional idea of the middle way, combining strength and flexibility. It signifies that those who can achieve a balance of strength and flexibility will enjoy a long life. I call this kind of artwork with a large tree set against the sky "grand."

These six works are characterized by the forms of "curved, straight, disconnected, connected, grand and detailed." I would classify "curved, disconnected and detailed" as Yin, and "straight, connected and grand" as Yang.

Since the use of brushstrokes belongs to the most subtle alteration of lines, to facilitate a clear understanding of these textural effects, I will now refer to examples from Chinese calligraphy.

From my Couplet in Seal Script 篆書對聯 (fig. 12), we can see that most of the lines start from a rounded position, which is caused by the brush tip wrapping around the edge of the brush. This method is called hiding the edge of the brush, and it can create a well-rounded texture, which I refer to as "hidden."

SHE Xueman 佘雪曼 (1908–1993), a native of Ba County, Chongqing, Sichuan province, promoted calligraphy education in Hong Kong after moving in 1949. In his Couplet in Slender Gold Script 瘦金書對聯 (fig. 15), the script was created by Zhào Jí 趙佶, Emperor Huīzōng of the Song dynasty 宋徽宗 (1082–1135). This has the beauty

of being both strong and sharp. To produce this texture, the strokes need to be made in such a way that the brush is exposed to the naked eye and the hair is laid down. I call this method "exposed."

SUN Xingge 孫星閣 (1897–1996), a native of Jieyang, Guangdong province, known as Shi-manshanren, was a poet, calligrapher and painter who moved to Hong Kong in 1949. The type of texture in his Couplet in Cursive Script 草書對聯 (fig. 19) can only be produced when the brush is used with a reverse brush stroke and then the brush is shaken, which I call "reversed."

LIANG Qichao 梁啟超 (1873–1929), a native of Xinhui, Guangdong province, was a promoter of the Wushu Revolution, and a driving force behind the New Culture Movement.

From his Couplet in Running Script 行書對聯 (fig. 10): "To bind oneself with a rope, to receive others, use the oar; to compare virtue with jade, to defend one's intention is like a city." One can see that his strokes are closely and smoothly connected, as graceful as flowing water, which I call "fluid."

YIK Yuet Sek 易越石 (1912–2007), a native of Hengyang, Hunan province, devoted his life to the art of calligraphy and the verification of the

origins of the Shikuwen (Stone-Drum Script). His Couplet in Shikuwen 石鼓文對聯 (fig.16) is the best example of his academic achievements, in which "Good flowers are like virgins, and good trees are like singing birds." Many of the mottled strokes look like chiseled inscriptions. This texture is created by using the brush against the grain, slowly moving the brush tip against the rice paper, which is like running against the wind. I call this method "bitter."

TING Yin Yung 丁衍庸 (1902–1978), from Maoming, Guangdong province, who moved to Hong Kong in 1949, was known both as the Modern Bada Shanren and one of the three out-standing artists of Guangdong. He is known for his simplicity, plainness and freehand style in his paintings and calligraphy.

From his Couplet in Cursive Script 草書對聯 (fig. 21): "A cup of wine for the wind and rain, and a heart for the rivers and mountains," we can see his typical freehand style in which the strokes are as quick as the wind and are made in a single stroke, which I call "swift."

These six types of strokes are categorized by the relationship between Yin and Yang, with "hidden, reversed and bitter" being Yin, and "exposed, fluid and swift" Yang. Having briefly analyzed the elements of "brushwork, form, composition and color"—does an artwork contain one single contrasting relationship or a diversity of contrasts?

To answer this we must return to the Yin-Yang relationship of Tai Chi; in Yin there is Yang, and in Yang there is Yin. This point of view is deeply rooted in Chinese cultural beliefs, so whether it is the use of brush, form, structure or color, the contrasting relationship they contain is never single, but a blend of various contrasts. When there is a "hidden" element there is also an "exposed"; when there is "curved" there is "straight"; when there is "dynamic" there is "static"; when there is "cold" there is "warm." With these types of contrasting relationships, the work becomes more vivid and lively.

Therefore, the more contrasting elements that a work contains, the more attractive it can become to the audience. Let us have a look at my painting *Inspired by Zen Master Zhiqin's Poems* 志勤禪師詩意圖 (fig. 97), in terms of the four elements of form:
Color: mountain is cold, wall is warm.
Composition: mountain is quiet, clouds are moving.
Modeling: mountain is straight, clouds are curved.
Brushwork: mountain is bitter, clouds are swift.

Now compare this with Lù Yǎnshào's 陸儼少 *The Great River in Autumn* 大江秋易盛圖, which has been mentioned before:
Color: warm mountains, cold water.
Composition: quiet mountain, moving water.
Modeling: straight mountain, curved water.
Brushwork: bitter in the mountains, swift in the water.

As I commented earlier, the more contrasting elements that a work contains, the more attractive it can become. Does this mean that more contrasts are inherently better? Of course not. A single piece of music would not be pleasing to the ear if all the notes of the different scales were included. On the contrary, this would be harsh and boring.

To compose a good piece of music, you must first unify the notes into a tune, and then express various rhythms with different emotions. If we translate this into the language of painting, the mood is equal to the tune, and the strokes are the notes. Only by using appropriate contrasts can the work fully express the mood.

Let's reconsider Zhào Chāng's 趙昌 painting *New Year's Day* 歲朝圖 at the National Palace Museum in Taipei again. The painting is decorated with plum blossoms, camellias, daffodils, periwinkle flowers, bamboo leaves, Taihu Lake

stones and so on. The pigments include rouge, cinnabar, white, ochre, green, aqua and blue. In the contrast of colors, there are the warmth and coldness of blue and red, the wetness and dryness of the earth and the bamboo leaves, and the splendor of the flowers and the withered stones of Taihu Lake. Compositional contrasts include the dynamic and static nature of the flowers and the Taihu Lake stones, the gathering and scattering of the flowers and ground, and the primary and secondary elements of the flowers and Taihu Lake stones. The contrast of modeling also includes the straight and curved nature of the Taihu Lake stones and daffodils, the connection between the flowers and the earth and the size of the Taihu Lake stones and plum blossoms. In terms of brushstrokes, if we zoom in and study them carefully, there are also the contrasts of "hidden, exposed, fluid, reversed, bitter and swift" brushstrokes. Because this painting was used in the royal palace to celebrate the Lunar New Year, the artist has nearly exhausted all of the techniques and colors available to him to please the royal family, forming an intricate combination of contrasts.

If Zhào Chāng's 趙昌 painting *New Year's Day* 歲朝圖 is considered kitsch, then **LIU Haisu**'s 劉海粟 painting *The Lone Pine at Huangshan Mountain* 黃山孤松圖 (fig. 77) is a work of solitude and clarity, a much different style from *New Year's Day*. There is no color in the painting, just ink, and a lone pine tree stands on the mountainside, which is like cooking tofu in water without any seasoning. However, there is still the contrast between wet and dry colors; the contrast between gathering and scattering and the contrast between primary and secondary elements in the composition; as well as the contrast between straight and curved, connected and disconnected, large and small shapes. To realize the spirit of the lone pine in defying adversity, besides "hidden, exposed, fluid and swift," the most frequently used strokes are the "reversed" and "bitter" strokes. Even a simple painting can contain numerous contrasting combinations.

Why does an artwork need to be represented in a particular form? Is it because this shape best expresses a specific texture? And does this texture evoke a certain mood?

This assumption is correct. Form and spirit are interdependent, and the so-called spirit must rely on form to be realized, which is similar to a person's temperament. The form and spirit of a painting can guide us to feel the artistic conception behind the work. This is the voice of the artist when he is creating, and it is also what we often call the voice off-screen. Only by understanding such off-screen voices can we truly understand the work's artistic concept. Taking *New Year's Day* and *The Lone Pine on Huangshan Mountain* as examples, the tone of *New Year's Day* is about celebrating the New Year, while *The Lone Pine on Huangshan Mountain* is about self-reliance in the face of adversity.

What is the most crucial part of the artistic process—money? Although money can provide a stable life for artists and allow them to create art without financial concerns, it is not the most important aspect.

Within the creative process, a mood is brewing in the mind, and when this mood is gradually perfected, there comes an impulse to pick up a brush, which is initiated by a specific emotion. It is precisely this emotion that allows the artist to enter into a state of passion. Throughout the entire creative process, the artist will be led by this emotion. This demonstrates that emotion is the most important.

Without emotion, Wang Xizhi 王羲之 (303–361) could not have written the preface to the *Collection of Poems Collected at the Orchid Pavilion* (Lántíngjí Xù, 蘭亭集序), nor could Yán Zhēnqīng 顏真卿 (709–785) have written the draft of a *Requiem to my Nephew* (祭姪文稿). The strokes generated by the artist act as a bridge between the artist and viewer. How can you tell the difference between an artwork and a craft?

The most important basis for this judgment is the degree of emotion carried by the object.

All of the contrasts in form are relative, and they routinely change over time and space. A heavy color in one work might appear as a lighter color when it is placed next to another. That's why we often say, "No comparison, no harm!" Or, "It's better to compare than not to know." When we are not sure about the artistic value of a certain work, we can use comparison to gain a clearer understanding. This type of comparison can be between different parts of the same work, a comparison between neighboring works in the same gallery, a comparison between works by the same author in different periods, a comparison between different authors in the same period or a comparison between different authors in different periods.

A few days ago, during a Christie's auction preview, I went with some students to view the works of Lù Yǎnshào 陸儼少, Huáng Bīnhóng 黃賓虹 (1864–1955) and Qí Báishí 齊白石 (1864–1957), and they quickly realized that the changes in their brushstrokes and the speed of the strokes were quite different, and that the strokes of all three had specific characteristics and frequencies. So, are comparisons simply black and white? No. If this were the case, the world would be boring.

The space between black and white can be even more fascinating.

When Harald Kraemer, the curator of this exhibition, explained his curatorial concept to me, he kept repeating in front of my two blue and yellow works, "What is between day and night?" If we convert "day and night" into "black and white," then what is between "day and night" is equivalent to what is between "black and white." Let's take "day and night" as an example.

In Chinese Taoist practice, the relationship between time and the movement of qi and the blood in the body is extremely important. The Taoist monks found that during a day, four hours are particularly important, which are called "Zǐ Wǔ Chōu Tiān (子午抽添) Mǎo Yǒu Mù Yù (卯酉沐浴)," which means 11 pm and 1 pm are for adding and taking, and 5 am and 5 pm are for bathing.

Zi runs from 11 pm to 1 am. During this time, the body's Yin energy, which is at its peak, begins to descend, and the Yang energy begins to rise, along with the saying, the "Zi hour gives birth to Yang." As the Yang energy gradually increases, it is called "additional."

Wu is from 11 am to 1 pm. At this time the body's Yang energy starts to decline from its peak and the Yin starts to rise, which is also known as "The Wu hour gives birth to Yin."

Since the Yang energy is gradually decreasing, as if being withdrawn, it is therefore known as "drawn." If the Zi hour is metaphorically "black," then Wu is "white." What exists between "black and white"?

This is also the "between day and night" that Harald Kraemer emphasizes. Four of the twenty-four hours fall between day and night, namely, Mao, which is between 5 am and 7 am, and You, which is between 5 pm and 7 pm.

Bathing at "dao-you" does not simply mean taking a shower, although this time of day is very good for the body. It is more important to bathe your mind at these hours when the Yin and Yang are in harmony within the body. Letting go of distracting thoughts and allowing the mind and body to be in a state of tranquility is helpful for cultivation. This is why Taoists emphasize the four hours of "Zi Wu Mao You," as it is easier to enter a "state of tranquility." Therefore, in addition to "Zi Wu," the "Mao You" hours are crucial.

If we translate the concept of "black and white" into "grey," that which lies between "black and white" is "grey," and this "grey" is key. It can flow between black and white, it can produce a thousand different shades of grey, and it can produce different levels of contrast.

The Buddhist saying "Never fall between two extremes," tells us not to be obsessed with either black or white, and that the grey is the middle way. This is also the meaning of "Between Day and Night" that Harald Kraemer asks us to consider, as well as the exhibition's overall message: "Through the contrasting relationship of different exhibits, we can come to realize what resides between and beyond the contrasts."

What is it that transcends contrasts? Consider *Not Coming, Not Going* 不來不去 by **Eric FUNG Yee Lick** 馮以力, which is arranged in a circle (fig. 85). Nearby hangs the drawing of Zen Master **THÍCH Nhất Hạnh** 釋一行禪師, also a circle (fig. 89). And the yellow/warm and blue/cold lightbulbs in the center of the exhibition hall—a work by **Joseph LEUNG Mong Sum** 梁望琛—are also circles (fig. 90). The two wall objects with colored glass filters for photo cameras by **Christoph DAHLHAUSEN** on the opposite wall are also circles (figs. 70, 71). A circle is a kind of cycle; so, what is the cycle between this coming and going? What is it that circulates in the warm and cold light? What circulates between the heaven and earth symbolized by these landscape paintings? What is it that transcends this cycle?

Let me first mention the Buddhist practice of Zen, that is, the two methods of movement and stillness: stillness, meditation in Zen; and movement, observing Zen wherever one lives, sits or sleeps. Meditation begins with observing the breath, that is, watching one's breath without disturbing it with one's consciousness. One's own breath is clear and distinct. As time passes, you will slowly realize that your breathing has changed from coarse and rapid to fine and long. As the breath becomes finer, longer, deeper and slower you will realize that there is a short pause between the breath and inhalation, and if you can grasp this pause, you will have entered a state of meditation. This is the trick of cultivation, the secret of the time between day and night, between black and white, between coming and going.

Zen does not tell you these things explicitly. It uses hints to remind you, so that you can realize them on your own. The same applies to Zen's other dynamic practice of observing Zen in the midst of living, sitting, lying and realizing the true meaning of transcending contrasts amid life. "When art moves towards philosophy," it is necessary to comprehend the interplay of contrasts and the connections that transcend contrasts in art, ultimately reaching and inspiring the audience through art.

This is also the purpose of the exhibition, which Harald Kraemer never reveals explicitly, but subtly reminds us to consider what resides be-

tween day and night, between heaven and earth, between coming and going.

My painting *Wang Changling's Poetic Painting* 王昌齡詩意圖 (fig. 84) contains mountains and water, and as there is white space between the mountains and water, let us borrow this particular stretch of mountain and water to tell a story about the three realms of Zen.
In Zen, there is a saying that

> "Seeing a mountain is a mountain,
>
> seeing water is water;
>
> seeing a mountain is not a mountain,
>
> seeing water is not water;
>
> seeing a mountain is still a mountain,
>
> seeing water is still water."

What does this mean?

The first stage: "Seeing a mountain is a mountain, and seeing water is water." Before one learns Zen, one looks at everything and sees only the surface of things, and so is trapped by falsehoods, is obsessed with superficial features.

The second stage: "Seeing a mountain is not a mountain, and seeing water is not water." After practicing Zen, one can see the essence of things, that everything is a result of karma, and one is no longer trapped by superficial features.

The third stage: "Seeing the mountain is still

a mountain, seeing the water is still water"—after understanding the true essence of things, we can treat things with a transcendental state of mind, no longer contained by the boundaries, responding to karma as it comes, and not staying when it goes. (According to Ch'ing-yüan Wei-hsin (Seigen Ishin). Jĭngdé Chuándēnglù (景德傳燈錄), in: Taishō Shinshū Daizōkyō, no. 2077, 51:614b-c. See also Suzuki 1926, 24; Watts 1957, 126).

By the same token, when looking at Chinese painting and calligraphy, we must utilize the relationship of contrasts to comprehend, and when we look at Chinese painting and calligraphy after understanding how to transcend the relationship of contrasts, these evoke three different feelings. The white space in this work reminds us to consider what resides between heaven and earth.

I would like to share two verses from the great Mahāyāna Mahāparinirvāna Sūtra (大般涅槃經):

> "All things change. This is the law of birth and death."
> "When birth and death are done away with,
> Quietude is bliss."
>
> Mahāyāna Mahāparinirvāna Sūtra
> 1973, vol. I, XIII, 19. ch., 352; 355.

The two verses from Chapter 19 on Holy Actions concern the worldly dharma, describing the true nature of time and space, where everything is in a state of constant change, between birth and death. Life and death are also a form of contrast, and we are surrounded by numerous contrasts. One type of contrast disappears and another contrast arises and continues endlessly. The final two sentences are about the supermundane dharma. Only by transcending this kind of contrast, by not being bound by it, can we achieve true happiness.

Because this world of contrasts is in a constant state of flux, how can we avoid being excluded in this environment? How can we keep pace with the times? How can we attain happiness? This brings us back to the origins of this exhibition, the "Gé" (革) hexagram in the *I Ching* (易經). Only through change and transformation can we achieve auspicious outcomes.

As an arts stakeholder, what is our cultural mission? The museum has fulfilled its function by organizing valuable and meaningful exhibitions to pass on culture and art. In these exhibitions, artists of the previous generation have left behind precious cultural treasures for the next generation, and contemporary artists have not only inherited traditional culture and art, but also made numerous innovations.

In this exhibition, SHUM Kwan-yi's breakthrough in composition, Eric FUNG Yee-lick's Zen calligraphy and my work have enhanced the use of color tones in traditional landscape paintings. In addition to these, there are many other creative works which convey the spirit of the "Gé" (革) hexagram, the inheritance and rebirth of culture. Harald Kraemer explained to me that each artwork in the exhibition not only has an independent identity, but is part of a whole, as the exhibition is itself a single artwork. This is in line with the Buddhist idea that "one is all, all is one," which is also the spirit of the "Gé" (革) hexagram.

Finally, I would like to explain to you the title of my painting *Inspired by Zen Master De Cheng's Poems* 德誠禪師詩意圖 (fig. 103). Chuánzǐ Dé Chéng 船子德誠 (820–858), also known as The Boatman Monk 船子和尚 has written: "The Ship returns empty with the Moon shining brightly." (滿船空載月明歸).

There is a Zen book titled *Record of Pointing at the Moon* (Zhǐyue Lù 指月錄) written by Qú Rǔ jì 瞿汝稷 (1548–1610) (see Cleary 2006; Holstein 1993, part 3; Lu 1961). It records cases of monks and great masters reaching enlightenment through the centuries. The Buddhist metaphor of the full moon denotes the state of enlightenment and the book *Record of Pointing at the Moon* shows the many possibilities of becoming enlightened.

The moment of enlightenment often takes place when the person in question realizes that there is nothing contradictory, but that everything is connected to everything else. Finally, we should not get caught up in opposites, but recognize the true meaning of overcoming opposites through our works and understand the "sound" behind the image. In this way, we will succeed in anchoring the spirit of the exhibition in our own actions.

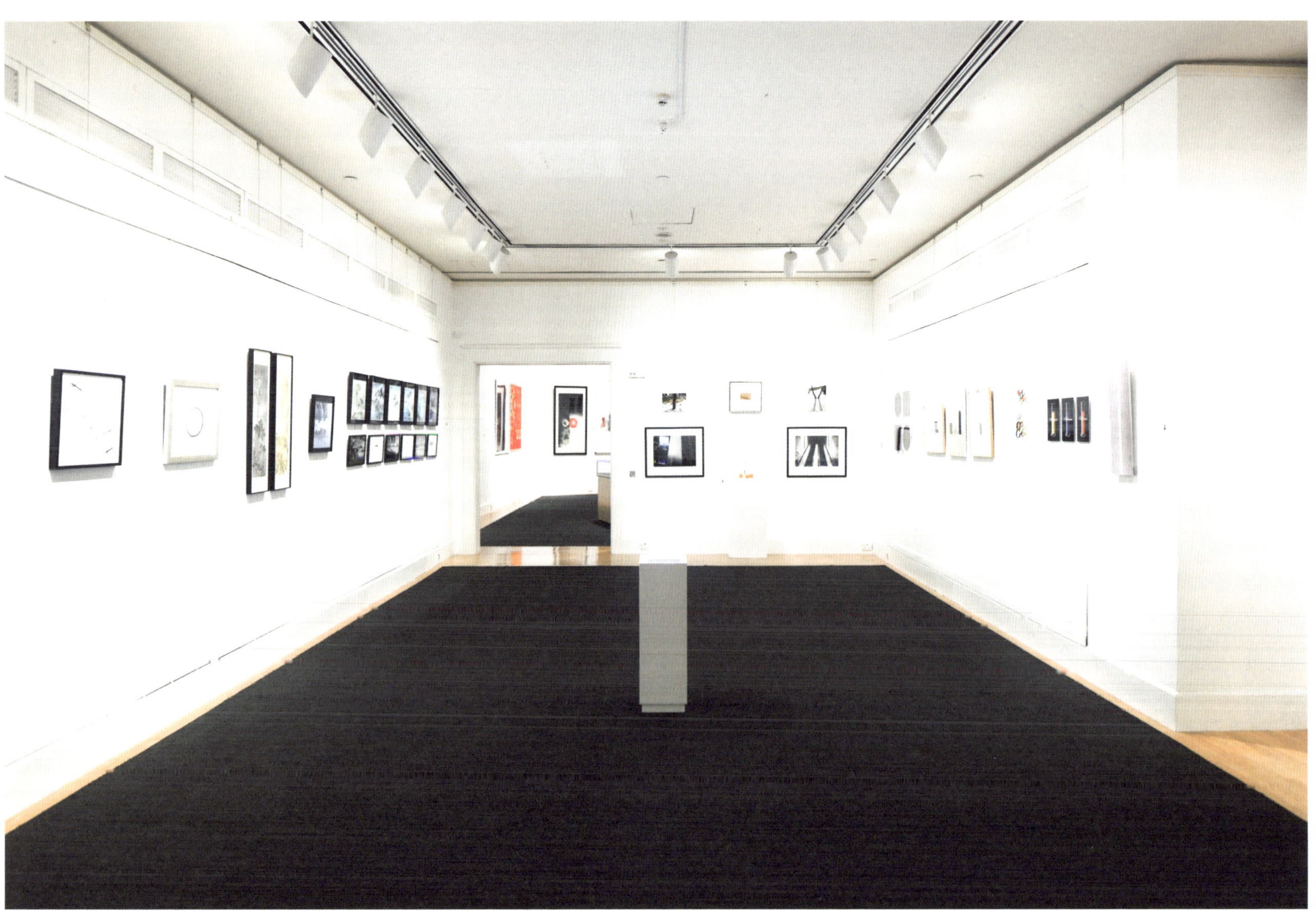

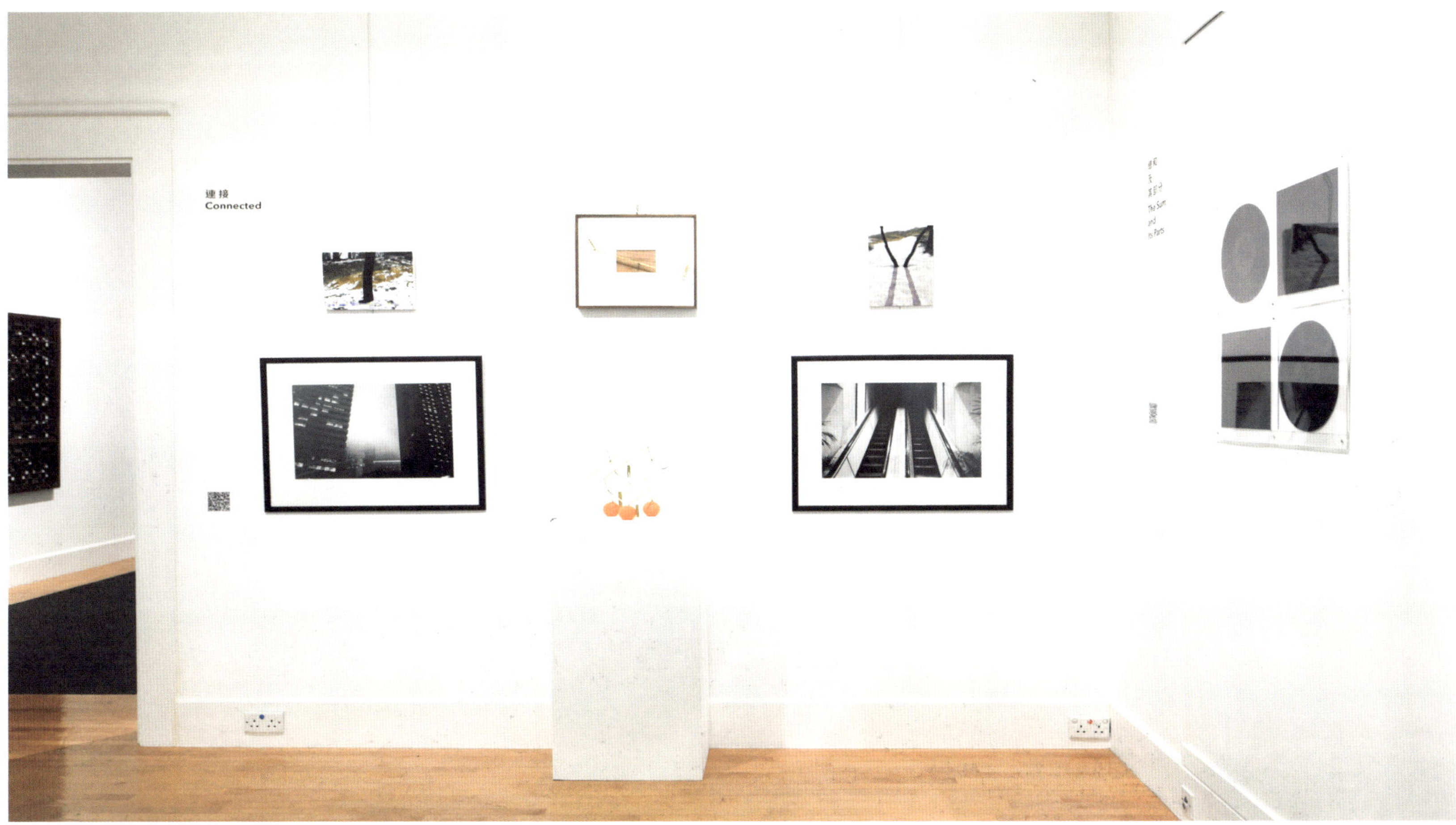

<table>
<tr><td>^ PAIR</td><td>> CONNECTED</td><td></td><td></td><td>THE SUM AND ITS PARTS ></td></tr>
<tr><td>LIAO Zenping 廖震平</td><td>Debe SHAM 岑愷怡</td><td>LIAO Zenping 廖震平</td><td></td><td>Herbert STAREK</td></tr>
<tr><td>David J. CLARKE 祈大衛</td><td>Debe SHAM 岑愷怡</td><td>David J. CLARKE 祈大衛</td><td></td><td></td></tr>
</table>

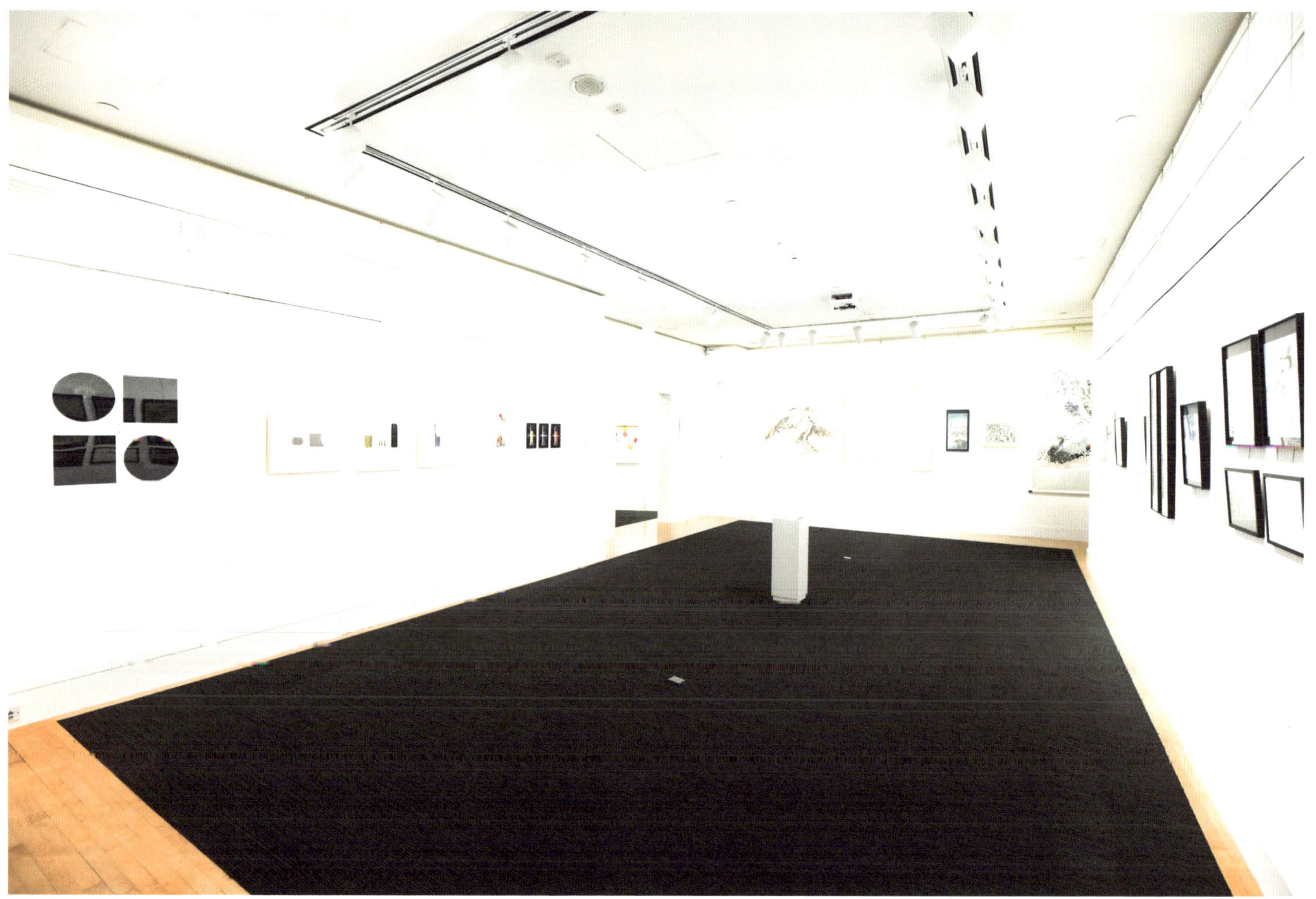

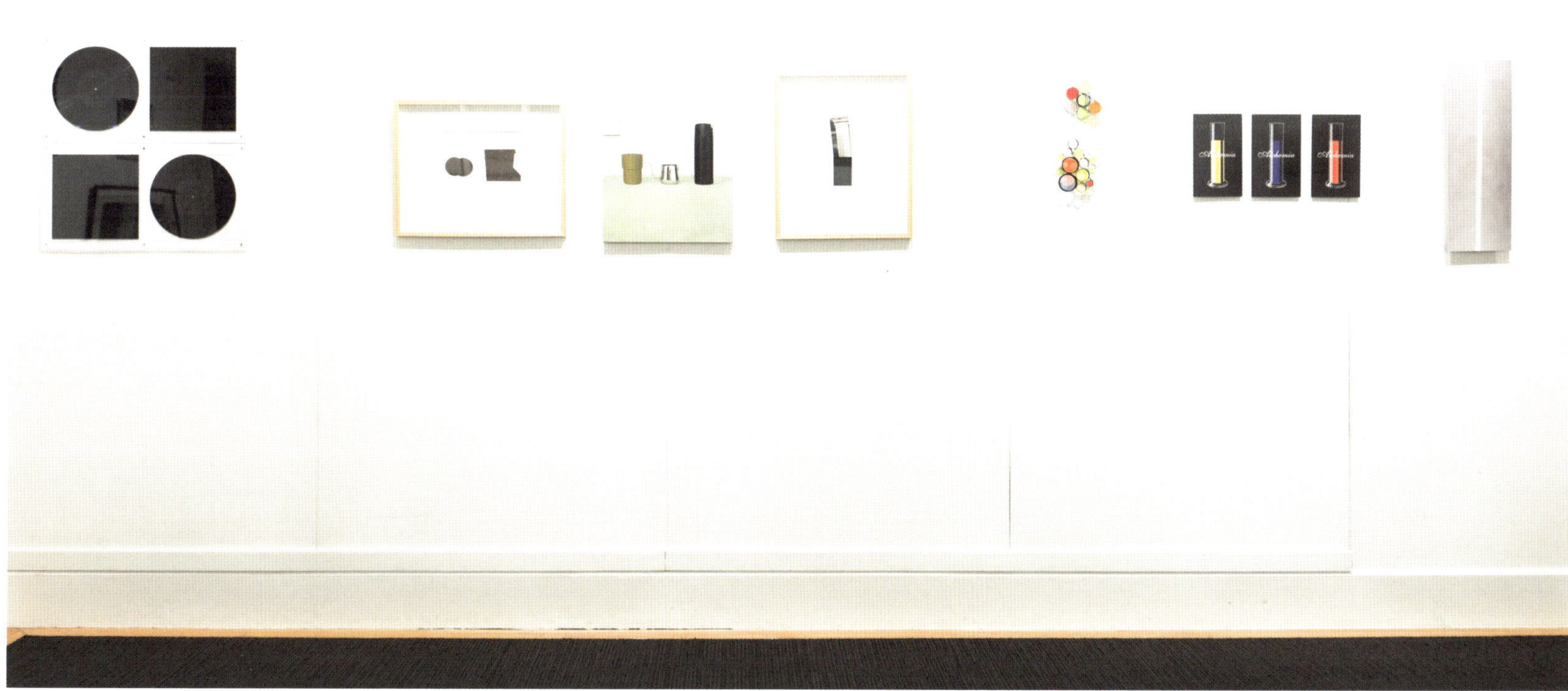

> THE SUM AND ITS PARTS

Herbert STAREK   Beat FELLER   LIAO Zenping   Beat FELLER   Christoph   Herbert STAREK   Christoph
                                       廖震平   DAHLHAUSEN   DAHLHAUSEN

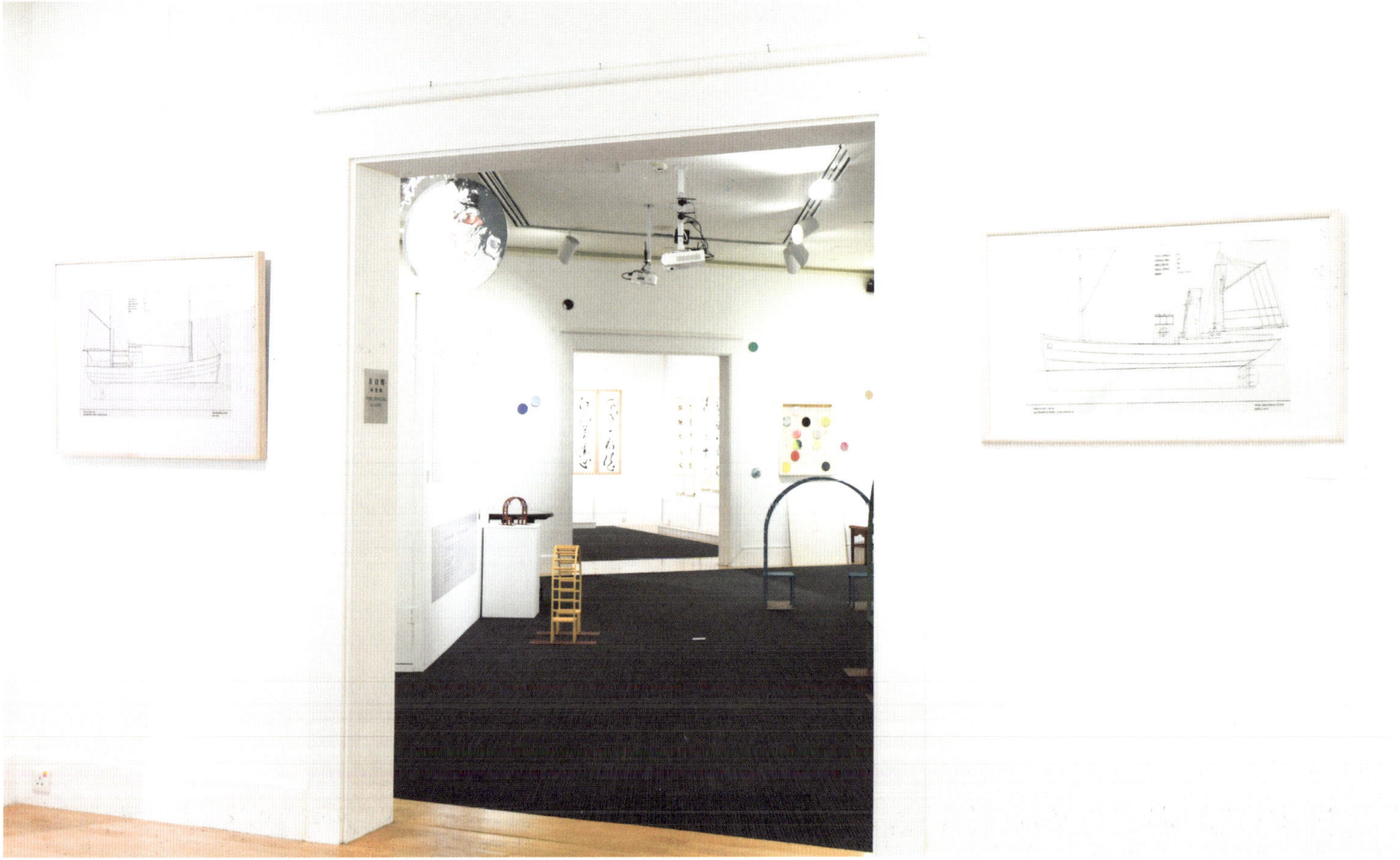

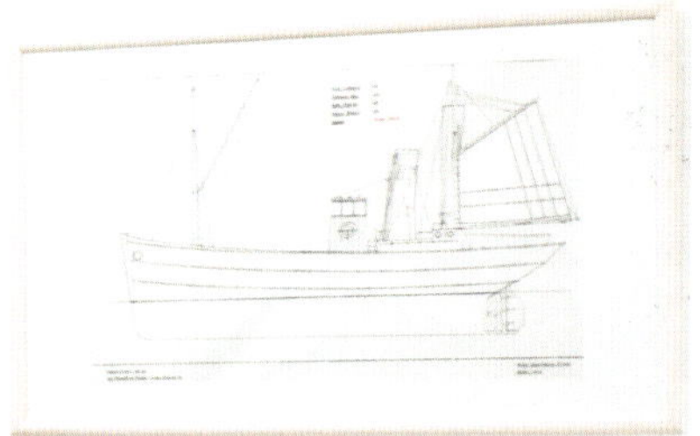

< THE SUM AND ITS PARTS >   ^ INTERACTIVE INSTALLATION ^ COUPLET

Ian Hamilton FINLAY   Mary Curtis   Debe SHAM   Christoph   Ian Hamilton FINLAY
                                   RATCLIFF   岑愷怡   DAHLHAUSEN

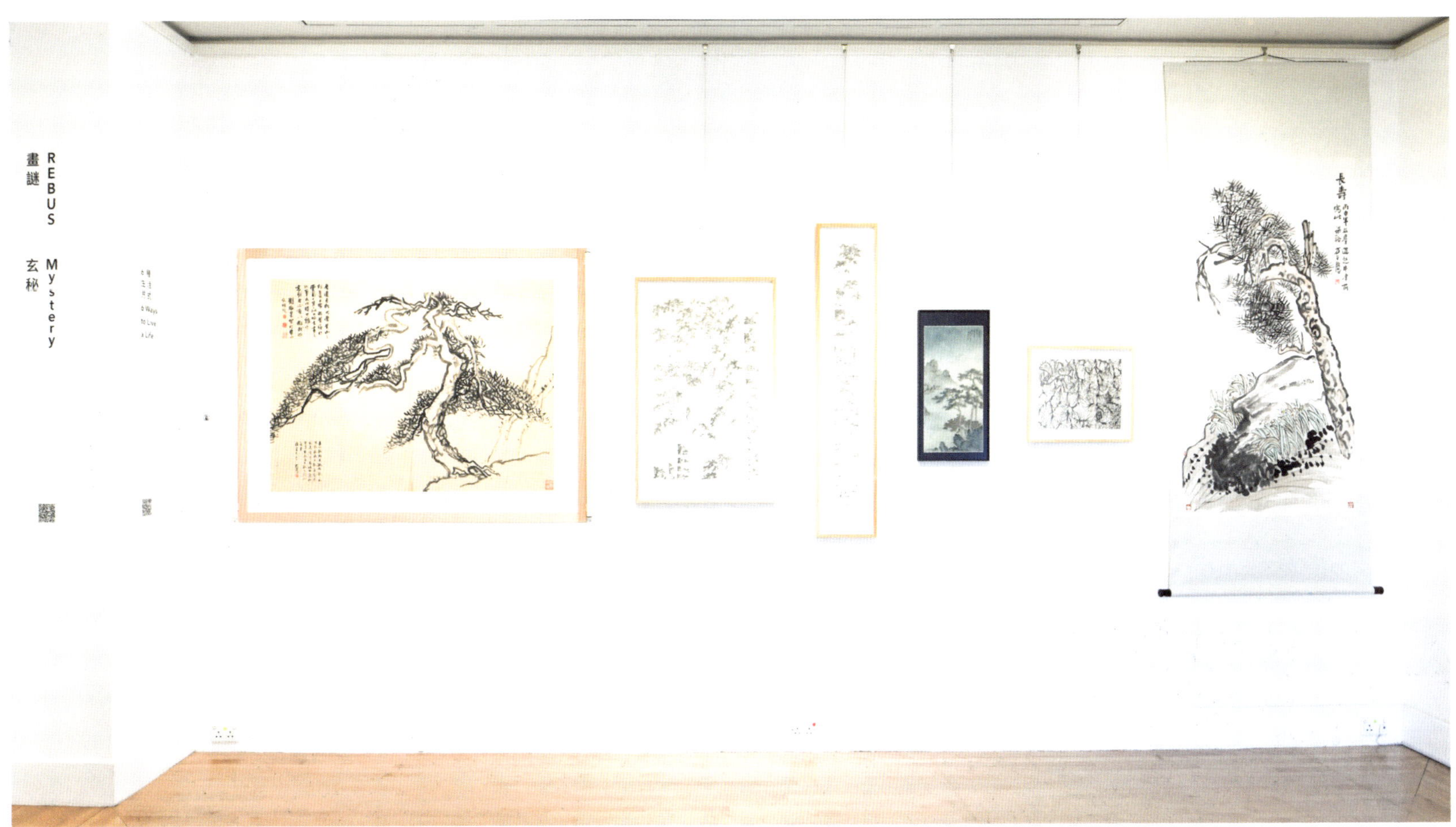

6 WAYS TO LIVE A LIFE >

LIU Haisu
劉海粟

Sim SHUM Kwan Yi 沈君怡

LI Jing
李淨

Robert
LETTNER

FANG Zhaoling
方召麐

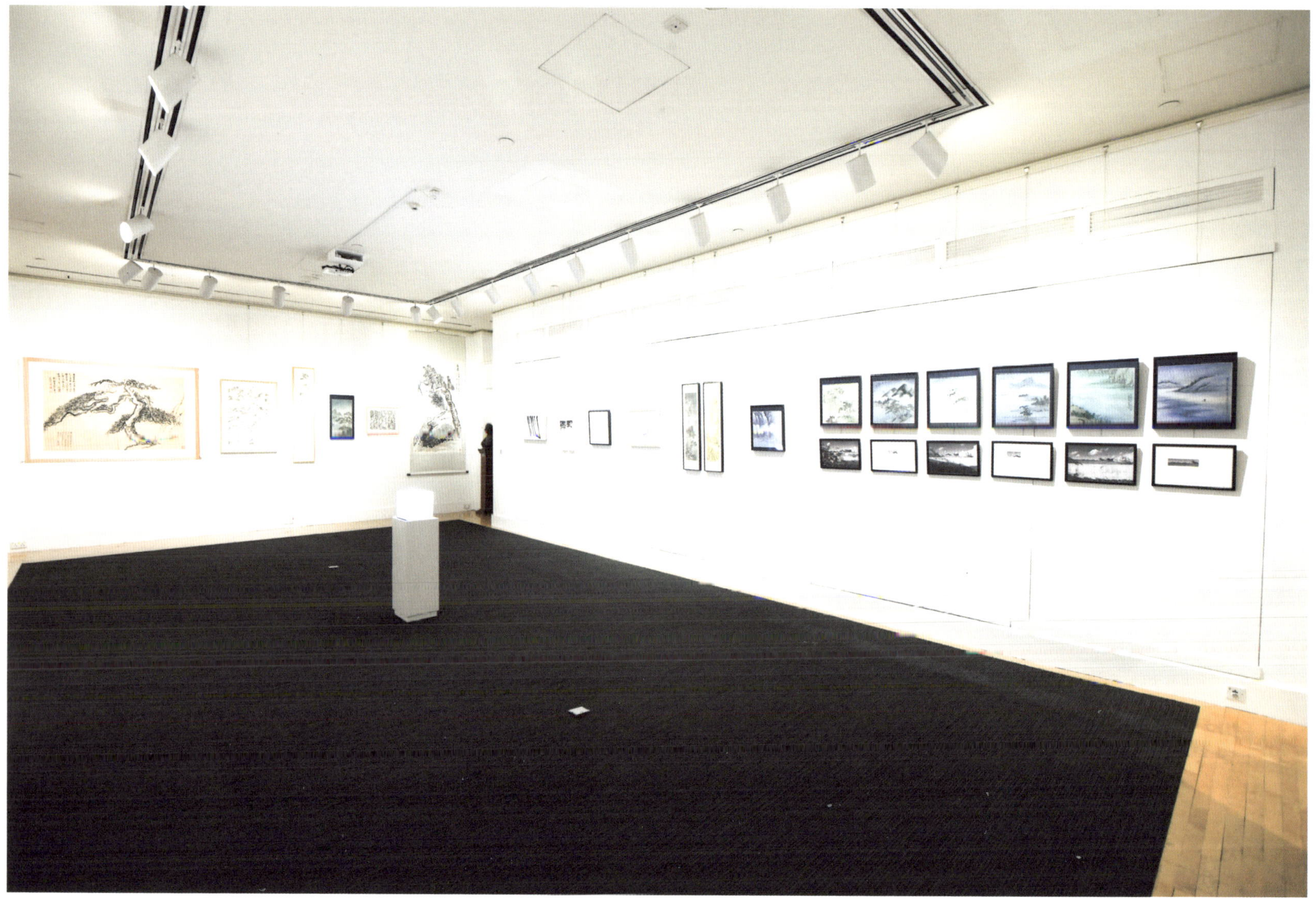

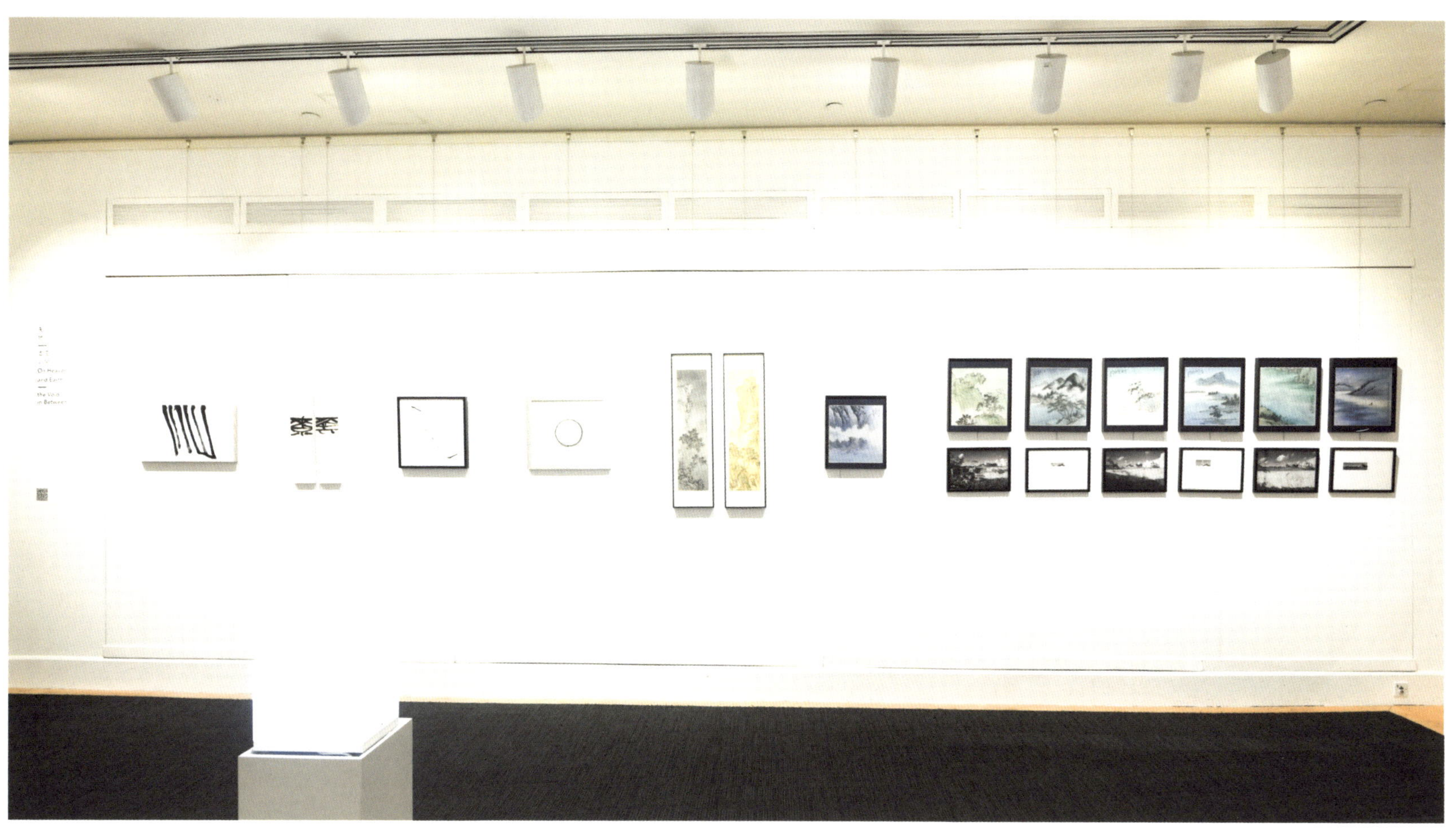

> ON HEAVEN AND EARTH – THE VOID IN BETWEEN

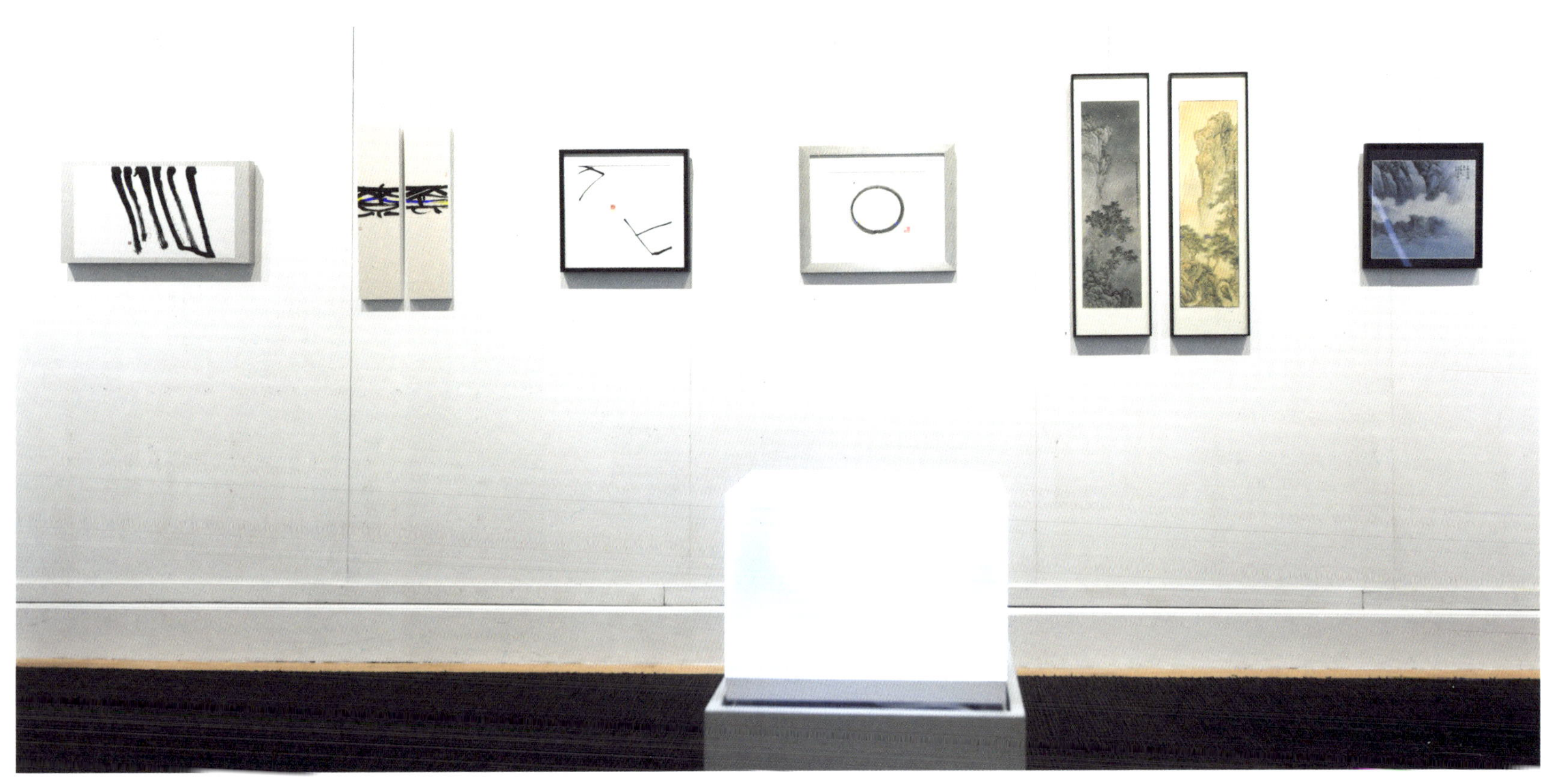

Eric FUNG 馮以力

Eric FUNG 馮以力

Eric FUNG 馮以力

THÍCH Nhất Hạnh 釋一行禪師

LI Jing 李淨

LI Jing 李淨

LI Jing 李淨

Joseph LEUNG Mong Sum 梁望琛

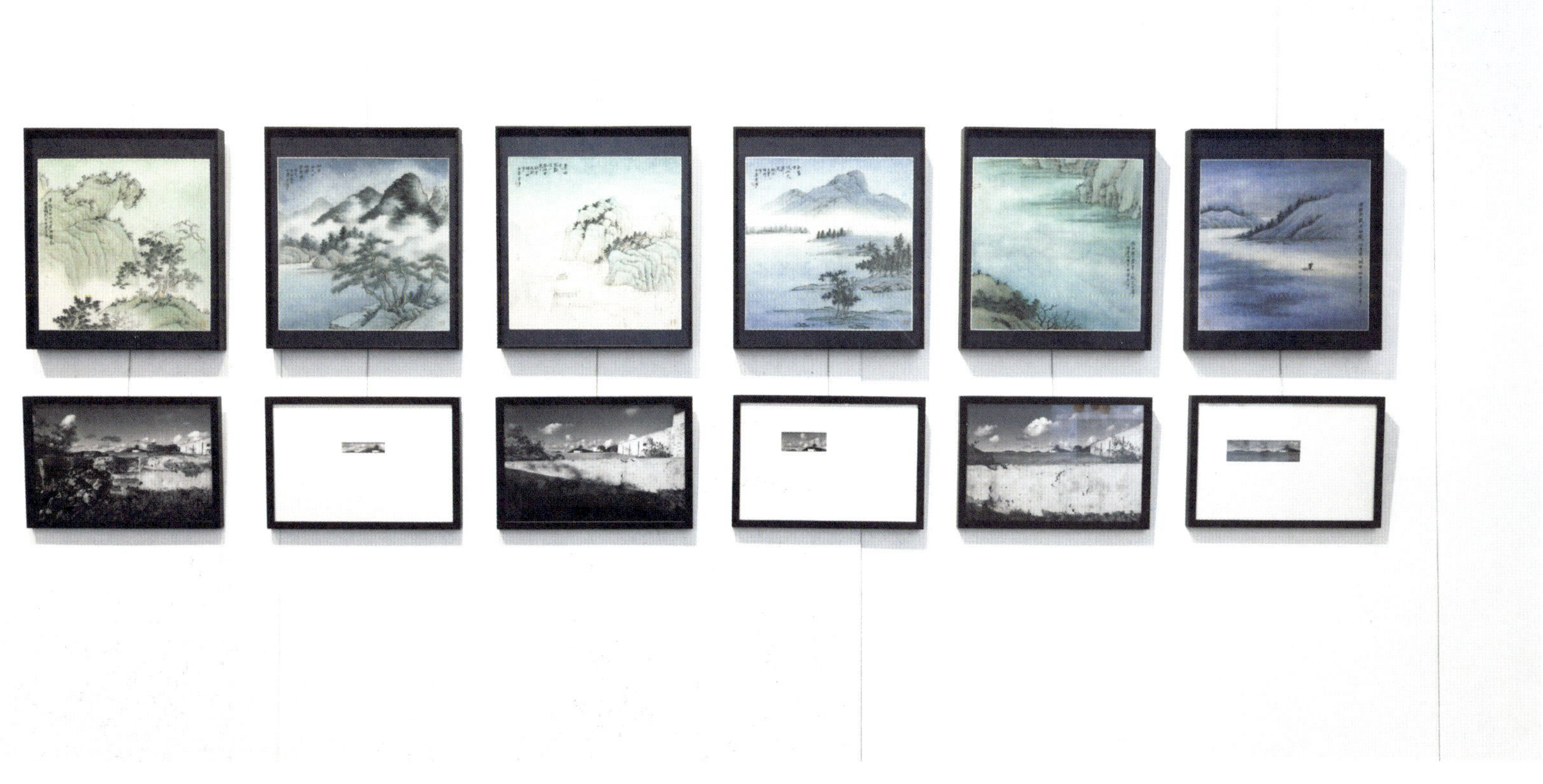

> ON HEAVEN AND EARTH – THE VOID IN BETWEEN

LI Jing	LI Jing	LI Jing	LI Jing	LI Jing	LI Jing
李淨	李淨	李淨	李淨	李淨	李淨
Peter SCHLÖR	Peter SCHLÖR	Peter SCHLÖR	Peter SCHLÖR	Peter SCHLÖR	Peter SCHLÖR

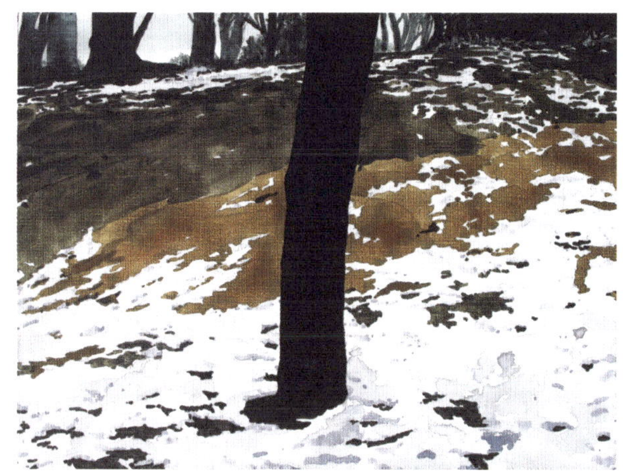

60 LIAO Zenping 廖震平

Snow and Tree Trunk | 2018

Aqyla on linen | H 24 x W 33.2 cm

Private collection, Hong Kong

61 David J. CLARKE 祈大衛

Central at night with low cloud – view towards the Cheung Kong Center, 1 December 1998 | 1998

Black and white photograph | H 40 x W 59 cm

HKU.Ph.2004.1546 | Gift of David J. CLARKE

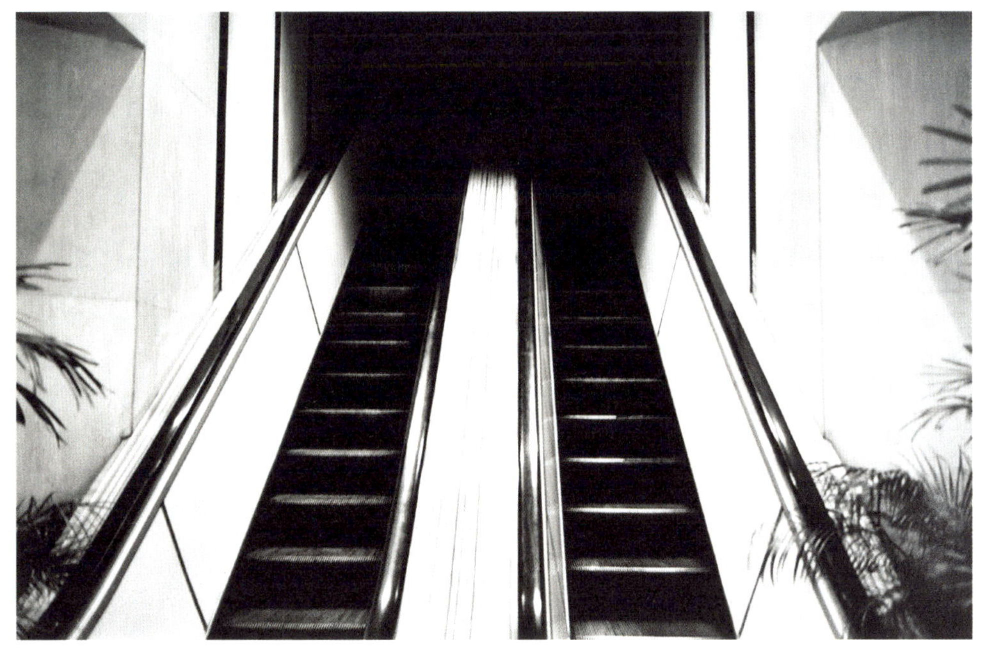

62 David J. CLARKE 祈大衛
Escalator at The Landmark, Night, 1 July 1996 | 1996
Black and white photograph | H 40 x W 59 cm
HKU.Ph.2004.1545 | Gift of David J. CLARKE

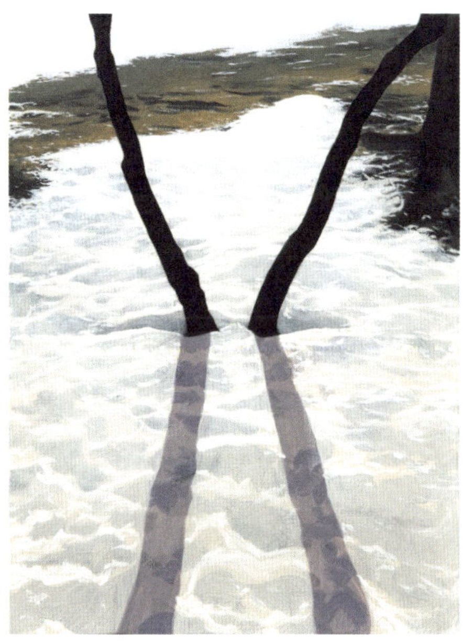

63 LIAO Zenping 廖震平
Snow and Tree Trunks-2 | 2019
Oil on linen | H 33.2 x W 24 cm
Private collection, Hong Kong

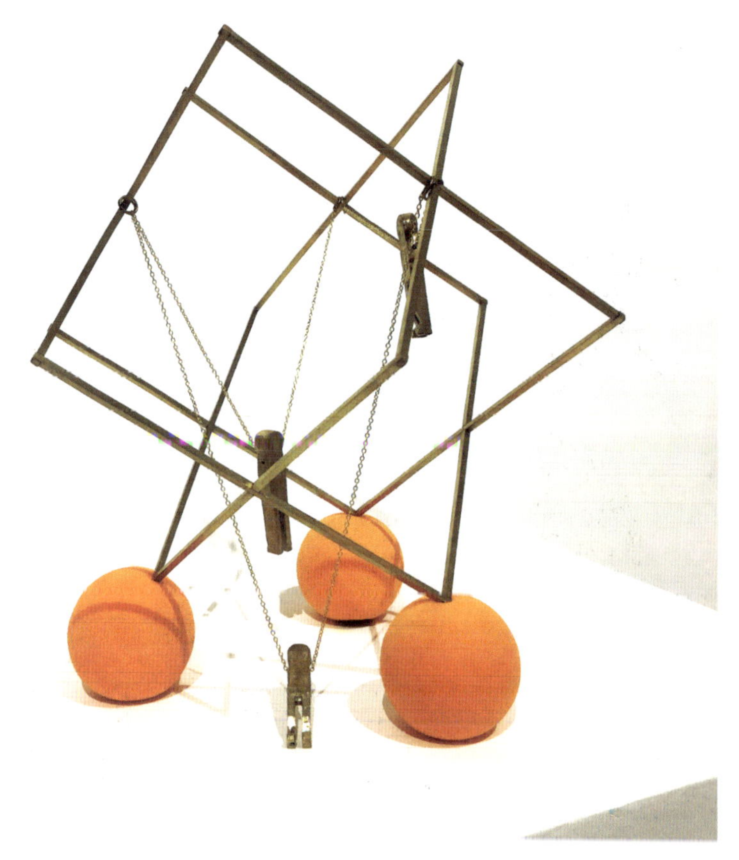

64 Debe SHAM 岑愷怡
Clothespin Doll Series—Still Flying | 2022
Brass, foam sponge and lead | H 31 x W 25 x D 25 cm
Collection of Grotto Fine Art Ltd

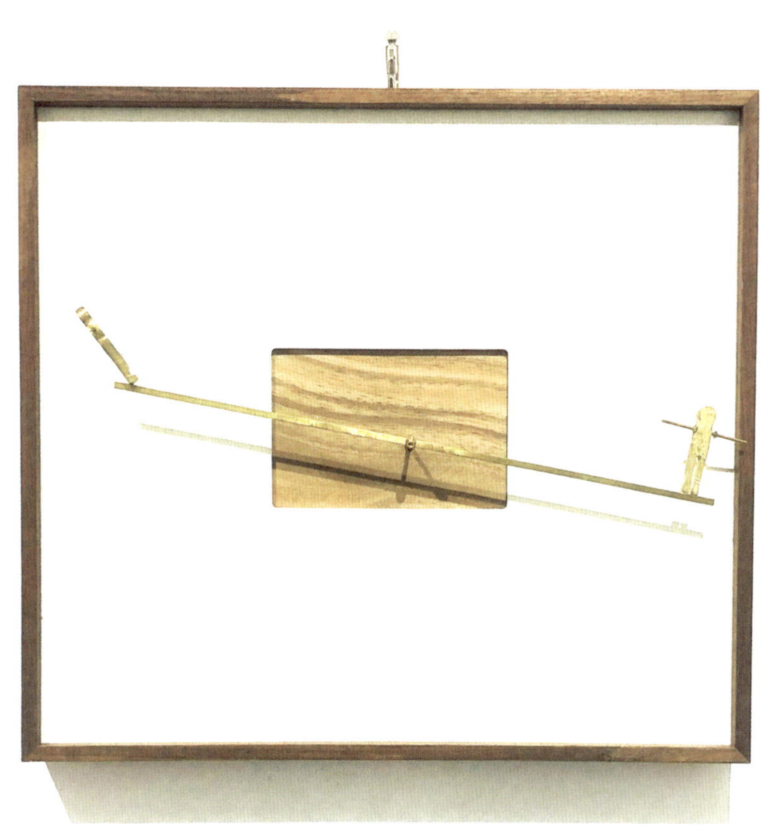

65 Debe SHAM 岑愷怡
Clothespin Doll Series—Clothespin Doll 02 | 2022
Brass and wood | H 39 x W 44 x D 6 cm
Collection of Grotto Fine Art Ltd

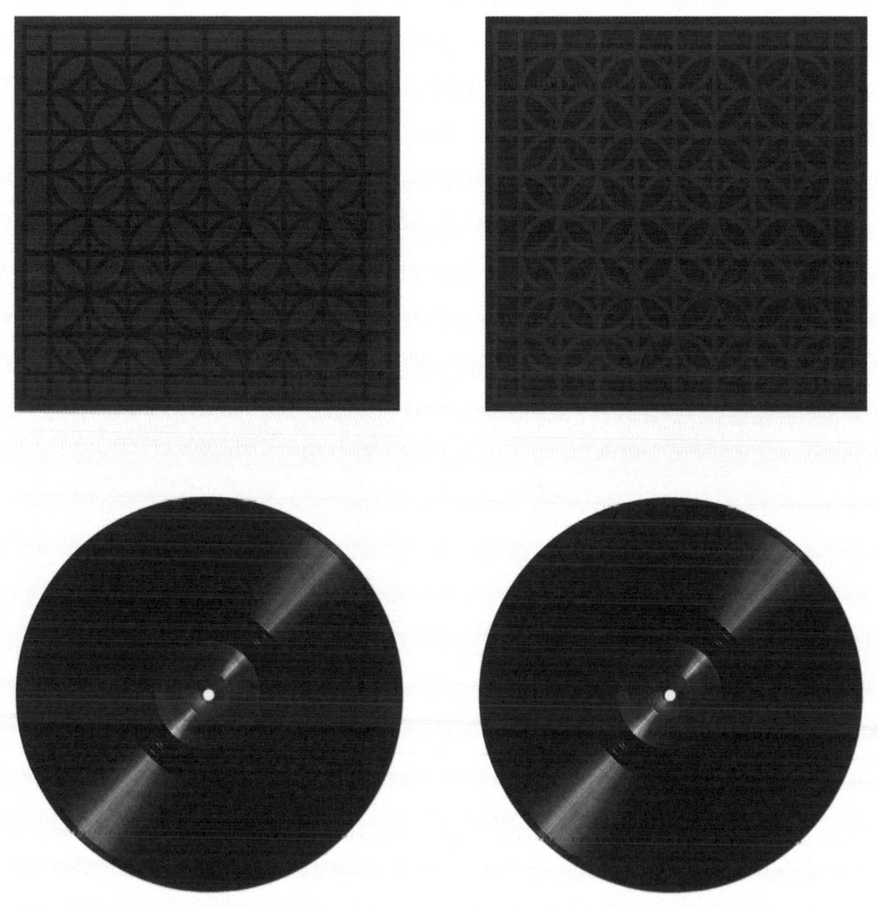

66 Herbert STAREK
HATTAH | 1994
Multiple, Vinyl, Ø 12 inches, screen printing on both sides on
plexiglass | Each H 30 x W 30 cm | Edition of 40
Collection of the artist

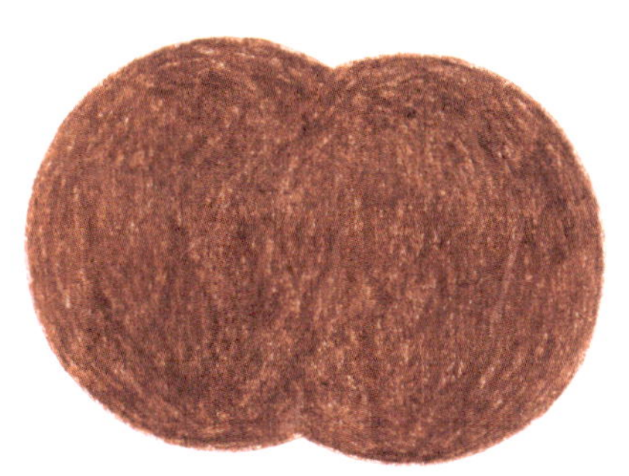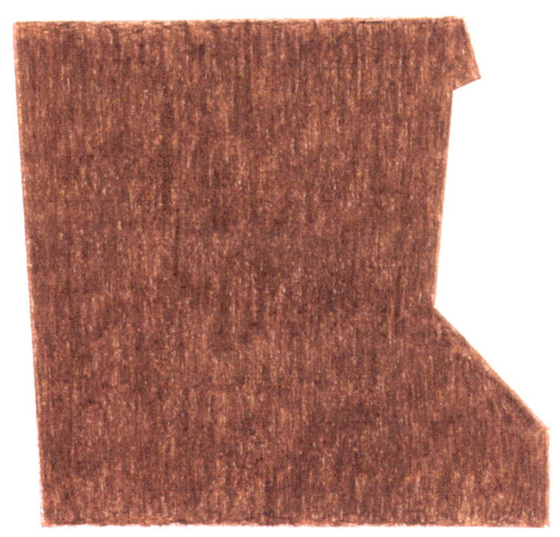

67 Beat FELLER
Dos Amigos (Two Friends) | 2008
Drawing, brown pencil on paper | H 29.7 x W 38.5 cm
Collection of the artist

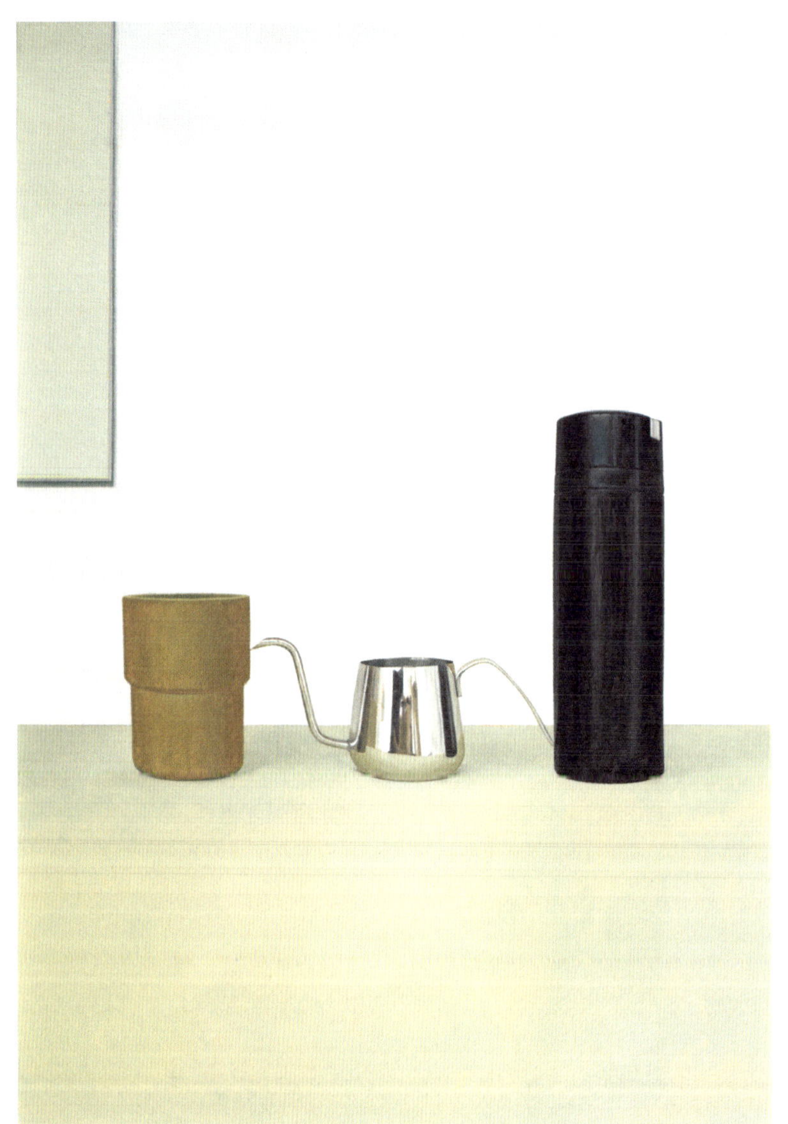

68 LIAO Zenping 廖震平
Still Life-4 | 2019
Oil on linen | H 65.2 x W 45.5 cm
Private collection, Hong Kong

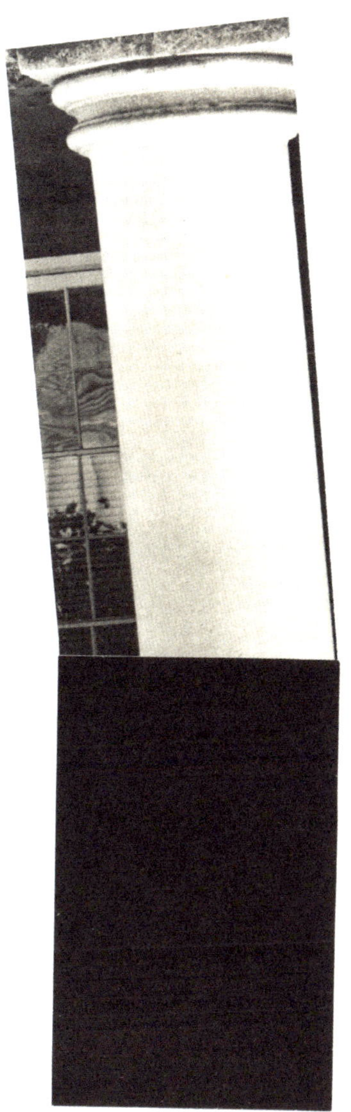

69 Beat FELLER
Dimensiones | 2010
Collage, colored paper on repro photo
H 30.5 x W 20.8 cm
Collection of the artist

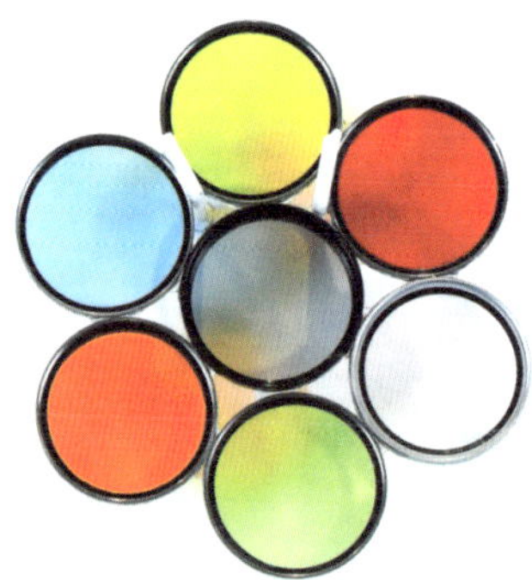

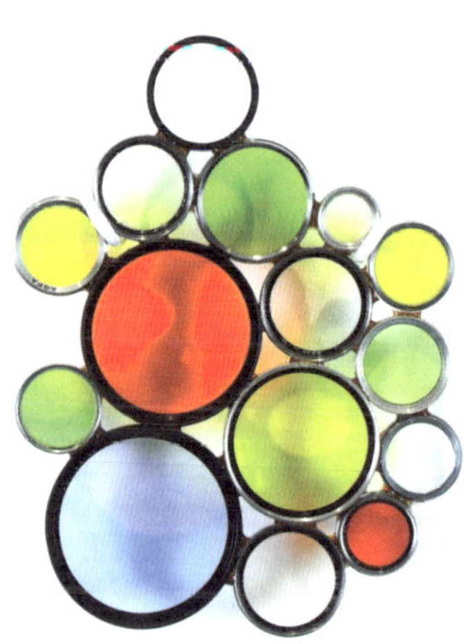

70 | 71 Christoph DAHLHAUSEN
Small Windows | 2013
Colored filters for photo cameras, 2 parts
H 14 x W 14 cm / H 19.7 x W 14.7 cm
Collection of the artist

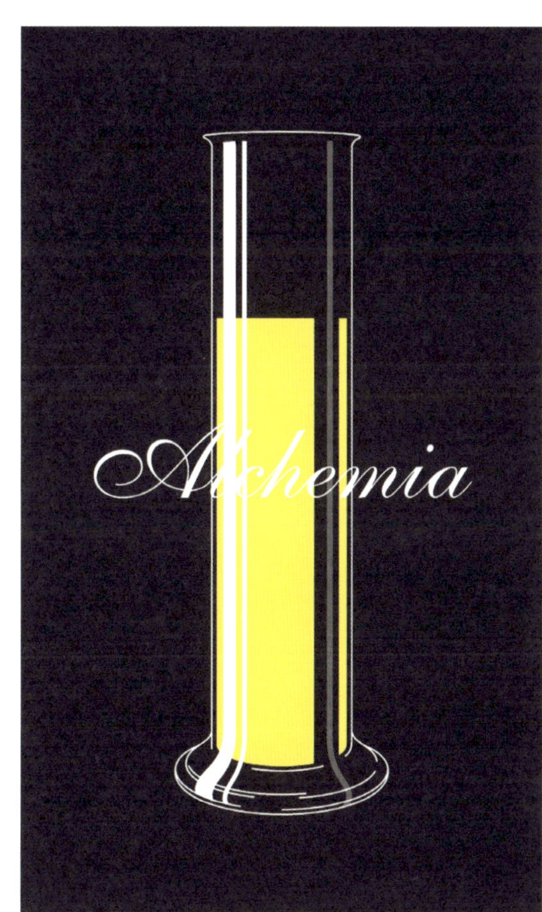 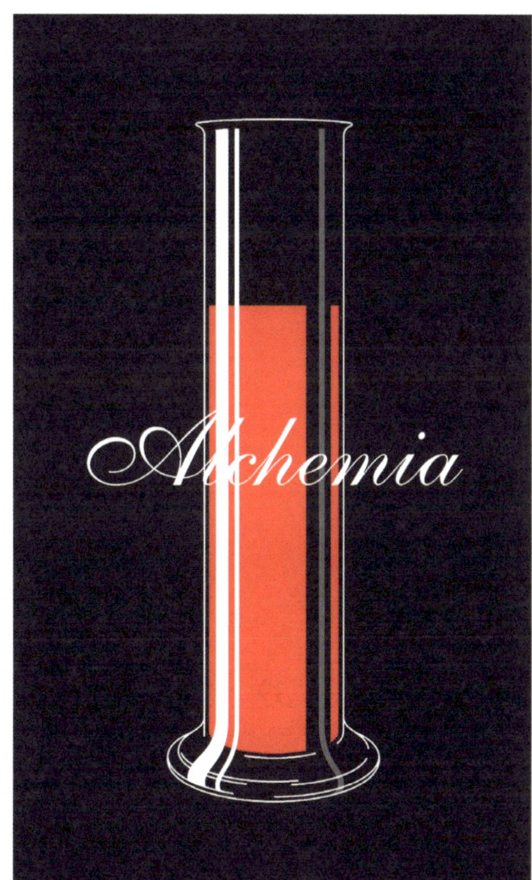 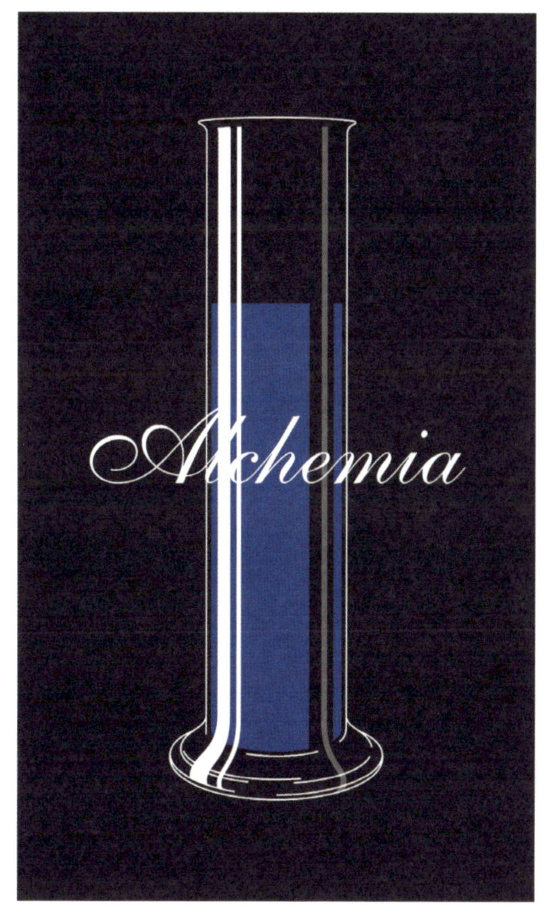

72 | 73 | 74 Herbert STAREK

Alchemia | 1999
Pigment print, 3 parts | Edition of 7
Each H 30 x W 18 cm
Collection of the artist

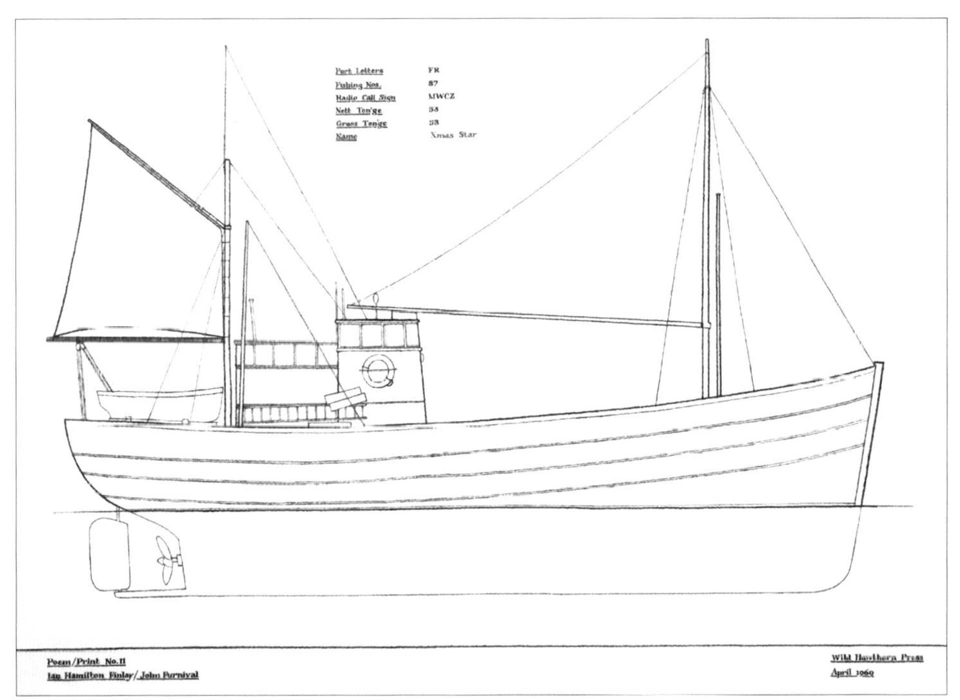

75 Ian Hamilton FINLAY with John FURNIVAL

Poem/Print No.11 Xmas Star | 1969

Silkscreen | H 51.1 x W 71.6 cm

Wild Hawthorn Press, The Archive of Ian Hamilton Finlay,

Dunsyre, Scotland

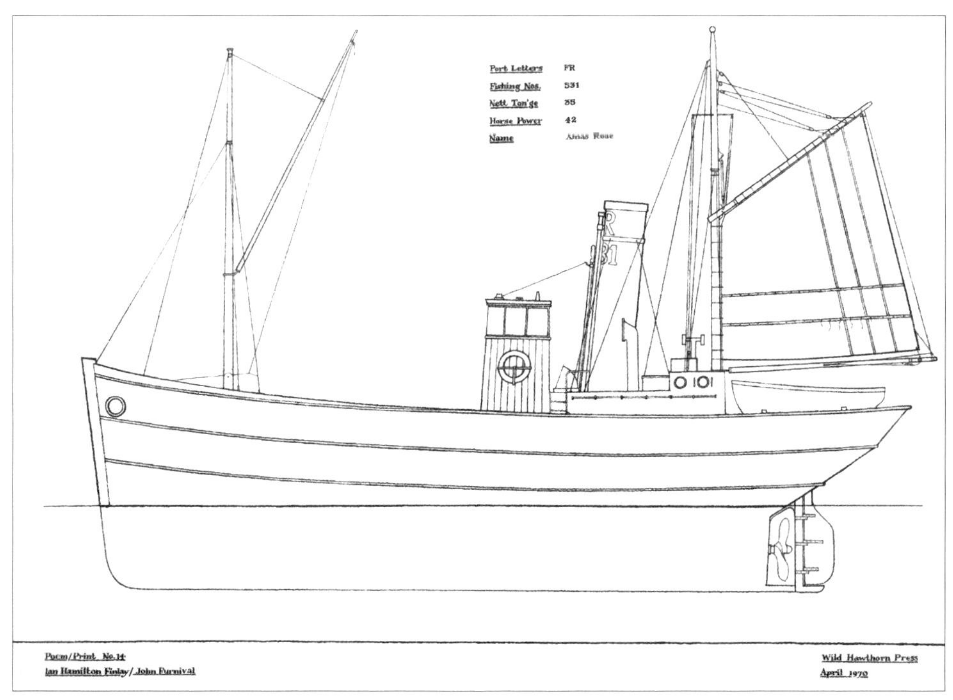

76 Ian Hamilton FINLAY with John FURNIVAL

Poem/Print No.14 Xmas Rose | 1970

Silkscreen | H 51 x W 71 cm

Wild Hawthorn Press, The Archive of Ian Hamilton Finlay, Dunsyre, Scotland

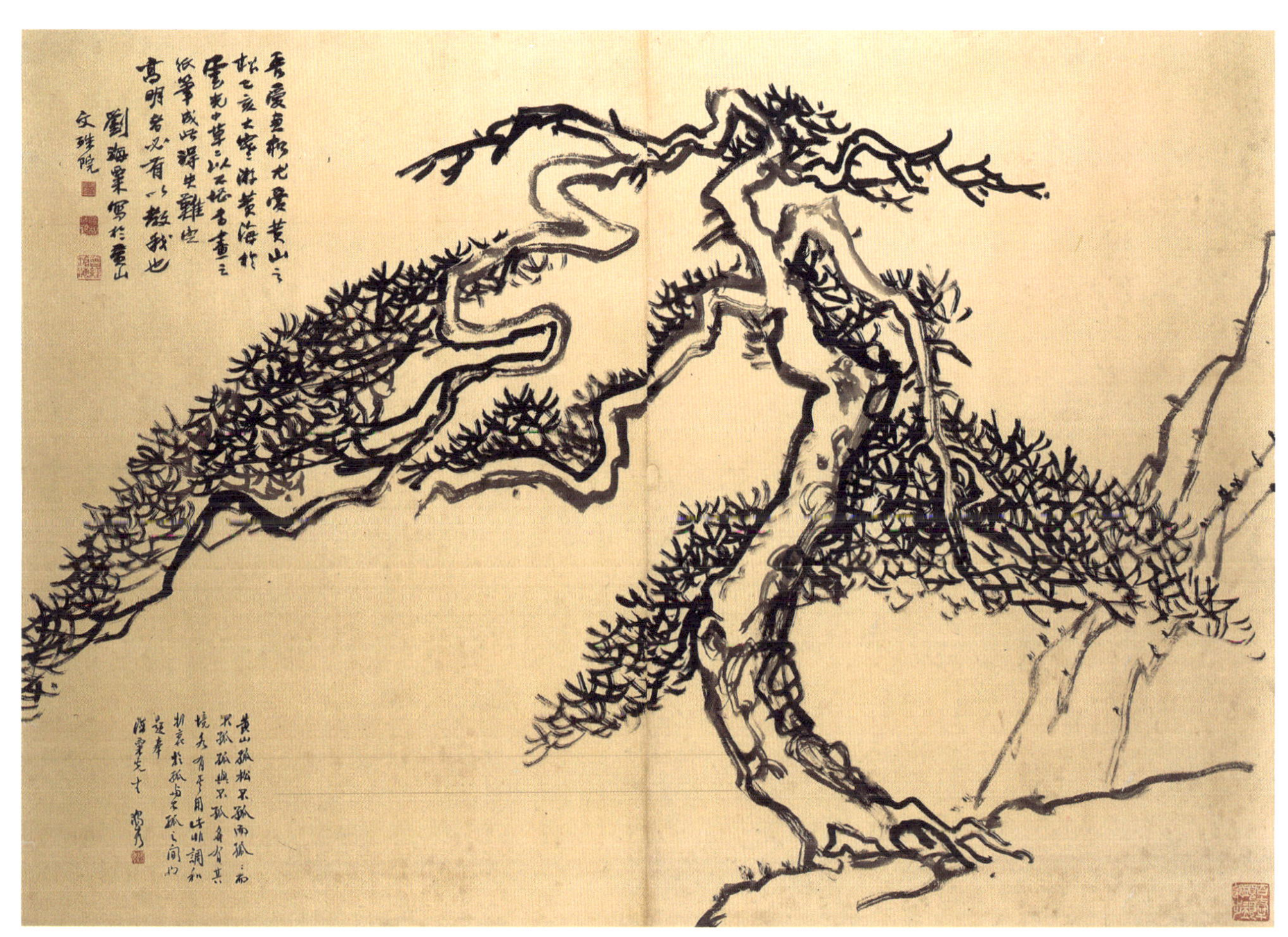

77 LIU Haisu 劉海粟

Pine at Huangshan | 1935

Hanging scroll, ink on paper | H 107 x L 154 cm

HKU.P.1997.1116 | Gift of LIU Haisu

152

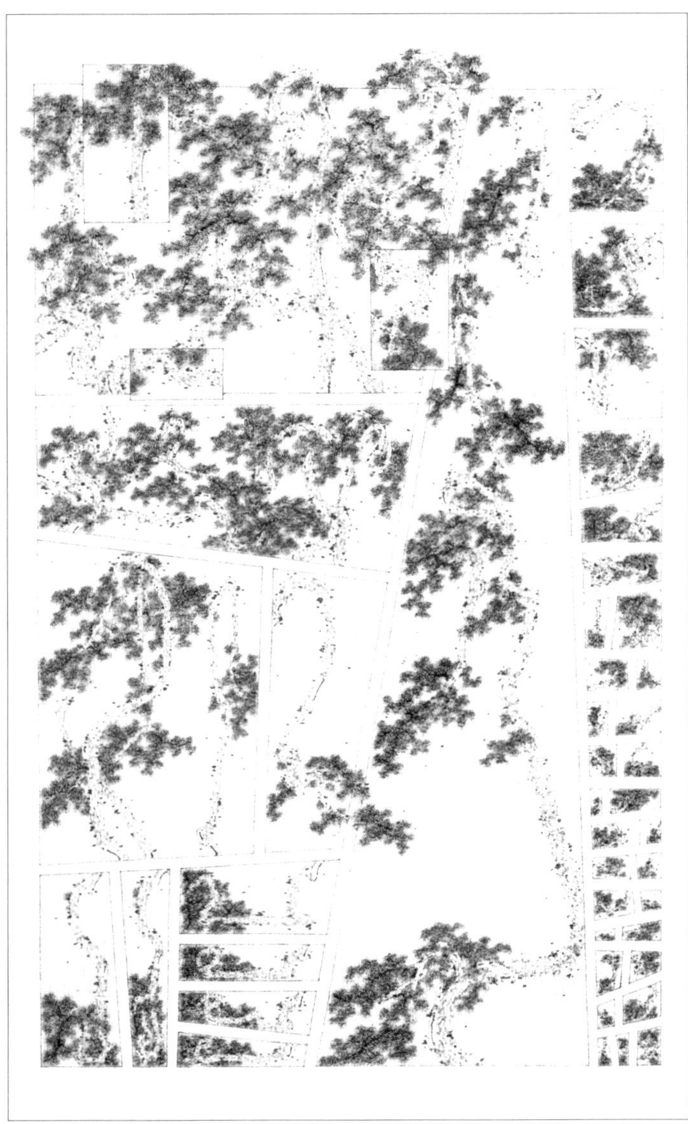

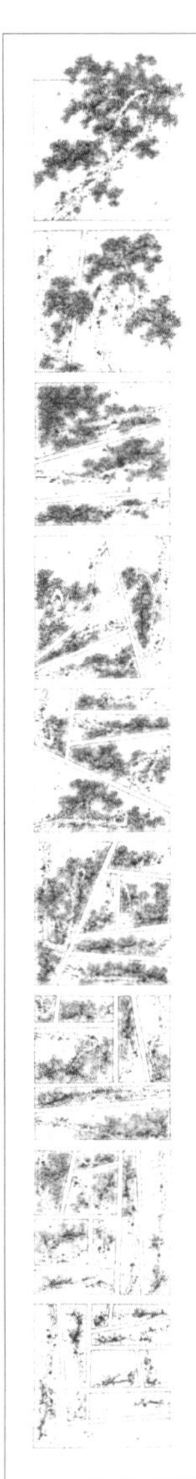

78 | 79 Sim SHUM Kwan Yi 沈君怡
The Comic Strip of Tree I | The Comic Strip of Tree II | 2023
Ink on paper | H 100 x W 63.5 cm | H 144 x W 20 cm
Collection of the artist

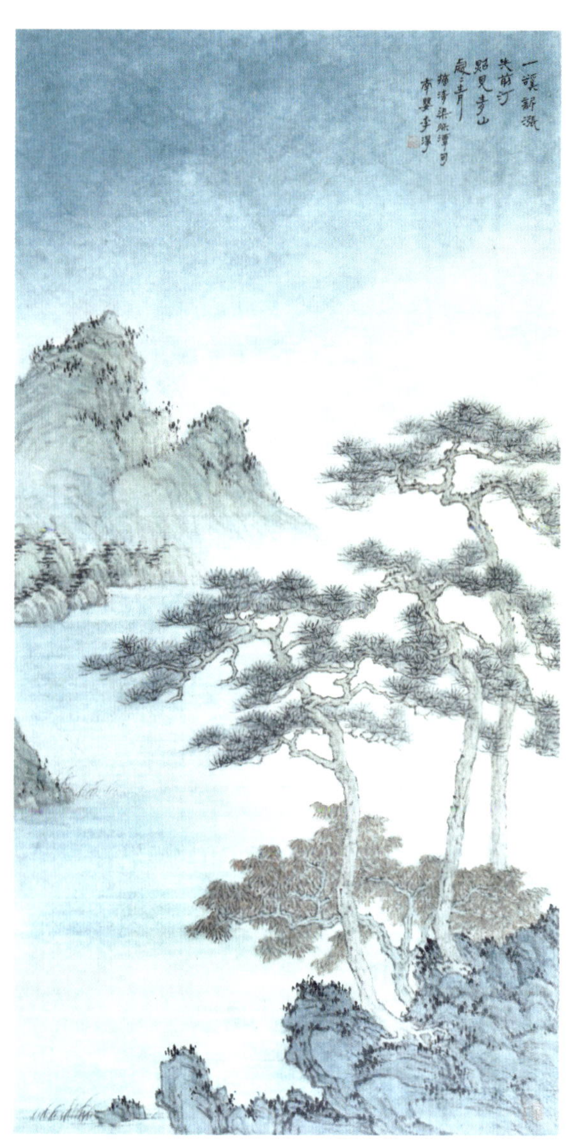

80 LI Jing 李淨

Liang Qiu Tan Poetic Painting | 2023

Ink, color on paper

L 62 x W 32 cm

Collection of the artist

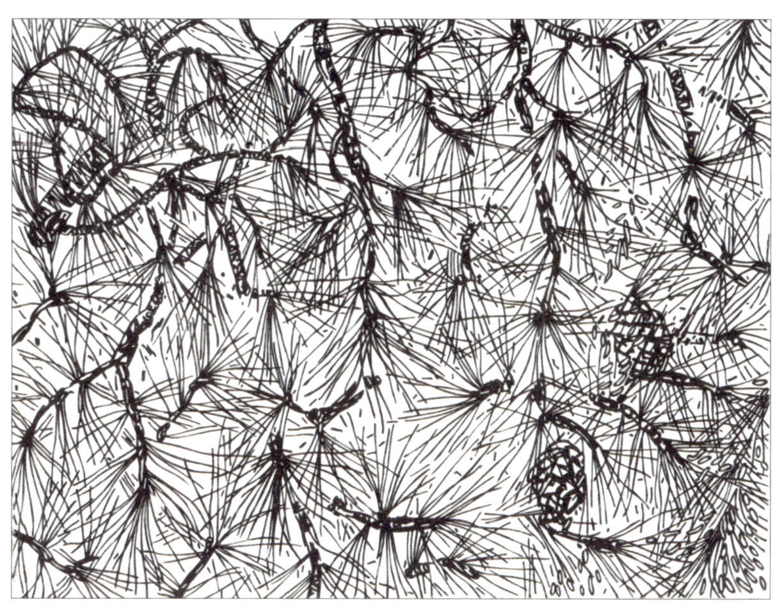

81 Robert LETTNER

Pines (Aalfang, Lower Austria) | 2010

Ink on paper

H 36 x W 48 cm

Private collection, Basel, Switzerland

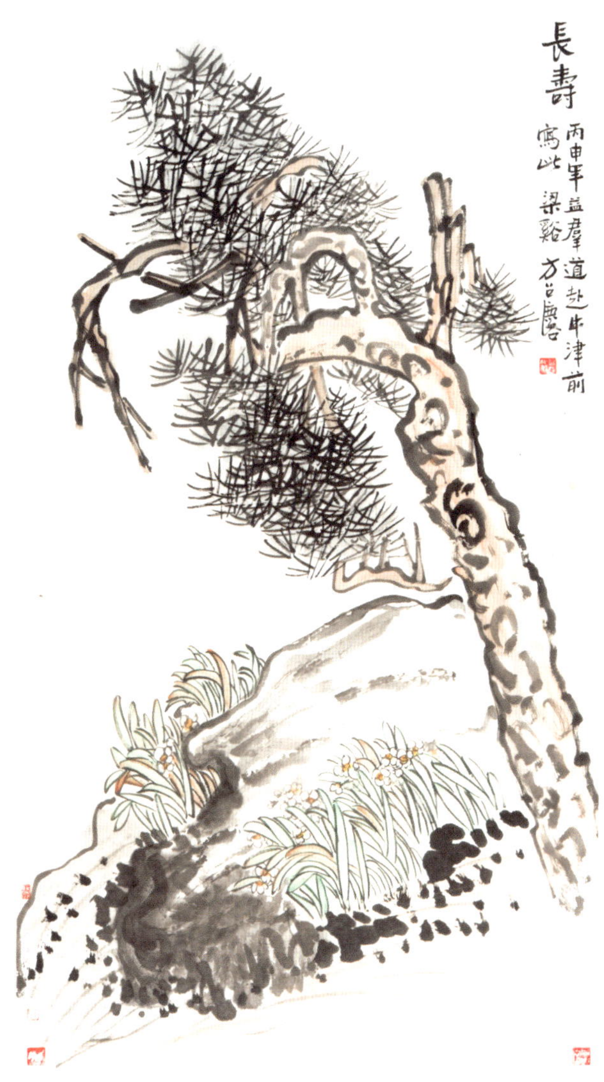

82 FANG Zhaoling 方召麐

Pine of Longevity | 1956

Hanging scroll, ink and color on paper

L 181 x W 97 cm (L 270 x W 124 cm)

HKU.P.1996.1197 | Gift of FANG Zhaoling

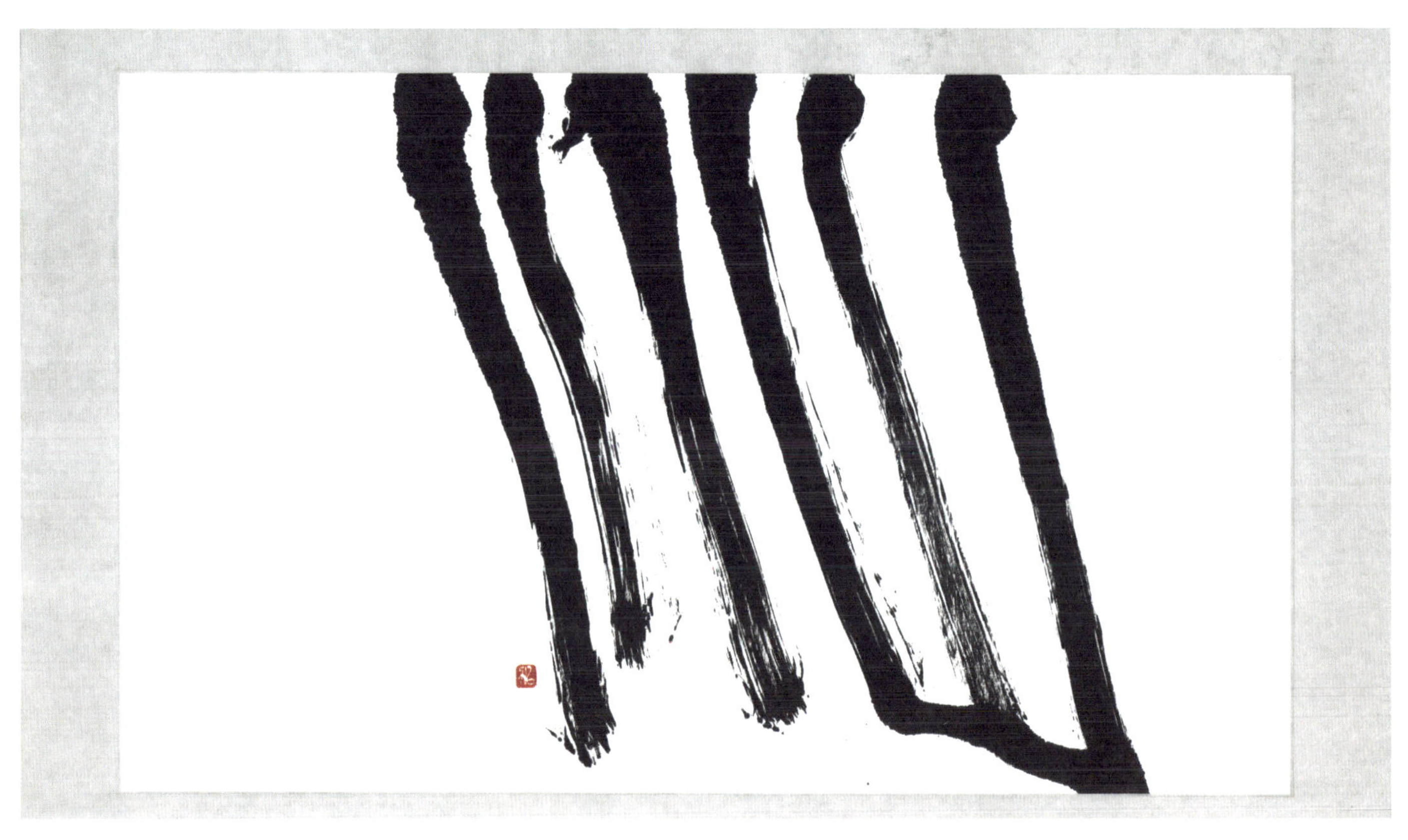

83 FUNG Yee Lick Eric 馮以力
Mountains and Rivers 《山川》 | 2022
Ink on rice paper
H 34.5 x W 57.5 cm
Private collection, Hong Kong

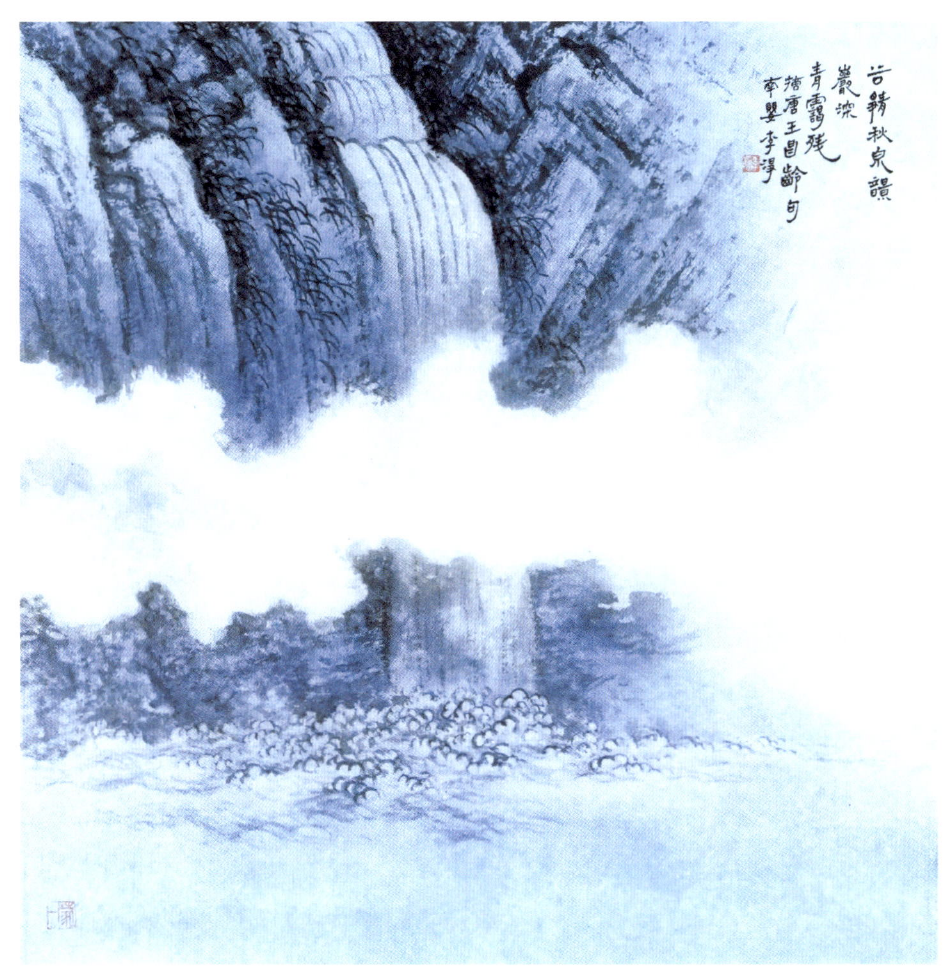

84 LI Jing 李淨
Wang Changling's Poetic Painting《王昌齡詩意圖》| 2023
Color on paper
H 35 x W 35 cm
Collection of the artist

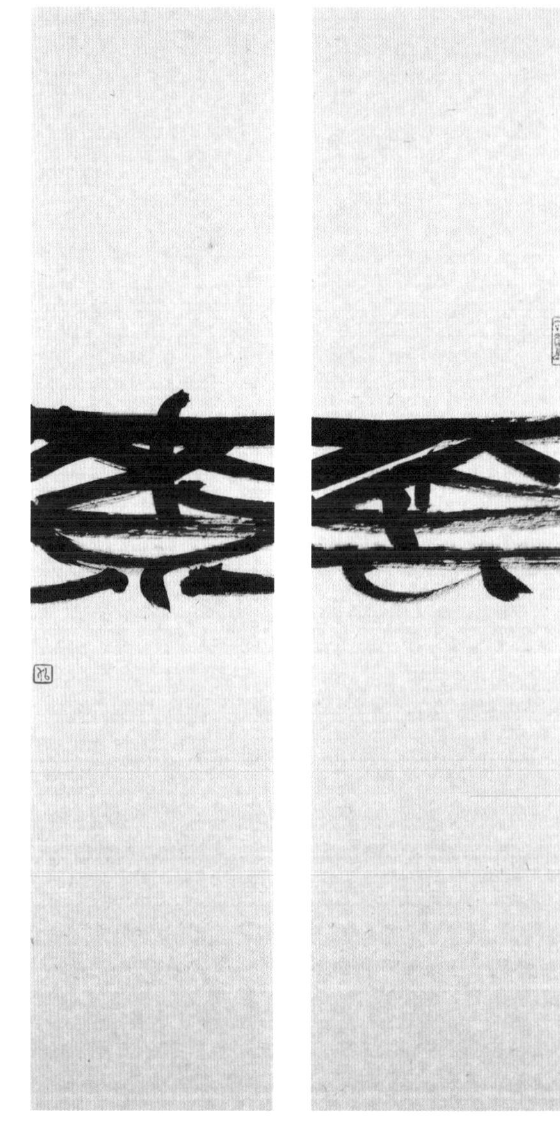

85 FUNG Yee Lick Eric 馮以力
Not Coming, Not Going 《不來不去》| 2023
Diptych, ink on paper
H 69.5 x W 34 cm
Private collection, Hong Kong

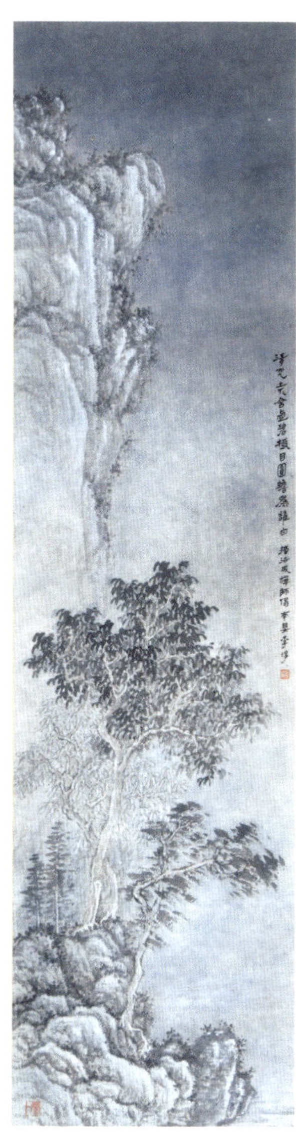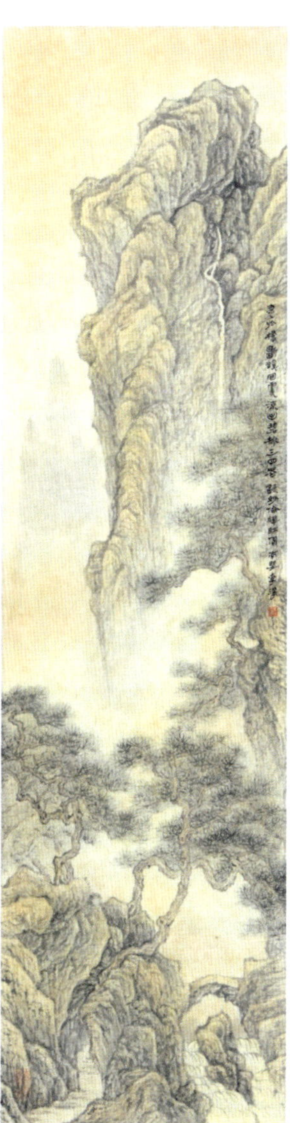

86 | 87 LI Jing 李淨

Inspired by Venerable Fa Cheng's Poems 《法成禪師詩意圖》 | 2018

Inspired by Venerable Miao Lun's Poems 《妙倫禪師詩意圖》 | 2018

Color on paper | Each H 75 x W 20 cm

HKU.P.2024.2662 | HKU.P.2024.2663 | Gift of LI Jing

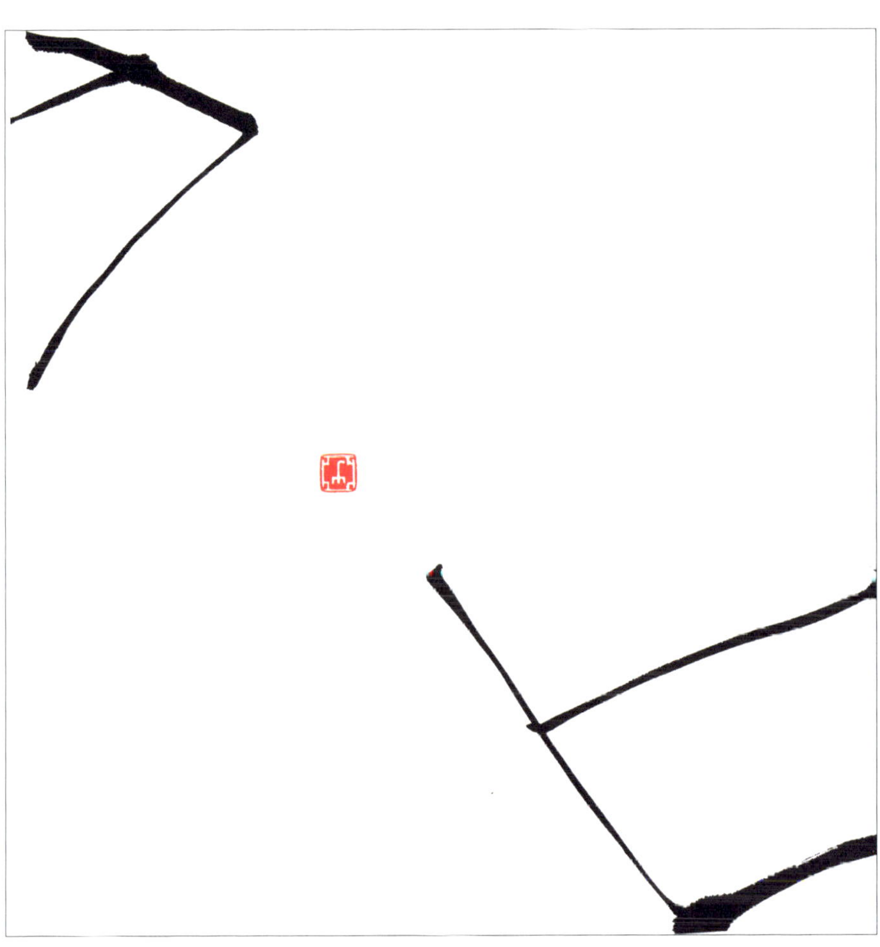

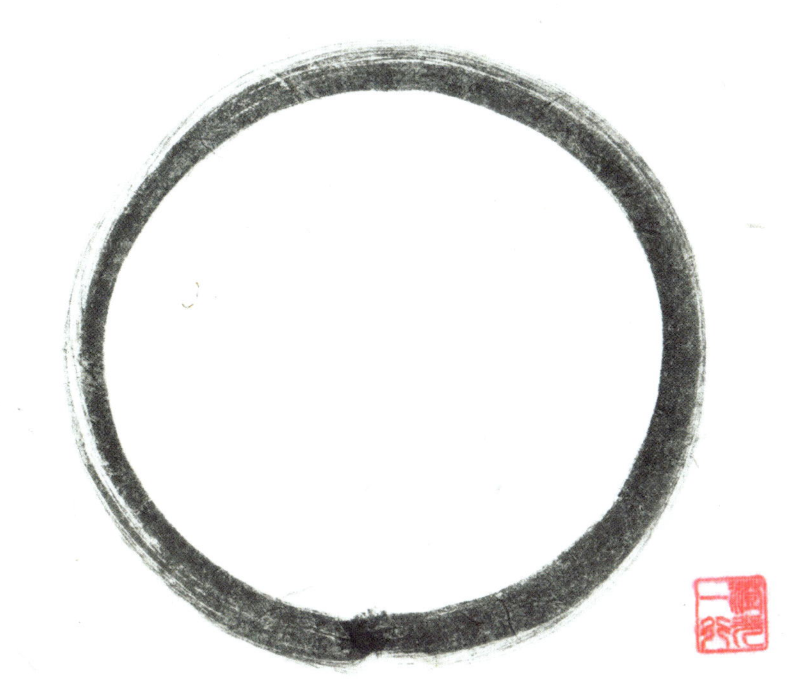

89 THÍCH Nhất Hạnh 釋一行禪師
Zen Circle 《圓禪》 | 2010
Ink on paper
H 54 x W 48 cm
HKU.Ca.2011.1905 | Gift of THÍCH Nhất Hạnh

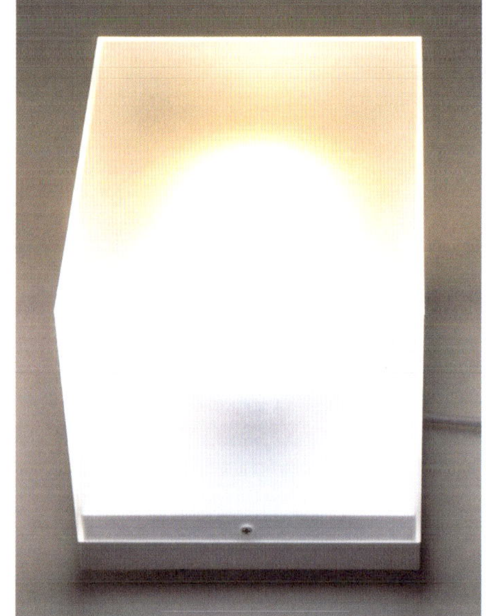

90 Joseph LEUNG Mong Sum 梁望琛

Untitled (Hong Kong, Hong Kong) 無題 (香港 香港) | 2020

Two lightbulbs from the opposite sides of the spectrum, plexiglas box

H 20 x W 30 x D 24 cm

Collection of the artist

91 Christoph DAHLHAUSEN

Bardos IV, 3 | 1999

C-print on aluminium

H 68 x W 23 cm

Collection of the artist

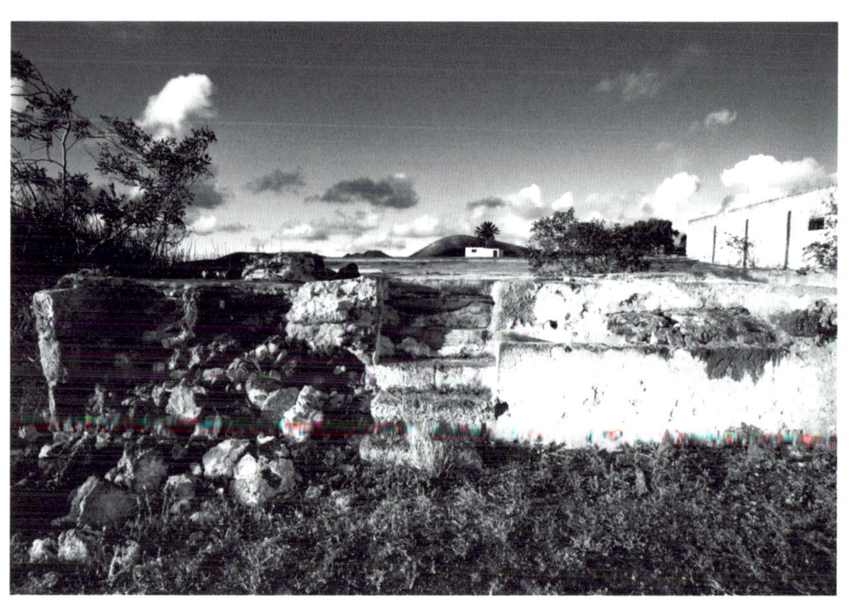

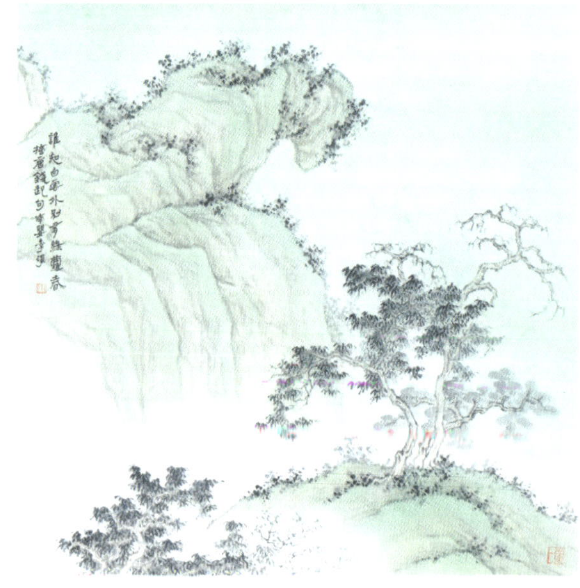

"Who knows that beyond the white clouds
is a green radish in spring."

Qian Qi 錢起 (710–782)

92 Peter SCHLÖR
La Geria I (Diptych) | 2003
Edition 12 + 3 AP | Fine art pigment print | H 25 x W 38 cm
Collection of the artist

93 LI Jing 李淨
Inspired by Qian Qi's Poems 《錢起詩意圖》 | 2023
Color on paper | H 35 x W 35 cm
Collection of the artist

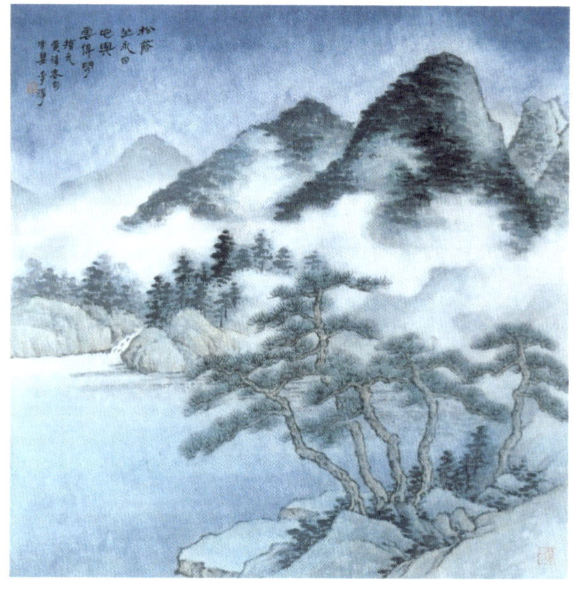

"Pines sit in the eternal sun.
My mind is at ease with the clouds."

Huang Qinglao 黃清老 (1290–1348)

94 Peter SCHLÖR
La Geria I (Diptych) | 2003
Edition 12 + 3 AP | Fine art pigment print | H 25 x W 38 cm
Collection of the artist

95 LI Jing 李淨
Inspired by Huang Qinglao's Poems 《黃清老詩意圖》 | 2023
Color on paper | H 35 x W 35 cm
Collection of the artist

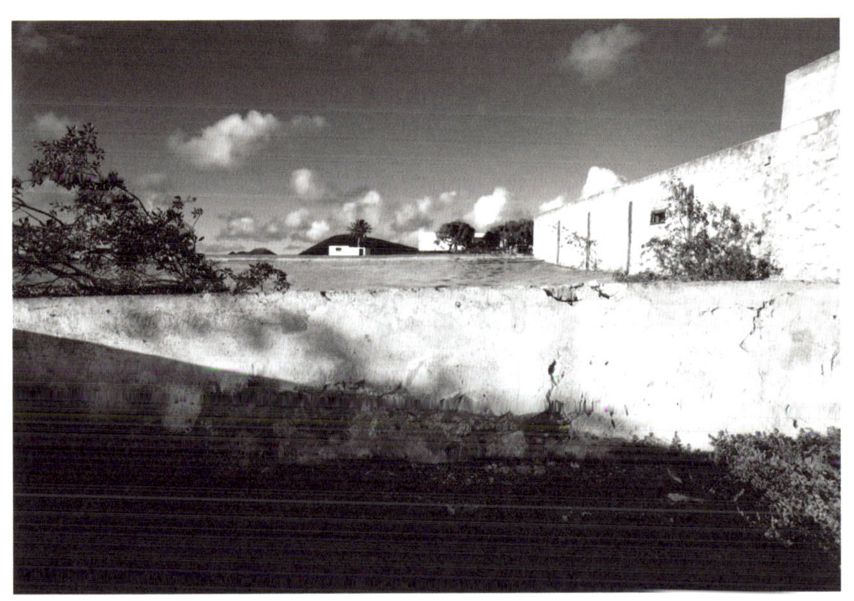

96 Peter SCHLÖR
La Geria II (Diptych) | 2003
Edition 12 + 3 AP | Fine art pigment print | H 25 x W 38 cm
Collection of the artist

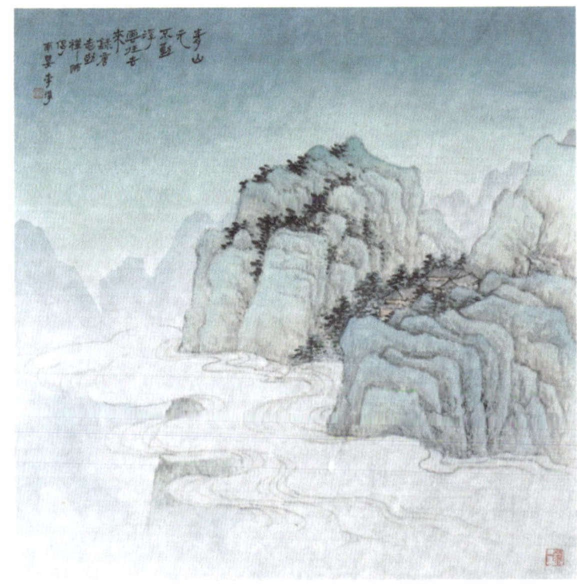

"The green mountain is immovable.
The floating clouds come and go as they please."
Lingyun Zhiqin aka Master Sacred Cloud

97 LI Jing 李淨
Inspired by Zen Master Zhiqin's Poems 《志勤禪師詩意圖》 | 2023
Color on paper | H 35 x W 35 cm
Collection of the artist

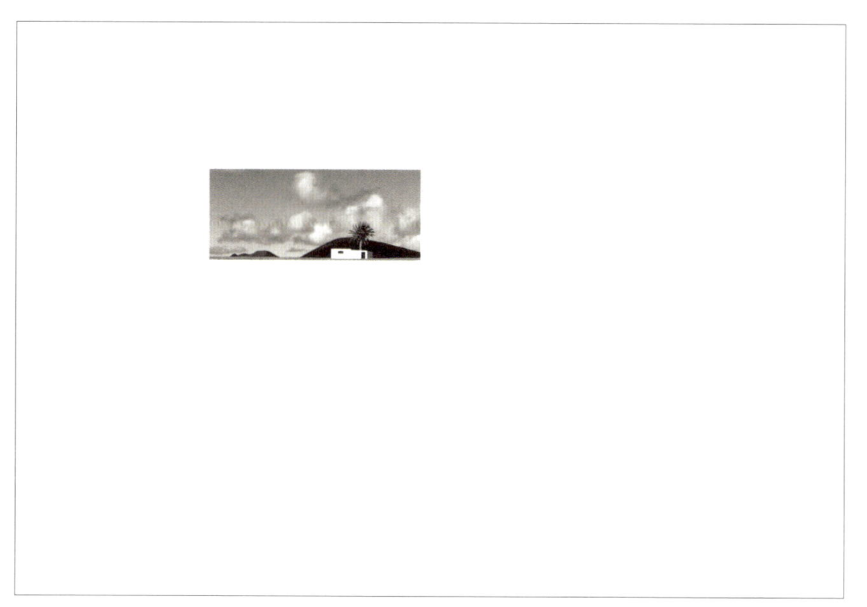

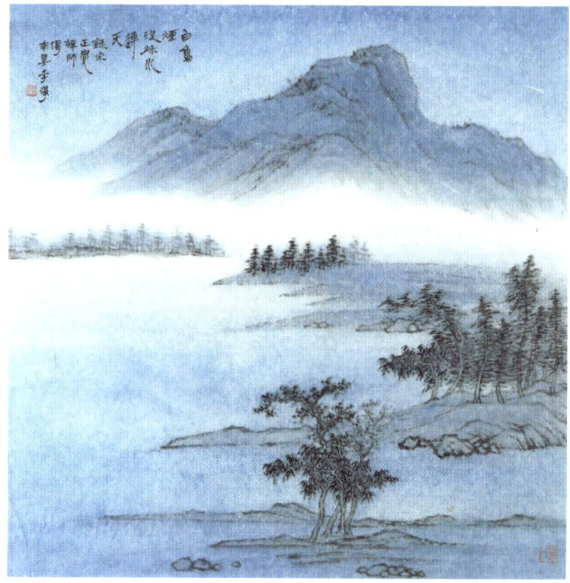

Hongzhi Zhengjue 宏智正覺禪師 (1091–1157)

98 Peter SCHLÖR
La Geria II (Diptych) | 2003
Edition 12 + 3 AP | Fine art pigment print | H 25 x W 38 cm
Collection of the artist

99 LI Jing 李淨
Inspired by Zen Master Zhengjue's Poems 《正覺禪師詩意圖》 | 2023
Color on paper | H 35 x W 35 cm
Collection of the artist

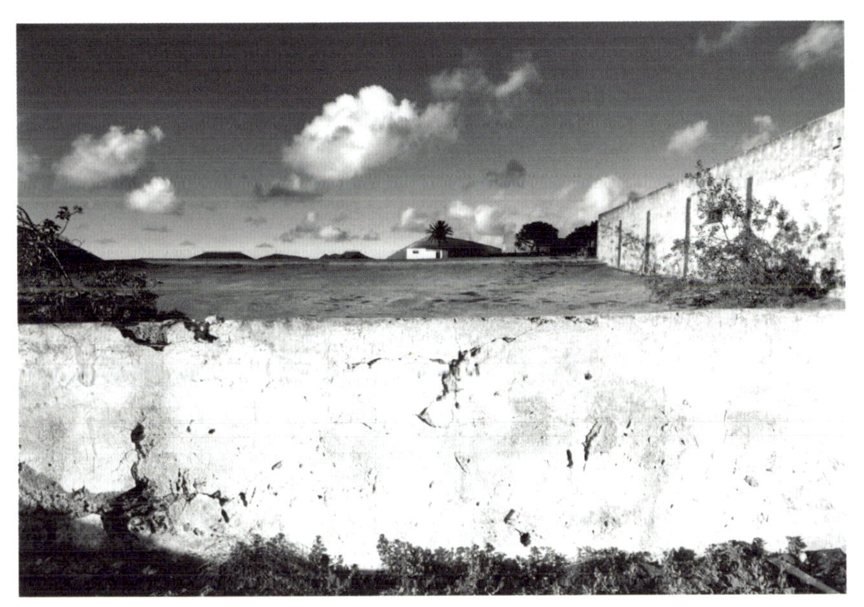

"The cold mountains turn pale and verdant.
The autumn water gurgles."

Wang Wei 王維 (699–759)

100 Peter SCHLÖR
La Geria III (Diptych) | 2003
Edition 12 + 3 AP | Fine art pigment print | H 25 x W 38 cm
Collection of the artist

101 LI Jing 李淨
Inspired by Wang Wei's Poems 《王維詩意圖》 | 2023
Color on paper | H 35 x W 35 cm
Collection of the artist

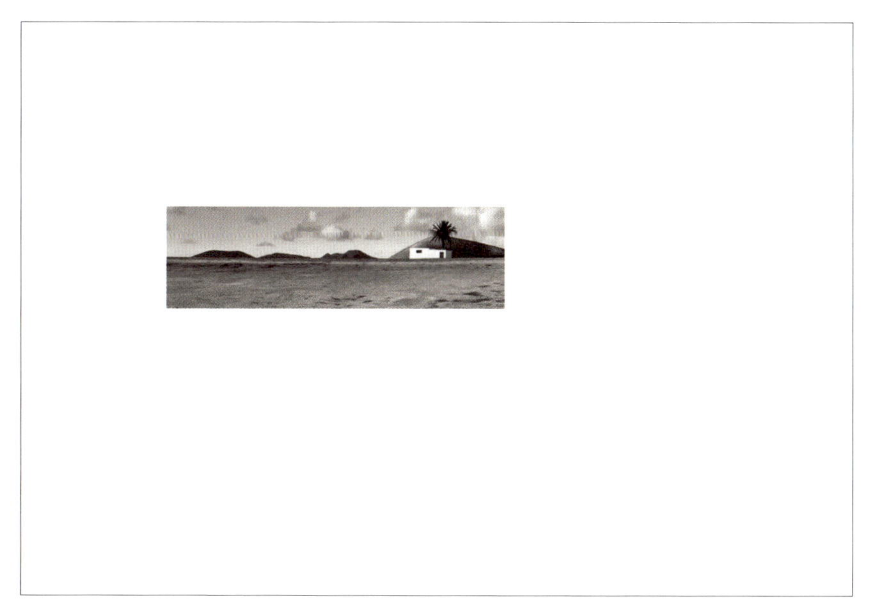

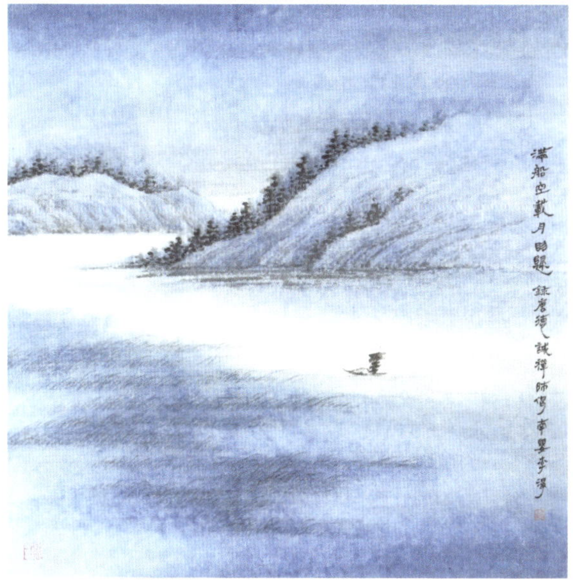

"The boat returns, empty of fish
but full of moonlight."

Chuanzi De Cheng 船子德誠 (820–858)

102 Peter SCHLÖR
La Geria III (Diptych) | 2003
Edition 12 + 3 AP | Fine art pigment print | H 25 x W 38 cm
Collection of the artist

103 LI Jing 李淨
Inspired by Zen Master De Cheng's Poems 《德誠禪師詩意圖》 | 2023
Color on paper | H 35 x W 35 cm
Collection of the artist

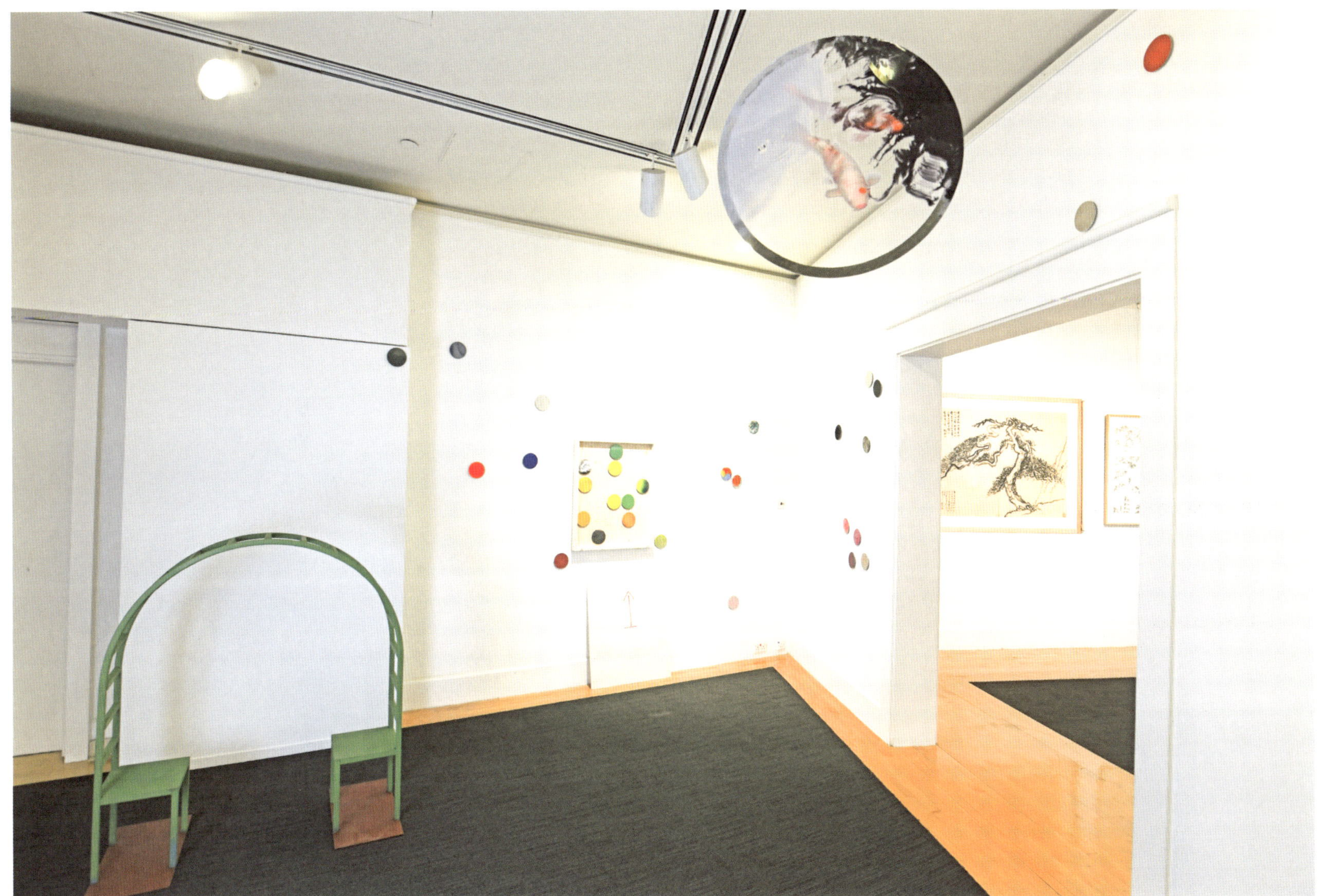

Introduction

A common feature of the exhibited works is their correlation with Oscar Niemeyer's declaration for architecture, "based on eternally valid rules of balance, proportion and harmony, rules that can be found in all works of the past: in the alternation of fullness and emptiness, smooth and transparent surfaces, straight lines and curves." (Niemeyer 2012, 28). To showcase the inherent unity in diversity and diversity in unity, the four exhibition rooms offered multiple visual languages.

COUPLET presented itself as a space for reading. As viewers wandered from poem to poem, this room was seen as a cohesive whole. The multi-layered content not only showed how diverse voices can be used to describe both nature and our world, but also how content can be richly visualized through different forms of calligraphy.

PAIR, or in the room of constellations, the works hanging on the wall formed a balanced equilibrium through their visual languages. On the other hand, the objects in the display cases demonstrated that the human endeavor to create objects in symmetrical harmony can be found in all arts and crafts.

REBUS was created as a space of associations. A network of diverse references was created to connect the objects in the room that require decoding by the viewer. As the opposite walls were also integrated, the entire room could be understood as a 3D picture puzzle.

The last room of the exhibition was dedicated to sensory experience. **INTERACTIVE INSTALLATION** featured works by three artists that also referenced the previous rooms.

The interactive work *New Ways to Colour the Wall* by German artist **Christoph DAHLHAUSEN**, produced in ever-new iterations since 2012, creatively addressed the process of cause and effect, actively engaging viewers (Dahlhausen 2021, 118–123).

In two corners of the exhibition space, 60 magnetic discs were mounted on the walls and placed in two wooden boxes (fig. 104). The positions at which the magnets were fixed to the wall were precisely specified by the artist. The wooden box contained additional colored metal discs, while more discs were distributed on the wall and held in place by magnets. As there were several magnets without discs (free to play with) it was possible to swap the colored discs and change their position on the wall or in the box. Visitors were invited to contribute their creative impulses— some selected discs in a single color, created strong color contrasts or grouped discs with different surfaces. Almost all the visitors placed their discs neatly inside the two wooden boxes when done. One unusually creative four-year-old boy from Chengdu broke with convention and placed all the discs he could reach on the floor in front of him, ultimately arranging them into a rainbow.

Through this interactive installation, DAHLHAUSEN created a minimalist wall of color that also examined visitor behavior as individuals were confronted with a range of questions:

Am I allowed to change something that has been created by someone else as a work of art?

Do I become an artist if I change it?

If I create something new by destroying or changing something that has been created, how is this to be assessed?

What happens to the old work of art?

And what will happen to my artwork when the next visitor changes it?

Every decision, whether passive or active, has a series of consequences. Through the continuous process of changing the discs on the wall, this work made it clear that the principle of causality has both creative and destructive moments, and that these alternate. By overwriting the old version of what has been found, something new is temporarily created, and inevitably this will also be destroyed to create something new. By learning to understand themselves as co-creators along with the artist, visitors also come to understand their passive or active participation within social systems. DAHLHAUSEN's installation offers

the opportunity to experience creative potential and become aware of one's role in the surrounding environment.

In her 2015 created *Rainbow Series* (fig. 107)—sculptures that are reminiscent of playground equipment—Hong Kong-born artist **Debe SHAM** 岑愷怡 also provided visitors with an unusual place to sit. The equipment was extremely popular with younger visitors for climbing, and also offered older visitors the opportunity for a direct exchange of memories. As soon as two people took a seat on the green or blue frame, there was a change in their behavior. Due to the cramped situation caused by the unfamiliar proximity of the seated persons and the shape of the device, both were forced to adopt a posture that was reasonably comfortable for both. This could only be achieved by taking a step back and giving the other person space.

SHAM's ingenious installation also focuses on balance. This is the result of mutual respect in interpersonal relationships. By valuing the other person, even if it is someone you are meeting for the first time, a basis for mutual recognition is created. In this way, communication can take place between equals. This installation was therefore directly related to the PAIR Balance room, picking up on the theme of the various constellations of male and female couples.

Two works by Berkeley-based artist **Mary Curtis RATCLIFF** (*1942 Chicago, Illinois) were selected for the exhibition. Her three-part kinetic sculpture *Koi* (fig. 105) from 2017 floated down from the ceiling and cast shadows on the wall. Koi are considered symbols of spiritual rigor and strength, while also standing for bravery, devotion, perseverance and modesty.

This kinetic sculpture was paired with the wall-based object *Waterborne Tree* (fig. 106) from 2016, which also consists of three parts. The upper disc shows a section of tree standing in water. The lower part of this disc along with the other two discs reveal branches and a patch of sky reflected in the water. The tree branches shown in the water look like well-trodden paths.

The shadows of *Koi* falling on the *Waterborne Tree* connect them. Shadows and reflections are illusions. These must be recognized and unmasked, as in Plato's Cave. To free yourself from illusions, you can take the koi as an example, as it is completely present in every movement. According to Zen philosophy, there is no yesterday or tomorrow for the koi; this fish lives in the here and now. And this presence in the present makes the here and now the key concept of Zen. (Deshimaru 1978).

Hidden in the contemplative rotation of Mary Curtis RATCLIFF's kinetic sculpture and wall piece is the realization that all things are interconnected and that the sequence of cause and effect is an endless movement that we can only experience in part, and only in the here and now. It is comforting that art can help us to recognize and understand these moments.

Finally. Adhering to the common cliché, the West bases its thinking on logos and reason, while the East focuses on feelings, emotions and holistic thought. However, this distinction is far too short-sighted and oversimplified. The West also has holistic views of the world and the East includes forms of rationalistic thinking. What is certain is that the success of modern technology has contributed to the world's interpretation as something calculable, fixed in numerical value and thus rational, causal and digital. This applies to both East and West. The fact that these innovations have been accompanied by a loss of aesthetics is impressively described by the Japanese author Tanizaki Jun'ichiro 谷崎 潤一郎 in his classic *In Praise of Shadows* (Tanizaki 2017).

Rational-logical thinking has an exclusive character. There is only one truth and it is either–or. From this conflict between thesis and antithesis, synthesis emerges victorious and makes us forget the opposites of thesis and antithesis. This dialectic of competition is contrasted with a dualism of simultaneity, interdependence and mutually dependent relationships. Thesis and antithesis are not mutually exclusive, but rather are related to each other in a fruitful interchange. This insight is the basis of classical Chinese philosophy. The balance of forces takes the place of exclusivity. This balance can also be understood as unity in contradiction. If we look at the processes of nature, chance takes its place alongside causality; rational-logical thinking is only one way of understanding the world.

Ultimately, it is also about grasping a thing not in its data, but in its essence. The Japanese philosopher Nishida Kitarō 西田 幾多郎 contrasts Western thinking, which sees everything as a development towards a better future, with thinking that knows no whence and no whither, which is pure eternity.

"Everything comes without a whence of its coming and goes without a whither of its going, and what is, is eternal as it is. Being and nothingness are opposites that constitute a unity."

Nishida 1956, 320.

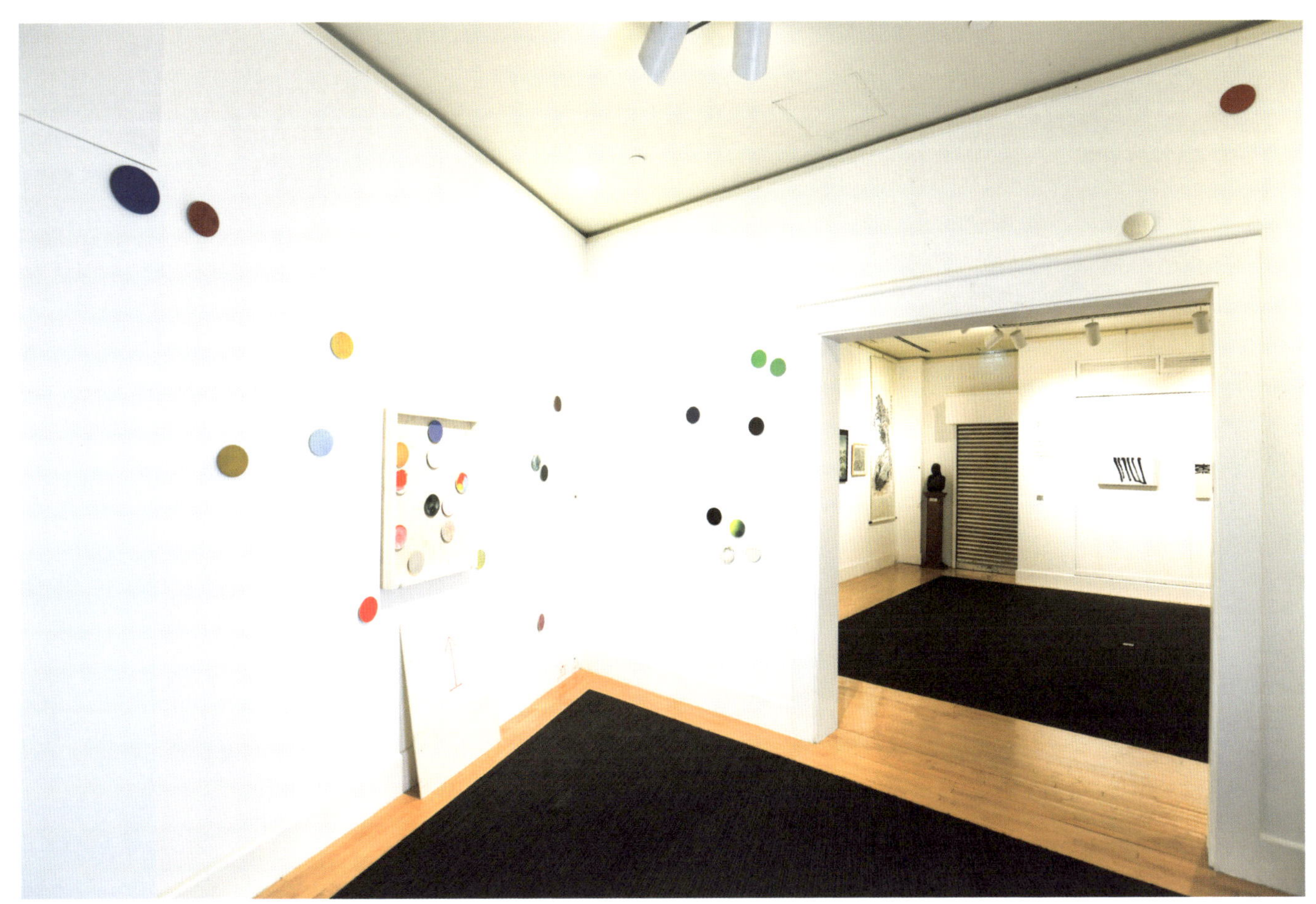

104 Christoph DAHLHAUSEN
New Ways to Colour the Wall | 2012
Interactive Installation, 2 x 30 cm colored metal discs
Dimensions flexible
Collection of the artist

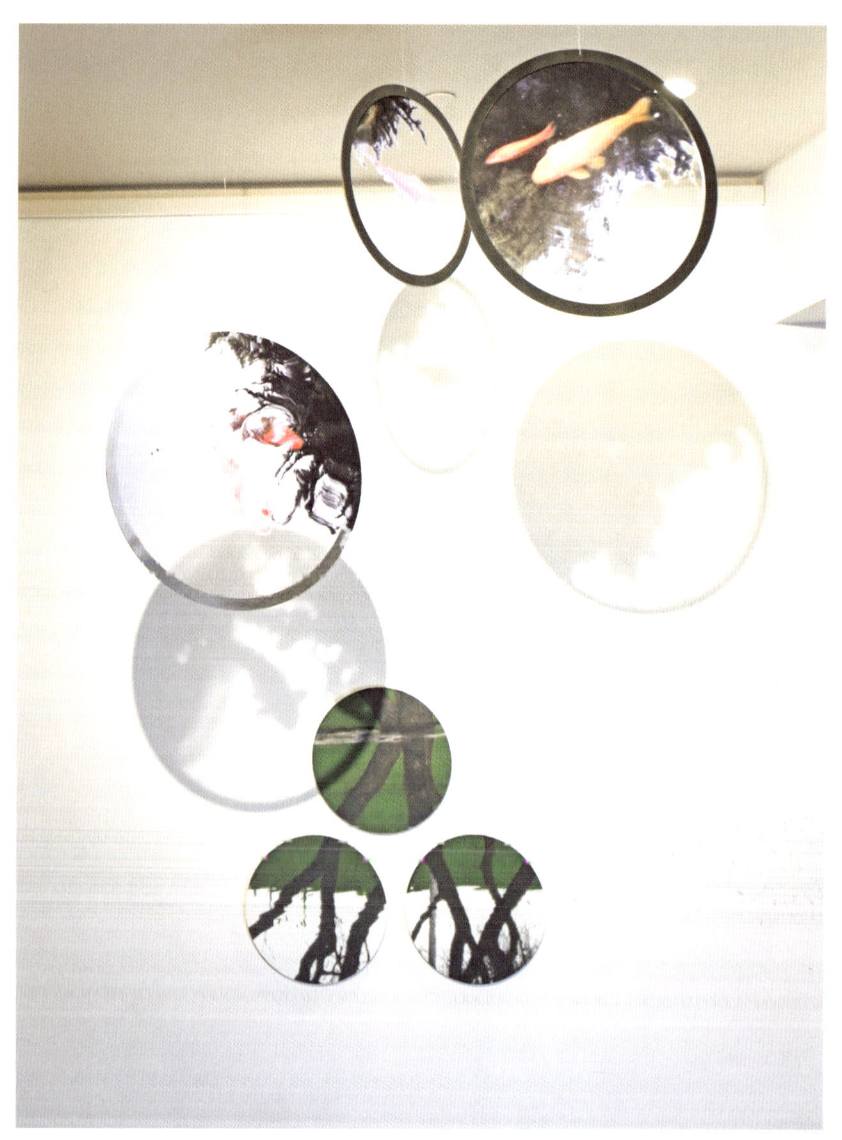

105 Mary Curtis RATCLIFF
Koi | 2017
Kinetic Sculpture, 3 parts, digital inkjet print on acetate, steel,
monofilament | D 96.5 cm / D 94 cm / D 48.2 cm
Collection of the artist

106 Mary Curtis RATCLIFF
Waterborne Tree | 2016
Bas relief, 3 parts, digital inkjet print on plexiglas, acrylic,
colored pencil, wood, steel | D 86.4 cm / D 83.8 cm / D 83.2 cm
Collection of the artist

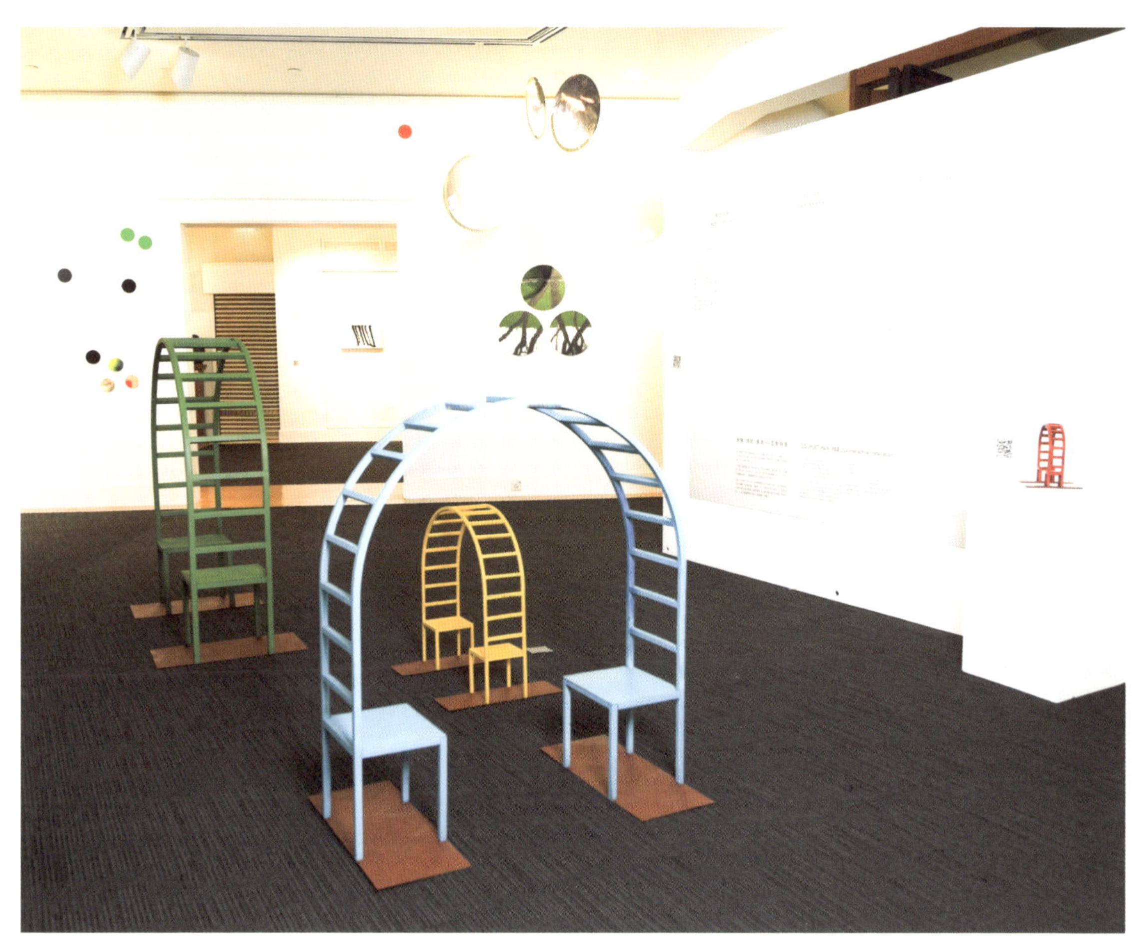

107 Debe SHAM 岑愷怡
Rainbow Series II (Red, Yellow, Blue, Turquoise) | 2015
4 parts, colored steel | Various dimensions
Collection of the artist

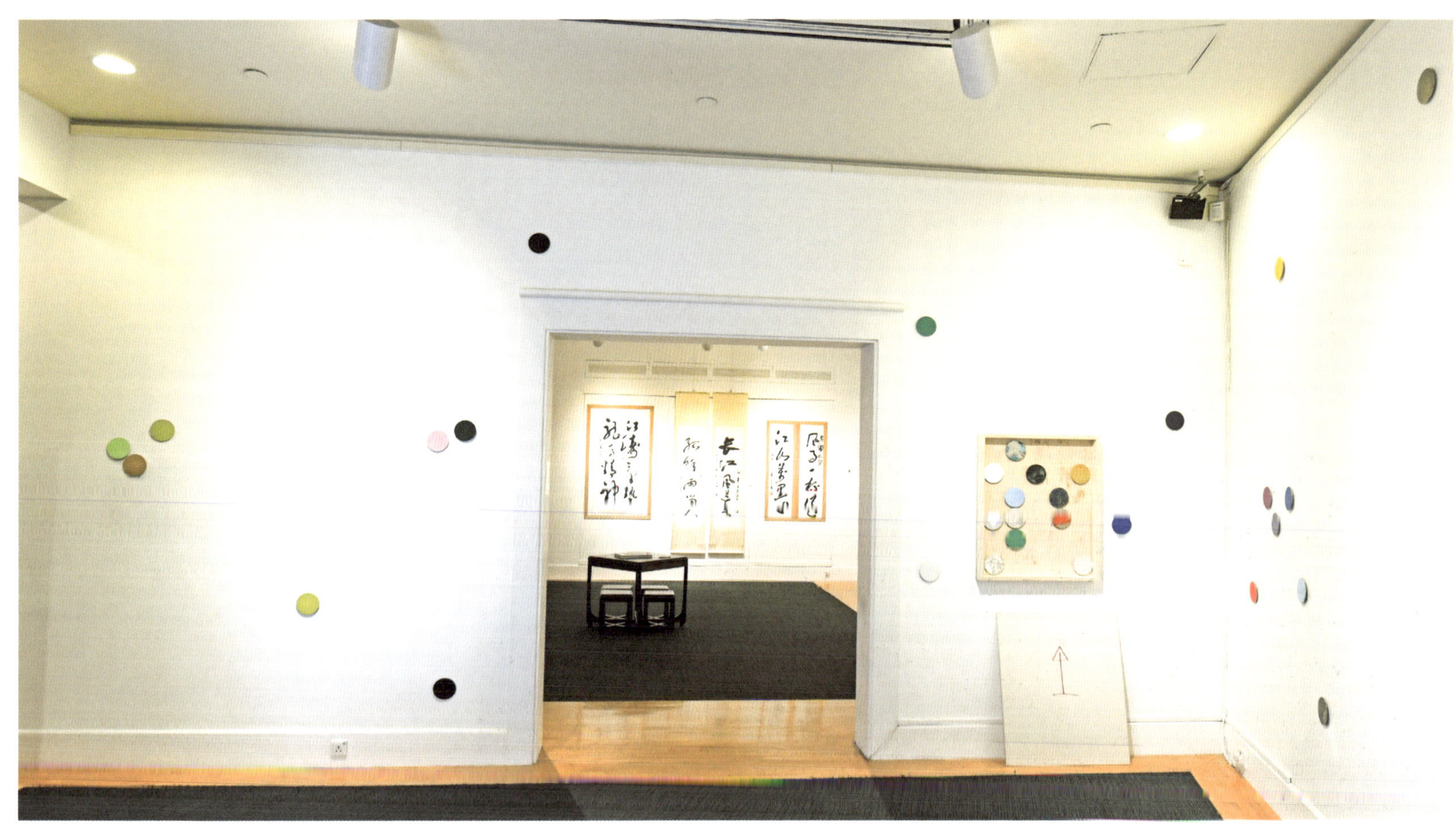

^ COUPLET

104 Christoph DAHLHAUSEN
New Ways to Colour the Wall | 2012
Interactive Installation, 2 x 30 cm colored metal discs
Dimensions flexible
Collection of the artist

References

Emil Angehrn (2007). *Die Frage nach dem Ursprung: Philosophie zwischen Ursprungsdenken und Ursprungskritik*. Munich: Fink.

Aristotle in 23 Volumes, vols. 17, 18, (1933, 1989). Transl. by Hugh Tredennick. Cambridge, MA: Harvard University Press; London: William Heinemann Ltd., see: *Metaphysics*, book VII.

Irene Bloom (2009). *Mencius*. New York: Columbia University Press.

Chan Wing-Cheuk (2006). "Mou Zongsan's Transformation of Kant's Philosophy". In: *Journal of Chinese Philosophy*, vol. 33, 21 Feb 2006.

François Cheng (1991). *Empty and Full. The Language of Chinese Painting*. Boston; London: Shambala [*Vide et plein. Le langage pictural chinois*, Paris: Éditions du Seuil, 1991].

Julia Ching; Willard G. Oxtoby (Eds.) (1992). *Discovering China: European Interpretations in the Enlightenment*. Rochester NY: University of Rochester Press.

The Way of Chuang Tzu (1965). Transl. by Thomas Merton. New York: New Directions.

Irene Chou (2006). *Universe of the Mind. Zhou Luyun (Irene Chou): A Retrospective Exhibition*, exh. cat., Hong Kong: University Museum and Art Gallery, The University of Hong Kong.

M. Tullius Cicero (1923). *De Senectute. De Amicitia. De Divinatione*. Transl. by William Armistead Falconer. Cambridge MA: Harvard University Press.

Kenneth Clatterbaugh (1999). *The Causation Debate in Modern Philosophy 1637–1739*. London; New York: Routledge.

J. Chr. Cleary (1977). "Records of Pointing at the Moon". In: *Swampland Flowers: The Letters and Lectures of Zen Master Ta Hui*. New York: Grove Press.

Derek Collins (2008). *Magic in the Ancient Greek World*. Malden, MA: Blackwell Publishing.

Confucius. Confucian Analects, the Great Learning, and the Doctrine of the Mean (2006). Transl. by James Legge, The Chinese Classics. vol. I., London: N. Trübner & Co. rev. 2nd ed. (1893). Oxford: Clarendon Press, repr. by New York: Cosimo Classics.

Daniel J. Cook; Henry Rosemont, Jr. (1992). "The Pre-established Harmony between Leibniz and Chinese Thought". In: *Discovering China: European Interpretations in the Enlightenment*, ed. by Julia Ching; Willard G. Oxtoby. Rochester NY: University of Rochester Press, 82–96.

Christoph Dahlhausen (2021). *Lightborn*. Milano: Skira.

Christoph Dahlhausen (2017). *Filter*, ed. by Kunstmuseum Ahlen, exh. cat., Ahlen: Kunstmuseum.

René Descartes. The Philosophical Writings of Descartes (1984–1991).Transl. and ed. by John Cottingham; Robert Stoothoff; Dugald Murdoch; Anthony Kenny, 3 vols. Cambridge: Cambridge University Press.

Taisen Deshimaru-Roshi (1978). *Za-Zen. Die Praxis des Zen*, Kristkeitz Verlag, [*Za-Zen. La Pratique du Zen*, 1974].

段建偉, 王宏建, 邵大箴, 鄒躍進, 李路明, & 鄧平祥 (1999). 鄉土中國：當代美術中的鄉村母題：段建偉, 湖南美術出版社.
Duan Jianwei; Wang Hongjian; Shao Dazhen; Zou Yuejin; Li Luming; Deng Pingxiang (1999). *Rural China: The Theme of the Rural Village in Contemporary Art*, ed. by Duan Jianwei. Hunan Fine Arts Publishing House.

Wolfram Eberhard (1983). *Lexikon chinesischer Symbole. Geheime Sinnbilder in Kunst und Literatur, Leben und Denken der Chinesen*. Cologne: Eugen Diederichs Verlag.

冯胜利 (2009). 汉语的韵律, 词法与句法, 北京大學出版社.
Feng Shengli (2009). *Interactions between Morphology, Syntax and Prosody in Chinese*. Beijing: Peking University Press.

Frank Fiedeler (1988). *Die Monde des I-Ging. Symbolschöpfung und Evolution im Buch der Wandlungen*. Düsseldorf; Munich: Diederichs.

Ian Hamilton Finlay (1997). *Ian Hamilton Finlay. Prints 1963–1997 Druckgrafik*, ed. by Rosemarie Pahlke; Pia Simig. Ostfildern: Cantz Verlag.

Jacques Gernet (2012). *Die Begegnung Chinas mit dem Christentum*, ed. by Roman Malek. Sankt Augustin: Steyler Verlag, [*Chine et christianisme: Action et réaction*, 1984].

Ernst H Gombrich (1984). *The Sense of Order. A Study in the Psychology of Decorative Art*, 2nd ed. [1979]. Oxford: Phaidon Press.

Marcel Granet (1963). *Das chinesische Denken*. Munich: Piper, [*La Pensée chinoise*. Paris: La Renaissance de livre, 1934].

Gu Pingdan (Ed.) (2001), *Zhongguo dui lian da ci dian*. Beijing: Xin hua chu ban she.

谷向阳 (2007). 中国楹联学概论, 昆仑出版社.
Gu Xiangyang (2007). *Theory of Chinese Couplets*. Beijing: Kunlun Press.

Robert J. Hankinson (1998). *Cause and Explanation in Ancient Greek Thought*. Oxford: Clarendon Press.

Chad Hansen (1983). *Language and Logic in Ancient China*. Ann Arbor: University of Michigan Press.

George L. Harris (1966). "The Mission of Matteo Ricci, S.J. A Case Study of an Effort at Guided Culture Change in China in The Sixteenth Century". In: *Monumenta Serica*, vol. XXV.

蘅塘退士 (1975). 唐詩三百首：中英對照, 五福出版社.
Hetangtuishi (1975). *Three Hundred Poems of the T'ang Dynasty 618–906*. Transl. by Witter Bynner; Kiang Kang-hu. Taipei Shi: Wu fu chu ban she.

John M. Hobson (2004). *The Eastern Origins of Western Civilization*. Cambridge: Cambridge University Press.

Alexander Holstein (1993). *Pointing at the Moon: One Hundred Zen Koans from Chinese Masters*. Rutland VT: Charles E. Tuttle.
David Hume (1777). *An Enquiry Concerning Human Understanding*. London: A. Millar, [1748].

David Hume (1882). *A Treatise of Human Nature: Being an Attempt to Introduce the Experimental Method of Reasoning into Moral Subjects*, ed. by Lewis Amherst Selby-Bigge, [1739/1740]. Oxford: Clarendon Press.

I Ching: The Book of Change (1992). Transl. by Thomas Cleary. Boston, MA: Shambhala.

Prospero Intorcetta et. al. (1687). *Confucius Sinarum Philosophus, sive, Scientia Sinensis Latine Exposita* [*Confucius, Philosopher of the Chinese, or, Chinese Knowledge Explained in Latin*]. Transl.; ed. by Prospero Intorcetta; Christian Herdtrich; François de Rougemont; Philippe Couplet. Paris: Daniel Horthemels.

Johannes Itten (1973). *Kunst der Farbe: Subjektives Erleben und objektives Erkennen als Wege zur Kunst: Arbeitsmaterial zur Farbenlehre*. 2 vols. [1961]. Ravensburg: Otto Maier Verlag.

Henrik Jäger (2012). *Zhuangzi: Mit den passenden Schuhen vergißt man die Füße*. Dettelbach: J.H. Röll Verlag.

Hans Jonas (1984). *The Imperative of Responsibility. In Search of an Ethics for the Technological Age*. Chicago: Chicago University Press. [*Das Prinzip Verantwortung. Versuch einer Ethik für die technologische Zivilisation*, 1979. Frankfurt am Main: Insel]

Jürgen Jost (2019). "Kausalität". In: *Leibniz und die moderne Naturwissenschaft*. Berlin; Heidelberg: Springer, 113–117.

Carl Gustav Jung (2011). "Zum Gedächtnis Richard Wilhelms". In: *Über das Phänomen des Geistes in Kunst und Wissenschaft*, Gesammelte Werke, vol. 15, chap. V, 2nd ed. [1995]. Ostfildern: Patmos Verlag, 63–74.

Carl Gustav Jung (2023). "Synchronizität als ein Prinzip akausaler Zusammenhänge". In: *Synchronizität: Der Sinn des Zufalls*, Edition C. G. Jung, [1952]. Ostfildern: Patmos Verlag, 7–126.

Immanuel Kant (1999). *Critique of Pure Reason*. Transl.; ed. by Paul Guyer; Allen W. Wood. Cambridge: Cambridge University Press. ["Kritik der praktischen Vernunft". In: *Immanuel Kant. Gesammelte Schriften*, ed. by Preussische Akademie der Wissenschaften, 1900ff., vol. 5, Berlin, AA V, 30].

Tobias Klein (2020). *Metamorphosis or Confrontation*, ed. by Florian Knothe; Harald Kraemer, exh. cat., 20 May–06 Dec 2020, Hong Kong: University Museum and Art Gallery, The University of Hong Kong.

Harald Kraemer (2022). *Future Memories: Utopia Dystopia Nature. Exhibition Strategy – Reflection – Documentation*, exh. cat., 10 Mar–06 Apr 2021. Run Run Shaw Creative Media Centre, Hong Kong, Barcelona; Hong Kong; Vienna: Ediciones Triton.

Harald Kraemer (2018a). *Robert Lettner: Das Spiel vom Kommen und Gehen*. Klagenfurt: Ritter Verlag.

Harald Kraemer (2018b). "Ornament and Transformation – the Digital Painting of Robert Lettner at the Interface of Analogue and Algorithmic Art". In: *Art Machines. Int. Symposium on Computational Media Art*, 04–07 Jan. 2019. Hong Kong: School of Creative Media, City University of Hong Kong, 2018, 42–56.

Harald Kraemer (2018c). "Painting Finds Me: Strategies of Composition in the Landscape Painting of Liao Zenping". In: *Liao Zenping: Daily Practice*. Taichung: Ke Yuan Gallery, 4–11.

Harald Kraemer (2015). *Beat Feller: Werke Wanderschaft Works Wanderings*. Basel: Transfusionen.

Harald Kraemer (2013). "Public Enemy? About the neo-informal painting by SMASH137 and some quotes by RB". In: *SMASH137 – Public Enemy*, exh. cat., 21 Mar–03 May 2013, Galerie Abtart. Stuttgart: Abtart, 80–83.

Harald Kraemer (2006). "Deep Black: The Transformation of Emptiness". In: *Peter Schlör: Deep Black*, ed. by Bernhard Knaus, Ostfildern: Hatje Cantz Verlag, 16–17.

Donald F. Lach (1992a). "Leibniz and China". In: *Discovering China. European Interpretations in the Enlightenment*, ed. by Julia Ching; Willard G. Oxtoby. Rochester NY: University of Rochester Press, 97–116.

Donald F. Lach (1992b). "The Sinophilism of Christian Wolff (1679–1754)". In: *Discovering China. European Interpretations in the Enlightenment*, ed. by Julia Ching; Willard G. Oxtoby. Rochester NY: University of Rochester Press, 117–130.

T. C. Lai (1976). *Chinese Couplets*. Transl. by T. C. Lai, repr. of 2nd ed. 1970, [1969]. Hong Kong: University of Hong Kong Press.

Lee Chun Yi (Ed.) (2001). *An Anthology of Hong Kong Modern Ink Painting*. Hong Kong: Hong Kong Modern Chinese Ink Painting Association.

James Legge (1861). *Confucian Analects, the Great Learning, and the Doctrine of the Mean*. The Chinese Classics, vol. I. Oxford: Clarendon Press. Repr. 2006, New York: Cosimo Classics.

James Legge (1882). *The Yî King (I Ching)*: Sacred Books of the East, vol. 16, 2nd ed. (1899). Oxford: Clarendon Press. Repr. 1963, New York: Dover Publications.

James Legge (1885). *The Lî Kî (Book of Rites)*. Sacred Books of the East, vol. 27, vol. 28. Oxford: Clarendon Press.

James Legge (1891). *The Texts of Taoism: The Tâo Teh King*. Sacred Books of the East, vol. 39. Oxford: Clarendon Press. Repr. 2001, Kent: Grange Books.

Gottfried Wilhelm Leibniz (2011). *Novissima Sinica: Das Neueste von China*. [1697]. Transl.; ed. by Heinz-Günther Nesselrath; Hermann Reinbothe. Munich: Ludicum Verlag.

Gottfried Wilhelm Leibniz (1998). *Monadologie [La Monadologie, 1720]*. Stuttgart: Reclam.

Gottfried Wilhelm Leibniz (1996). *Theodizee* [Essais de Théodicée, 1710, Amsterdam: I. Troyel]. Berlin: Akademie Verlag.

Gottfried Wilhelm Leibniz (1994). *Writings on China*. Transl. by Daniel Cook; Henry Rosemont. Chicago IL: Open Court.

Gottfried Wilhelm Leibniz (1863). "Explication de l'arithmétique binaire, qui se sert des seuls caractères 0 et 1, avec des remarques sur son utilité, et sur ce qu'elle donne le sens des anciennes figures Chinoises de Fohy" [1703, Mémoires de l'Academie des Sciences]. In: *Leibnizens gesammelte Werke*, ed. by Georg Heinrich Pertz, 3. Mathematik, vol. 7, XXI, 223–228. Halle: Verlag H.W. Schmidt.

Robert Lettner (2017). *In Dialogue with the Chinese Landscape: Utopia of Ornaments New Wunderkammer of Rococo*, ed. by Florian Knothe; Harald Kraemer, exh. cat. Hong Kong: University Museum and Art Gallery, The University of Hong Kong.

Leung Kui-ting (2005). *Transmutation of Vision and Resonance: The Works of Leung Kui Ting*, exh. cat., 04 Jun–07 Aug 2005. Hong Kong: University Museum and Art Gallery, The University of Hong Kong, Hong Kong: University Museum and Art Gallery.

Liao Zenping (2022). *Still Life*. Taichung: Ke Yuan Gallery.

Lin Shuen-Fu; Stephen Owen (2014). *The Vitality of the Lyric Voice: Shih Poetry from the Late Han to the T'ang*. [1987]. Princeton: Princeton University Press.

James J. Y. Liu (1962). *The Art of Chinese Poetry*. Chicago: University of Chicago Press.

劉勰 (1983). 文心雕龍
Liu Xie (1983). *The Literary Mind and the Carving of Dragons*. Transl. by Shih, Vincent Yu-chung. Hong Kong: The Chinese University Press.

龙榆生 (2010). 中国韵文史, 商務印書館.
Long Yusheng (2010). *Chinese Poetry. History and Criticism*. Shanghai: Commercial Press.

John Losee (2011). *Theories of Causality. From Antiquity to the Present*. New Brunswick; London: Transaction Publishers.

Lu K'uan Yü (Charles Luk) (1961). *Ch'an and Zen Teaching*. London: Rider.

John Randolph Lucas (1993). *Responsibility*. Oxford: Oxford University Press.

Adolf Lumpe (1955). "Der Terminus 'Prinzip' (ἀρχή) von den Vorsokratikern bis auf Aristoteles". In: *Archiv für Begriffsgeschichte*, no. 1, 104–116.

Knud Lundbæk (1991). "The First European Translations of Chinese Historical and Philosophical Works". In: *China and Europe: Images and Influences [from the] Sixteenth to Eighteenth Centuries*, Monograph Series, no. 12. Hong Kong: Chinese University Press, 29–44.

Knud Lundbæk (1992). "The Image of Neo-Confucianism in *Confucius Sinarum Philosophus*". In: *Discovering China: European Interpretations in the Enlightenment*, ed. by Julia Ching; Willard G. Oxtoby. Rochester NY: University of Rochester Press, 27–38.

Ansgar Lyssy (2016). *Kausalität und Teleologie bei G. W. Leibniz*, Studia Leibnitiana, vol. 48. Stuttgart: Franz Steiner Verlag.

马光仲 (2006). 中國對聯大觀, 深圳：海天出版社.
Ma Guangzhong (2006). *Chinese Couplets*. Shenzhen: Haitian Publishing House.

René Magritte (1981). *René Magritte. Sämtliche Schriften*, ed. by André Blavier. Munich; Vienna: Carl Hanser Verlag.

The Mahayana Mahaparinirvana-Sutra (1973–1975): *A complete translation from the classical Chinese language in 3 volumes*. Transl. by Kōshō Yamamoto. Ube, JP: The Karinbunko.

William E. May (1970). "Knowledge of Causality in Hume and Aquinas". In: *The Thomist*, April 1970, no. 34.

Denis McManus (2006). *The Enchantment of Words: Wittgenstein's Tractatus Logico-Philosophicus*. Oxford: Oxford University Press.

Nāgārjuna (2014). *Nāgārjuna's Middle Way: Mūlamadhyamakakārikā*. Transl. by Mark Siderits; Shōryū Katsura. Somerville MA: Wisdom Publications.

Oscar Niemeyer (2013). *Wir müssen die Welt verändern*, [*Il mondo è ingiusto*, 2012]. Munich: Verlag Antje Kunstmann.

Nishida Kitarō (2005). "Die Einheit der Gegensätze. Der metaphysische Hintergrund Gottes". In: *Japanische Geisteswelt: Vom Mythos zur Gegenwart*, ed. by Oscar Benl; Horst Hammitzsch. Baden-Baden: Holle Verlag, 316–320.

François Noel (Ed.) (1711). "Sinensis Imperii Liber Quartus Classicus Dictus Memcius, Sinice Mem Tsu, [The Fourth Classic Book of the Chinese Empire, Called the Mencius or, in Chinese, Mengzi]". In: *Sinensis Imperii Libri Classici Sex* [The Six Classic Books of the Chinese Empire]. Praque: Charles-Ferdinand University Press, 199–472.

Stephen Owen (1981). *The Great Age of Chinese Poetry: The High T'ang*. New Haven CT: Yale University Press.

Qiu Zhao'ao (1979). *Du shi xiang zhu*. Beijing: Zhonghua shu ju, 1979.

Stephen Palmquist (2010). *Cultivating Personhood: Kant and Asian Philosophy*. Hong Kong: De Gruyter, Inc.

Matteo Ricci (1985). *The True Meaning of the Lord of Heaven*, [Tianzhu shiyi (天主實義), 1603, Beijing] Transl.; ed. by Douglas Lancashire, St. Louis MO: Institute of Jesuit Sources.

Matteo Ricci (2005). *Über die Freundschaft (Dell' amicizia)*, [Jiāoyǒu lùn (交友論), 1595, Nanchang]. Transl. by Nina Jocher. Macerata: Edizioni Quodlibet.

Joachim Ritter; Karlfried Gründer; Gottfried Gabriel (Eds.) (2001). *Historisches Wörterbuch der Philosophie*, vol. 11, Basel: Schwabe Verlag, see *Ursache / Wirkung*, 378–411.

Heiner Roetz (2006). "Die chinesische Sprache und das chinesische Denken: Positionen einer Debatte". In: *BJOAF* (Bochumer Jahrbuch zur Ostasienforschung), ed. by Faculty of East Asian Studies, Ruhr-Universität Bochum, Bd. 30, 9–37.

Arnold H. Rowbotham (1966). *Missionary and Mandarin: The Jesuits at the Court of China*. New York: Russell & Russell.

James A. Ryan (1996). "Leibniz' Binary System and Shao Yong's 'Yijing'". In: *Philosophy East and West*. University of Hawai'i Press, vol. 46, no. 1, Jan 1996, 59–90.

Peter Schlör (2006). *Deep Black*, ed. by Bernhard Knaus. Ostfildern: Hatje Cantz Verlag.

Tad Schmaltz (2008). *Descartes on Causation*. Oxford: Oxford University Press

Arthur Schopenhauer (1903). *On the Fourfold Root of the Principle of Sufficient Reason* [Ueber die vierfache Wurzel des Satzes vom zureichenden Grunde. 1813 Diss., University of Jena, 2nd ed. 1847]. Transl. by Mme. K. Hillebrand. London: George Bell.

Hans Sedlmayr (1958). *Kunst und Wahrheit: Zur Theorie und Methode der Kunstgeschichte*. Hamburg: Rowohlt.

Shōbōgenzō (2023). *Treasury of the True Dharma Eye: Dōgen's Shōbōgenzō* (正法眼藏), ed. by Carl Bielefeldt. Tokyo: Sōtōshū Shūmuchō

沈君怡 (2024). 塵雜與蟬鳴. 香港：嘉圖現代藝術.
Shum Kwan Yi (2024). *Dust and Cicada Chirping*, Hong Kong: Grotto Fine Art Ltd.

Si Wing Zhou (2006). *Tang and Song Poetry: Chinese-English*. Taibei: Jiu Ge chu ban she, 2006.

Richard J. Smith (2002). "The Yijing (Classic of Changes) in Global Perspective: Some Reflections". In: *Book of Changes World Conference*, Proc., 28 Sep–2 Oct 2002. Taipei, Taiwan.
宋永红 (2008). 欲望广场：宋永红, 广东美术馆编 [广州]：广东美术馆.

Song Yonghong (2008). *Square of Desire*, exh. cat. Guangzhou: Guangdong Museum of Art.

Herbert Starek (2002). *Blinde Worte*. Vienna: Transfusionen.

Janine Stoll (2018). *La Salle Blanche: Marcel Broodthaers' gemaltes Alphabet. Rebus – Bühne – Index*, ed. by Harald Kraemer.Munich: edition Metzel.

Donald Sturgeon (2019). *Chinese Text Project: A Dynamic Digital Library of Premodern Chinese*. Digital Scholarship in the Humanities. < https://ctext.org/ >

Daisetz Teitaro Suzuki (1914). *A Brief History of Early Chinese Philosophy*, 2nd ed. London: Probsthain & Co.

Daisetz Teitaro Suzuki (1926), *Essays in Zen Buddhism*, publ. for the Buddhist Society. London: Rider.

The Taishō Shinshū Daizōkyō (1962), ed. by Junjirō Takakusu; Kaigyoku Watanabe, [1924 1935] Tokyo: Daizokyokai

Jun'ichirō Tanizaki (2017). *In Praise of Shadows*, [*In'ei-raisan*, 1933]. Transl. by Gregory Starr. Sora Books.

Thích Nhất Hanh (2010). *Calligraphic Meditation. The Mindful Art of Thích Nhất Hạnh*, exh. cat., 09 Sep–17 Oct 2004. Hong Kong: University Museum and Art Gallery, The University of Hong Kong.

Rolf Trauzettel (1990). "Denken die Chinesen anders? Komparatistische Thesen zur chinesischen Philosophiegeschichte." In: *Saeculum*, vol. 41, 79–99.

Tu Chen Tsui (2016). *Xi-Ruo-San Poetry and Couplets: A Critical Literary Commentary*. Xiamen: Xiamen University Press.

Yamamoto Tsunetomo (2002). *Hagakure. The Book of the Samurai*. Transl. by William Scott Wilson, [1716]. New York: Kodansha America.

UMAG (2020). *Pictorial Silks: Chinese Textiles from the UMAG Collection*, exh. cat., 18 Sep–6 Dec 2020. Hong Kong: University Museum and Art Gallery, The University of Hong Kong.

UMAG (2018). *Tradition to Contemporary: Ink Painting and Artistic Development in 20th century China*, exh. cat., 24 Aug–25 Nov 2018. Hong Kong: University Museum and Art Gallery, The University of Hong Kong.

UMAG (2017). *Objectifying China: Ming and Qing Dynasty Ceramics and Their Stylistic Influences Abroad*, exh. cat., 9 Dec 2017–27 Feb 2018. Hong Kong: University Museum and Art Gallery, The University of Hong Kong.

UMAG (2004). *Concepts in Wood: Contemporary Hong Kong Wood Sculpture* (2004), exh. cat., 09 Sep–17 Oct 2004. Hong Kong: University Museum and Art Gallery, The University of Hong Kong.

Wang Li 王力 (2000). *Shici gelü* 詩詞格律. [1977]. Beijing: Zhonghua Book Company 中華書局.

Wang Zigui (2012). "On the Philosophical Implications of Leibniz's Principle of Sufficient Reason". In: *China Social Science Net*. Chinese Academy of Social Sciences.

Eric Watkins (2005). *Kant and the Metaphysics of Causality*. Cambridge: Cambridge University Press.

Alan Watts (1957). *The Way of Zen*. New York: Pantheon Books.

Patricia Bjaaland Welch (2008). *Chinese Art. A Guide to Motifs and Visual Imagery*. North Clarendon VT: Tuttle Publishing.

Richard Wilhelm (2005). *I Ging: Das Buch der Wandlungen*. New ed. by Ulf Diederichs [Jena: Eugen Diederichs Verlag, 1924]. Munich: Deutscher Taschenbuchverlag, 2nd ed. 2005.

Richard Wilhelm (2003). *Laotse. Tao te king. Das Buch vom Weg des Lebens*. [Jena: Eugen Diederichs Verlag, 1910]. Bergisch Gladbach: Bastei Lübbe, 2nd ed. 2003.

Richard Wilhelm (1981). *Li Gi. Das Buch der Riten, Sitten und Gebräuche*. [Jena: Eugen Diederichs Verlag, 1930]. Munich: Diederichs Gelbe Reihe, vol. 31.

Thomas Wilson (2014). *The Swastika. The earliest known symbol, and its migrations: with observations on the migration of certain industries in prehistoric times* [Washington: Government Printing Office, 1896]. Calgary: Theophania Publishing.

Ludwig Wittgenstein (1922). *Tractatus Logico-Philosophicus*, Series: International Library of Psychology, Philosophy and Scientific Method. Transl. by Charles Kay Ogden; Frank Ramsey. London: Kegan Paul, Trench, Trubner & Co.

Ludwig Wittgenstein (1953). *Philosophical Investigations*. Transl. and ed. by G. E. M. Anscombe. Oxford: Blackwell.

Matt Hettche; Corey Dyck (2006). "Christian Wolff". In: *The Stanford Encyclopedia of Philosophy*, ed. by Edward N. Zalta.

Christian Wolff (1985). *Oratio de Sinarum philosophia practica*. [*Rede über die praktische Philosophie der Chinesen*] (Speech on the practical philosophy of the Chinese). Transl.; intr.; ed. by Michael Albrecht. Hamburg: Felix Meiner Verlag.

Christian Wolff (1720). "Vernünftige Gedanken von Gott, der Welt und der Seele des Menschen, auch allen Dingen überhaupt" [Rational Thoughts on God, the World and the Soul of Man, and on All Things in General], Halle, 7th edition, 1751. In: *Christian Wolff. Gesammelte Werke*, 1. div., Deutsche Schriften, vol. 3, Hildesheim: Olms, 1983.

Christian Wolff (1713). "Vernünftige Gedanken von den Kräften des menschlichen Verstandes und ihrem richtigen Gebrauch in der Erkenntnis der Wahrheit" [Rational Thoughts on the Powers of the Human Understanding and Its Proper Use in the Cognition of Truth], Halle, 14th edition, 1754. In: *Christian Wolff, Gesammelte Werke*, 1. div., vol. 1, repr. Hildesheim: Olms, 1965.

Xin Haizhou (2005). *Xin Haizhou 1987–2005*, exh. cat., 06 Sep–06 Oct 2005, Beijing: Beijing Art Now Gallery.

Yip Wai-Lim (Ed.) (1976). *Chinese Poetry: Major Modes and Genres*. Transl. by Wai-Lim Yip. Berkeley CA: University of California Press.

Yoshikawa, Kōjirō (1995), *Zhongguo shi shi*. Taibei: Ming wen shu ju.

Zhāng Dōngsūn (张东荪) (1939). "A Chinese Philosopher's Theory of Knowledge". In: *Yenching Journal of Social Studies*, vol. I, no. 2.

Zhao Lu (2021). "Richard Wilhelm's Book of Changes and the Science of the Mind in the Early Twentieth Century". In: *The Making of the Global Yijing in the Modern World*, ed. by Benjamin Wai-mong Ng, Chinese Culture, vol. 4. Singapore: Springer, 155–173.

Zhu, Guangqian (1993). *Shi lun*. Shanghai: Shanghai gu ji chu ban she, 1993.

Acknowledgements

We would like to thank the UMAG team as well as
Henry Au-yeung | Chen Haiqing | Kay Chiu Yan Ki |
David J. Clarke | Christoph Dahlhausen | Du Chenghan |
Adrian Falkner | Beat Feller | Ken Fung Long Him | Fung
Yee Lick Eric | Tobias Klein | Margit and Markus Lettner |
Joseph Leung Mong Sum | Li Jing | Liao Zenping | Fiona
Lui | Tony Maslić | Mary Curtis Ratcliff | Peter Samis |
Peter Schlör | Debe Sham | Sim Shum Kwan Yi | Pia
Simig | Philipp Stadler | Herbert Starek | Janine Stoll | To
Yeuk Hung | Tu Chen Tsui | Tsz-ching Wong | Xu Feng-
peng | Xu Yitian | Cynthia Yuen.

COUPLET PAIR REBUS The Principle of Cause and Effect in Art

27. October 2023–7. April 2024
University Museum and Art Gallery, The University of Hong Kong
1/F, T. T. Tsui Building, 90 Bonham Road, Hong Kong
http://www.umag.hku.hk

Curated, designed, written & edited by Harald Kraemer
Translation Couplets: To Yeuk Hung
© Texts by Florian Knothe, Harald Kraemer, Li Jing, To Yeuk Hung
© Photographs by Wenxin Wendy Zhang and the artists
Cover: Dish with Dragons and Phoenixes, Ming dynasty, Wanli period (1573–1620), Jingdezhen, Jiangxi province
Porcelain with underglaze blue and overglaze enamels, H 2.2 x Ø 11 cm | HKU.C.1959.0232

ISBN 978-988-74708-3-0
© University Museum and Art Gallery, The University of Hong Kong, 2024